GCSE
Leisure and Tourism
FOR OCR

DOUBLE AWARD

GCSE Leisure and Tourism FOR OCR

DOUBLE AWARD

Peter Hayward

Heinemann Educational Publishers
Halley Court, Jordan Hill, Oxford OX2 8EJ
Part of Harcourt Education

Heinemann is the registered trademark of Harcourt Education Limited

© Peter Hayward, 2002
First published 2002
07 06 05 04 03
10 9 8 7 6 5 4 3

British Library Cataloguing in Publication Data is available from the British Library on request.

ISBN 0 435 47122 8

All rights reserved. No part of this publication may be reproduced in any form or by any means (including photocopying or storing it in any medium by electronic means and whether or not transiently or incidentally to some other use of this publication) without the written permission of the copyright owner, except in accordance with the provisions of the Copyright, Designs and Patents Act 1988 or under the terms of a licence issued by the Copyright Licensing Agency, 90 Tottenham Court Road, London W1T 4LP. Applications for the copyright owner's written permission should be addressed to the publisher.

Designed by Artistix, Thame, Oxon
Typeset by Tek-Art Croydon, Surrey
Printed in Spain by Edelvives

Original illustrations © Harcourt Education Limited, 2002

Cover photo: © Corbis

Tel: 01865 888058 www.heinemann.co.uk

Websites
There are links to relevant websites in this book. In order to ensure that the links are up to date, that the links work, and that the sites aren't inadvertently linked to sites that could be considered offensive, we have made the links available on the Heinemann website at www.heinemann.co.uk/hotlinks. When you access the site, the express code is 1228P.

Contents

Acknowledgements · · · vii
Introduction · · · ix

Unit 1 Investigating leisure and tourism · · · 1

Chapter 1	The leisure industry	2
Chapter 2	The travel and tourism industry	55
Chapter 3	Links between leisure and tourism	87

Unit 2 Marketing in leisure and tourism · · · 95

Chapter 1	What is marketing?	96
Chapter 2	Target marketing	102
Chapter 3	Market research	108
Chapter 4	The marketing mix	121
Chapter 5	SWOT analysis	141
Chapter 6	Promotional campaigns	143

Unit 3 Customer service in leisure and tourism · · · 153

Chapter 1	What is customer service?	154
Chapter 2	Different types of customer	162
Chapter 3	External and internal customers	171
Chapter 4	Benefits of customer service	173
Chapter 5	Communicating with customers	182
Chapter 6	Personal presentation	188
Chapter 7	Handling complaints	195
Chapter 8	Keeping customer records	198

Appendix · · · 203
Index · · · 209

Acknowledgements

Many organisations have assisted in the writing of this book by providing information or agreeing for material to be reproduced. We would like to thank the following: Alton Towers, Beaulieu, Bluewater, British Airways London Eye, Council for National Parks Dukeries Leisure Centre, Eden Project, English Heritage, English Tourism Council, Jorvik, Meadowhall Centre, The Trafford Centre.

Crown Copyright material on pages 8, 9, 14 and 38 is reproduced under Class Licence Number C01W0041 with the permission of the Controller of HMSO and the Queen's Printer for Scotland.

The author and publisher would also like to thank the following individuals and organisations for permission to reproduce photographs:

Action Plus – page 9, 33
Alamy.com – page 30
Allsport/Stephen Dunn – page 13
Alton Towers – page 29, 88 (left)
Big Bus Company – page 88 (right)
British Travel Trade Fair 2002, Isle of Wight Tourism – page 133
Burlees Hotel, Blackpool – page 64 (top right)
Canterbury Tourist Information – page 163
Chewton Glen Hotel, Health & Country Club – page 1 (middle), 64 (bottom left)
Corbis/Sygma – page 85
Cosmos Holidays – page 164
Fin Costello/REDFERNS – page 123
The Dome – Doncaster Leisure Park – page 35
EMPICS Sports Photo Agency – page 11, 48, 58, 126, 134
Ffestiniog Railway – page 72
Getty Images – page 1 (right), 5, 7 (top), 7 (middle), 7 (bottom), 23 (top), 45, 51, 60, 61, 64 (bottom right), 70, 79, 105
Richard Greenhill – page 108
Guildford Spectrum – page 1 (left), 189, 192
Robert Harding/Mark Mawson – page 39
John Heseltine/Corbis – page 20
Legoland Windsor – page 43
Peter Morris – page 139
Science Museum/Science & Society Pic Lib – page 16
Somecoasters.com – page 25
Trafford Centre, Manchester – page 57
Travel Ink/Tony Page – page 23 bottom.

Every effort has been made to contact copyright holders of material published in this book. We would be glad to hear from unacknowledged sources at the first opportunity.

Introduction

How to use this book

This book has been written for students who are working to the 2002 National Standards for the GCSE in Leisure and Tourism. It covers the three compulsory units:

1. Investigating leisure and tourism
2. Marketing in leisure and tourism
3. Customer service in leisure and tourism.

Individual chapters within each unit use the same headings as the GCSE units to make it easy for you to find your way around. By working through the units, you will find all the knowledge and ideas you need to successfully complete both your external assessment for Unit 1 and your portfolio coursework for Units 2 and 3.

The Appendix at the end of the book contains information on work experience and building your portfolio.

Special features

Throughout the book, there are a number of features which are designed to encourage discussion and group work, and to help you to see how the theory is put into practice in leisure and tourism. These activities will not only help you achieve your GCSE in Leisure and Tourism, but will also enable you to build up a portfolio of key skills. This can be done by carrying out the activities provided, which include the key skills of numeracy, communication and information and communications technology (ICT).

The features are:

Group exercises involving research, discussion and/or a writing activity.

Thought provoking questions or dilemmas about issues in leisure and tourism. They can be used for individual reflection or group discussion.

Interesting facts and snippets of information about the leisure and tourism industries.

Activities that encourage you to apply the theory in a practical situation. These include core activities and extension activities:

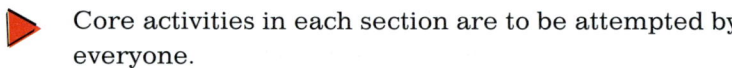 Core activities in each section are to be attempted by everyone.

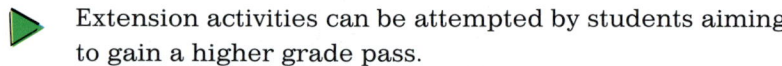 Extension activities can be attempted by students aiming to gain a higher grade pass.

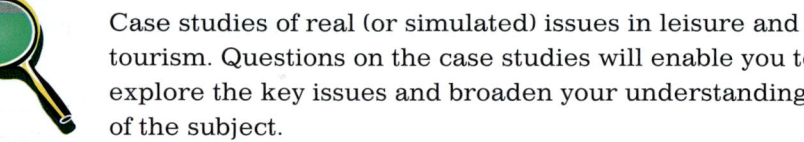 Case studies of real (or simulated) issues in leisure and tourism. Questions on the case studies will enable you to explore the key issues and broaden your understanding of the subject.

Snapshot Close-ups of people working in the leisure and tourism industries and the problems and challenges they face.

 Definitions of key terms.

The aim of this book is to give you the opportunity to achieve your full potential. All the special features and information are geared towards increasing your knowledge of the leisure and tourism industries and helping you to gain a relevant qualification for working in these industries.

What are leisure and tourism?

Leisure and tourism together make up one of the biggest and fastest growing industries in the world. Successful completion of your GCSE in Leisure and Tourism could lead to an exciting and interesting career within these industries.

As the leisure and tourism industries are so vast, there are a lot of job opportunities in leisure and recreation and travel and tourism. Examples of jobs include: travel consultants, sports centre managers, air cabin crew, holiday reps, sports coaches, tour guides, hotel managers, conference organisers, marketing executives, public relations officers and many more. These jobs can offer you a rewarding career in terms of promotion and salary, as well as variety and interest. Your studies and qualifications can help you achieve your ambitions, so work hard, enjoy your course and believe in your abilities. This way of thinking will impress any future employer.

One of the most important qualities you need is the ability to get on with people and to be able to work as part of a team. This book will help you develop your customer care skills and show the importance of teamwork.

You may already have a part-time job, perhaps working in a supermarket, a restaurant or a shop. The work may be hard, the hours long and the pay may not be that good. But also there may be variety, responsibility, friendship and fun. These parts of the job make up the 'feel good' factor – when you enjoy your work, you like the people you work with and you know you are doing a good job for your customers.

The leisure and tourism industries offer this 'feel good' factor. It can be an excellent way to make a living and develop a career. You will find that you probably have to start your career at the lowest level, commonly known as 'the bottom of the ladder'. You must then be prepared to do anything (within reason), learn as much as you can and be enthusiastic in your work. This way you will climb the ladder and maybe reach the top.

Another positive aspect of the work you will be doing is that you have the opportunity to make people happy. Customers you look after may thank you and recommend your organisation. This will most certainly impress your manager.

Realistically, however, it will not be all fun and games. You will have to deal with complaints and calm those customers who want to let off a little steam. You will learn to cope with this – it's all part of the job.

This book covers all the topics required for you to complete your qualification. There are plenty of interesting and motivating case studies which bring the world of work alive for you.

Your course will include some or all of the following:

- teamwork tasks and activities
- learning new skills
- listening to guest speakers
- giving presentations
- building self-confidence
- achieving things you never thought you could.

How you will be assessed

Assessment is by means of portfolio evidence and an external test. Unit 1 has an external test which is set and marked by the exam board. Assessment material similar to that which you will be expected to complete in order to pass the unit can be found at the end of each unit. Units 2 and 3 are assessed by means of a portfolio which is marked by your teacher/tutor and is moderated by the exam board.

Finally, good luck with your studies and have an exciting journey in your chosen career.

Unit 1 Investigating leisure and tourism

The leisure and tourism industries consist of many different facilities, products and services ranging from swimming pools and sports centres to travel agents and tour operators. This unit looks at the key components of each industry and discovers how leisure and tourism are linked.

The leisure and tourism industries offer a variety of facilities

The knowledge you gain from learning about the characteristics of the leisure industry will be put into practice during your investigation into the leisure industries in an area. The information you gather will enable you to match the facilities you investigate to the key components of the leisure and tourism industries.

This unit also looks at the travel and tourism industry and you will find out about the tourist destinations that people visit and how they spend their leisure time at these places. It also examines the key components that make up the travel and tourism industry. These components consist of products and services for people in the UK who visit tourist destinations.

Your studies will also include an investigation into a selection of the popular tourist destinations in the UK including their location, how best to reach them and what they offer visitors when they arrive there.

Unit 1 provides a good foundation for more detailed study of the leisure and tourism industries that you will carry out in other sections of your GCSE in Leisure and Tourism.

Assessment

Unit 1 is assessed through an external assessment. You will find more details about this at the end of the unit.

What you will learn

- Chapter 1 The leisure industry
- Chapter 2 The travel and tourism industry
- Chapter 3 Links between leisure and tourism

Chapter 1: The leisure industry

This chapter looks at the definition of leisure and examines the seven components of the leisure industry.

The leisure industry offers many different facilities, products and services ranging from leisure centres to libraries. It's worth remembering that people like to spend their personal disposable income – the money left over after paying for essentials such as food, clothing and rent – on doing things they enjoy, for example going to the cinema, eating out or ten-pin bowling.

You can imagine when someone has done a hard day's work at the office or on the factory floor they want to unwind in their leisure time. For many people, especially those who don't like their jobs, their leisure time activities are more important than work.

This chapter also looks at the employment opportunities in the leisure industry, which might give you an idea about the type of career you may wish to follow.

What you will learn

- What is leisure?
- Leisure time activities
- The growth of leisure time
- Why is there a leisure industry?
- What makes up the leisure industry?
- Meeting leisure needs in different areas
- How different parts of the leisure industry interrelate
- Meeting people's leisure needs – leisure facilities
- Main factors influencing how people spend their leisure time
- Other factors affecting choice of leisure activities
- Employment opportunities in the leisure industry

Talk about it

In your group, decide on your own definition of leisure.

What is leisure?

Fact file

Leisure is the time remaining after work, travel to and from work, sleep and household chores. In other words, leisure time is that time when you can choose to do what you want. Leisure can also be described as the range of activities that individuals do in their free time.

How do you spend your leisure time?

Talk about it

Many people go to work purely for the pay. In your group, suggest other reasons why people go to work.

Investigating leisure and tourism · Unit 1

Activity

▶ Find some information about a job you could do in the future that would motivate you to go to work and enjoy it. You may be able to talk to someone doing that job now. Present your findings to the rest of your group.

▶ Ask three people (family or friends) you know who work full time why they go to work. Tell your group what you discovered.

Snapshot

Dan

Dan is 27 and single. He is a biker and spends hours working on his beloved 900 cc Honda Fireblade. He also supports Manchester United and hasn't missed a game in two years. Any time left over is spent playing computer games or going down to the pub with his mates.

Leisure time activities

Case study

Bob and Beryl

Bob and Beryl have been married for 40 years. They have three grown-up children who have all left home.

Bob is a home improvements fanatic who spends hours building wall units, making garden furniture and decorating every nook and cranny in the house.

Beryl loves gardening, throwing dinner parties for friends and playing bowls. Together they go ballroom dancing every Tuesday and Thursday evening and spend every other weekend at their caravan on the coast.

1. Do you know other retired couples who have similar lifestyles?
2. What seems to be the secret of their relationship?

Fact file

Facilities are the places where people can carry out their leisure activities. Both active and passive leisure activities take place in a wide range of facilities such as cinemas, clubs, libraries, leisure centres, restaurants and the home. They even include natural features like mountains and lakes where you can take part in outdoor pursuits such as climbing, walking, canoeing and sailing.

Products include food and drink, sports clothing, gifts, souvenirs or a holiday.

Services may include information given by a receptionist, coaching or supervision provided by leisure centre staff or the use of facilities like the car park, changing rooms or even the bar.

Facilities – places where people carry out leisure activities, e.g. health and fitness club, theme park, swimming pool

Leisure industry provides:

Products, e.g. sports equipment, food and drink, souvenirs

Services, e.g. coaching, information and advice

The leisure industry provides facilities, products and services

Snapshot

Jasmine

Jasmine is 17 and has just started work as a junior travel consultant after successfully completing her GCSE in Leisure and Tourism. She enjoys aerobics, horse riding and going to the local nightclub with her friends. She hopes to spend her future leisure time travelling abroad.

To sum up the meaning of facilities, products and services, we can say:

A leisure centre (*facility*) sells sports equipment (*products*) and offers coaching courses (*service*).

A restaurant (*facility*) serves fast food (*products*) and also has a 'drive-thru' for customers (*service*).

Activity

▶ Write a sentence similar to the above examples showing your meaning of facilities, products and services.

Leisure is one of the fastest-growing industries in the UK. People are always looking for new ways to spend their leisure time, which means that leisure activities are many and varied, and include activities such as those shown in Figure 1.1.

Figure 1.1 *Ways of spending your leisure time*

Talk about it

In your group, talk about which of these leisure activities you do.

Let's look at these activities in a little more detail.

Reading

Believe it or not, in these days of 24-hour television, reading is still a very popular leisure time activity. As well as books, there are newspapers and numerous glossy magazines which can be read, for example, on the bus or train to work.

Talk about it

'Reading does to the mind what exercise does to the body.' In your group, discuss what you think this means.

Sport

Fact file

Sport involves all forms of physical activity aimed at improving physical fitness and well-being.

We now live in an age of healthy lifestyles and 'image' so anything to improve fitness, like sport, has become increasingly popular. The UK is a sports-loving nation and if we are not taking part in sport we are often watching it – on the touchline or the television.

Talk about it

In your group, talk about why you think many students give up sport when they reach the age of 16.

Going to the cinema or disco

In the 1980s watching videos at home largely replaced going to the cinema. This has now changed. Cinema attendances are as high now as they were in their heyday before everyone had a television.

Luxury seating, a wide choice of films and the quality of the films themselves are three factors which now attract people more and more to the cinema. Films with hi-tech special effects and surround sound can be appreciated better on the big screen.

Talk about it

In your group, talk about how often you each go to the cinema. Which types of films are the most popular? What's your favourite film?

Going to a disco on a Friday or Saturday night is the highlight of the week for many people. The attractions are socialising with friends, dancing and meeting new people. Discos are not exclusive to the over-18s as many youth clubs hold regular Friday night discos. Some clubs hold discos on other evenings from 7.30 pm to 10.00 pm for the 14–16 age group. Soft drinks only are served as people dance to the latest chart sounds.

Talk about it

In your group, which of you regularly goes to a disco? What are the attractions? Is the term 'disco' a little out of date?

Going for a walk

Going for a walk remains a popular leisure time activity. After all, it's healthy, it's free and you can walk anywhere and at any time of the year. There are even walking clubs.

Watching television or listening to music

The average weekly television viewing time per person is 25 hours. Soaps, sport, cooking, DIY and gardening programmes dominate television. Add to that the endless quiz shows and you have the basic make-up of what we watch.

Listening to music on the radio or CD players or personal stereos is an everyday activity.

Activity

> Just for fun, work out how many televisions, radios and CD players there are in your home! Make a list and compare with it the rest of your group.

Eating out

Did you know?

Eating out is one of the most popular leisure activities. People now spend more money than ever before on eating out.

Eating out is one of the most popular leisure activities

There is a wide variety of restaurants which promote special offers like 'two meals for the price of one' or discounts for party bookings. Food is not only served in restaurants. Nearly all pubs now serve food. This attracts more customers and so increases income.

Activity

> Working in your group, identify a range of restaurants in your local area. You will realise there are many types, including fast food, à la carte, wine bars, bistros, family or ethnic (Chinese, Indian, Thai, Italian and so on). Put the names and types of restaurant into a chart.

Playing computer games

Sometimes it's a case of 'when there's nothing much on television, let's go and play on the computer'. Some people are addicted to computer games, especially around Christmas time when a brand new game has just been launched.

> **Think about it**
> How much time do you spend playing games on the computer? Why do people spend so much time playing computer games? Do you think there are any harmful effects from spending too much time playing computer games?

> **Did you know?**
> Nearly one in two households has a computer.

Visiting a tourist attraction

Visitor attractions cover a wide range of facilities. The English Tourism Council describes visitor attractions as 'Historic buildings, museums and galleries, wildlife attractions, gardens, country parks, steam railways and leisure parks'.

People visit these attractions for fun, interest and entertainment. Many visitors from overseas are attracted to the UK because of its history and culture. Other visitors like to explore the countryside with its natural attractions such as lakes, mountains and rivers.

Milestones in the development of leisure

1815 – first steam-driven sea voyage (Glasgow to Dublin)
1830 – first passenger train service (Manchester to Liverpool)
1841 – Thomas Cook's first 'day' excursion

> **Did you know?**
> Thomas Cook is known as the 'grandfather' of the travel industry. By 1885 he was running his own travel company, arranging trips and tours both at home and abroad.

1860 – invention of bicycle (independent travel for the masses)
1870 – 60-hour working week became the standard. Half-day holiday introduced on Saturday afternoon, later termed the 'weekend'

> **Talk about it**
> Imagine you worked 60 hours a week in a factory. How would this affect your life?

1871 – Bank Holiday Act establishes four public Bank Holidays, see Figure 1.2.

> **Activity**
> ▶ Find out how many Bank Holidays we have in the UK. List them all and give the dates.

1900s – vast improvement in road, rail, sea and air transport
1938 – Holidays with Pay Act introduced paid holidays for employees
1952 – first jet airline passengers
1960s – introduction of 37-hour week
1968 – first cross-Channel hovercraft service
1976 – Concorde goes into service
1980s – leisure technology takes off in the home
1990s – Eurotunnel carries first passengers
2000 – Millennium Dome opened (and closed)

The 1960s, 1970s and 1980s were influenced by a youth culture that was dominated by music, dancing and fashion. Television took over from the cinema and crazes like ten-pin bowling and skateboarding came and went. Indoor leisure activities including computers and watching videos tended to replace the outdoor activities of the early twentieth century.

During the 1980s wealthier young people began to enjoy sports which cost a lot of money to take part in such as hang-gliding, ballooning and powerboat racing. The terms 'yuppie' (young, free and single) and 'dinky' (double income', no kids) were coined in this decade.

Most leisure activities have become available to all, although it is still apparent, as we have seen through history, that the more wealth and status people have, the greater amount of leisure they enjoy. This repeated itself in the 1990s and there is no reason to suggest it will change in the twenty-first century.

> **Talk about it**
>
> In your group, discuss how you see leisure developing over the next ten years.

The growth of leisure time

There is now more leisure time available to the individual than ever before. This is due to factors such as:

- early retirement
- a reduction in working hours
- greater paid holiday entitlement
- new technology, for example microwaves and dishwashers, enabling people to spend less time on household chores
- an increase in life expectancy
- an increase in disposable income – the money left over after you have paid for essentials, like rent, food and clothing
- the growth in employment.

Not surprisingly, retired people have most leisure time. The unemployed have greater flexibility over their leisure time but less choice in the activities they can afford. Generally, people in work have more money to spend on leisure activities and take part in these activities between 5.00 and 11.00 pm on weekdays and at weekends.

These sports have been enjoyed by wealthier people. Name some sports that cost little or no money to enjoy

> **Think about it**
>
> Study the chart on page 8 showing how people in the UK spend their leisure time. How do people's leisure activities change as they get older?

Activity	Age				
	16–24	25–34	35–44	45–59	60+
	Hours per week				
Television or radio	14	15	13	17	26
Visiting friends	7	5	4	4	4
Reading	1	1	2	3	6
Talking, socialising and phoning friends	3	3	3	4	4
Eating out and drinking	6	4	4	4	2
Hobbies, games and computing	2	2	1	3	3
Walks and other recreation	2	2	1	2	3
Doing nothing (may include illness)	1	1	1	2	2
Sports participation	3	1	1	1	1
Religious, political and other meetings	–	1	1	–	1
Concerts, theatre, cinema and sports spectating	1	1	–	–	–
Other	1	–	–	–	–
All free time	40	37	33	40	42

How people in the UK spend their leisure time, by age
Annual Abstract of Statistics, ONS, 2002

Activity

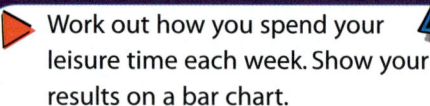

- Work out how you spend your leisure time each week. Show your results on a bar chart.
- Analyse your group's average weekly amount of leisure time.

Talk about it

Does anyone in your group have an unusual hobby?

Did you know?

Some people may not be able to take part in some leisure activities because of religious and cultural traditions. For example, Muslim women following Islamic laws are not allowed to show any part of their bodies. Obviously, this restricts their sporting activities. In some areas, for example Birmingham, a compromise has been reached at some leisure centres for Muslim women who want to swim. Women-only swimming lessons using female lifeguards have been introduced and have been very popular.

Why is there a leisure industry?

People now work fewer hours per week than ever before. Trade union pressure and government legislation have resulted in the working week being reduced from 45 hours to, on average, 37 hours.

Leisure has developed as a direct improvement in technology and improved transport systems that have enabled people to travel for education and pleasure.

Activity

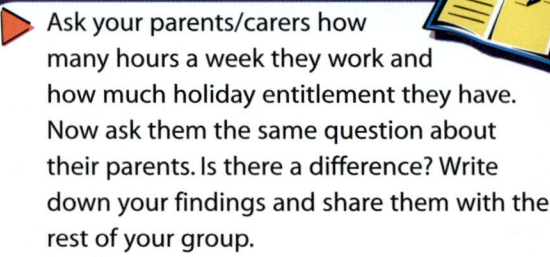

- Ask your parents/carers how many hours a week they work and how much holiday entitlement they have. Now ask them the same question about their parents. Is there a difference? Write down your findings and share them with the rest of your group.
- Find out about the European Union directive on the working week.

Investigating leisure and tourism   Unit 1

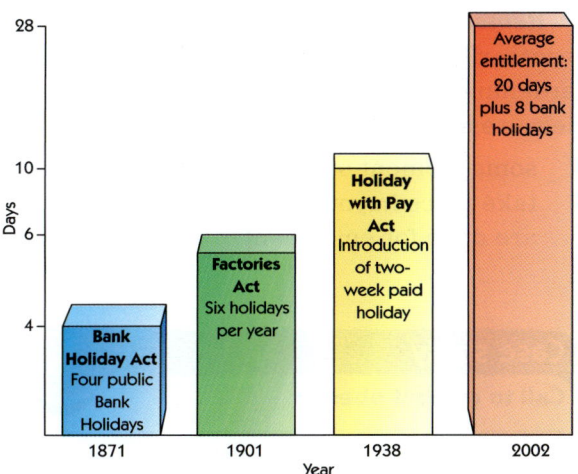

Figure 1.2 Holiday entitlement since 1871

What makes up the leisure industry?

As we have seen, the leisure industry covers a vast range of activities, from train spotting to bungee jumping. It also offers a wide variety of facilities, from the local authority swimming pool to huge sports stadia. It is therefore useful to divide the industry into the following components, or parts:

- sport and physical recreation, e.g. football, badminton, trampolining
- arts and entertainment, e.g. clubs, cinemas, theatres
- countryside recreation, e.g. climbing, hiking, cycling
- home-based leisure, e.g. home improvements, gardening, watching television
- children's play activities, e.g. play parks, adventure playgrounds, play schemes
- visitor attractions, e.g. Alton Towers, Buckingham Palace, Hadrian's Wall
- catering, e.g. fast-food outlets, pubs, cafés.

Sport and physical recreation

Trampolining is a popular physical recreation. What sport or physical recreation do you enjoy doing and how often do you take part?

Talk about it

In recent decades, new technology has reduced the need for human labour. This has led to a rise in unemployment. The resulting enforced leisure time could possibly lead to growing crime and social disorder. This may be especially so where people affected do not have the necessary work skills for today's society. In your group, discuss this issue.

Nowadays, people tend to have more time and money to spend on leisure (Figure 1.2) and with both parents working, families often want to spend their leisure time together. This has led to:

- family tickets at theme parks, heritage centres and so on
- pubs with family rooms
- fast-food restaurants aimed at families
- package holidays which provide activities for the whole family.

	1987	1988	1989	1990	1991	1992	1993	1994/5	1995/6	1996/7	1997/8	1998/9	1999/2000
Leisure services	18.11	18.13	19.02	21.54	22.20	27.56	25.56	31.20	32.05	33.95	38.81	41.90	43.90
Leisure goods	9.03	9.65	10.97	11.28	12.06	13.32	13.26	13.89	13.23	15.17	16.35	17.80	18.00

Average weekly household expenditure on leisure activities and goods, 1987–2000 (£)
Annual Abstract of Statistics, ONS, 2002

Activity

▷ Let's have some fun. Who is the fittest student in the room? Who can do most press-ups?

▷ List the benefits of exercise.

Fact file

Sport means all forms of physical activity, either casual or organised, usually with some element of competition aimed at improving well-being and social participation.

Some people enjoy playing badminton two or three times a week where they know they will meet their friends and enjoy being part of a group. This is one of the most important aspects of sport – meeting people and enjoying their company. That explains why there are so many sports teams in the UK.

Sport can also be an individual activity; for example, a runner may want to achieve a personal best time or a snooker player may want to achieve a century or even a maximum break.

Whatever the reason, the popularity of sport and physical recreation is growing all the time. Thirty years ago, someone running alone on a dark winter's night would have been considered slightly eccentric. Not any more. Today, joggers can be seen pounding the pavements everywhere come rain, hail or shine. Just look at the popularity of the London Marathon and the Great North Run.

Did you know?

Sport England is part of the Department for Culture, Media and Sport (a government department) and plays a major part in developing sport in England.

Activity

▷ Look up the website for Sport England or Sport Scotland or The Sports Council for Wales and list the aims of the organisation you have chosen.

▷ 1. How many people take part in the Great North Run?
2. What is the distance of a half marathon?

Remember: Physical recreation doesn't necessarily have to be sport. Activities like gardening, home improvement and walking for pleasure all have:

- some element of physical activity
- take place in your leisure time
- are done for enjoyment.

Case study
Call to combat obesity

Obesity in the UK has reached shocking levels and contributes to 30 000 deaths each year, a committee of MPs said yesterday.

Products such as Sunny Delight and Walker's Crisps – as well as a host of chocolate bars, snacks and sugary drinks – are advertised heavily on television.

Most adults in the UK are overweight and around 8 million are obese. The problem is estimated to cost £2.6 billion in NHS bills and working days lost.

Paul Kendall, 'Call to combat obesity', Daily Mail, *7 January 2002*

1. Do you think that as a nation we are overweight?
2. If you were the minister responsible for health care, how would you tackle the problem of obesity?

Talk about it

How do you feel about PE being a compulsory subject at school?

Activity

▷ How many local sports clubs are in your area? Who do you think runs them?

▷ Local sports clubs usually have committees to ensure the club runs smoothly. Give the official title of the person who:
  a acts as the co-ordinator
  b organises the money
  c takes the minutes
  d informs the media.

Did you know?

There are four 'S' factors in fitness: stamina, strength, speed, suppleness.

Aerobics, circuit training and keep-fit classes promote the ideas that exercise:

- is good for you
- helps you lose weight
- makes you feel good
- helps you make friends.

All these claims are true providing you exercise regularly, perhaps three times a week.

Talk about it

Someone once said that teenagers rarely break sweat, tend to be overweight and are more likely to be chauffeured by car than walk. In your group, say whether you think this is a fair view.

Talk about it

In your group, discuss the dangers of watching too much television.

Sport as a business

Sport and physical recreation are big business and form a significant part of the national economy. There are many businesses, both local and national, servicing the sports industry, including:

- the media, e.g. football magazines
- merchandising, e.g. souvenirs, flags, pendants
- transportation, e.g. coach trips to sporting events
- clothing, e.g. football strips, training shoes
- catering, e.g. food for supporters on the way to and at venues
- venues, e.g. racecourses, football grounds.

Did you know?

Total consumer expenditure (the things we buy) on sport and physical recreation was £15 billion in the UK in 2000. We spent £6 million on sportswear and £4 million on sports participation.

Business organisations recognise the value of sport to their business. In 2000, they spent £355 million on sports sponsorship. Examples of sponsorship from business sectors include car, insurance, computer, sports clothing and alcoholic drinks companies.

Talk about it

Sponsorship attracts big money for top sportsmen and sportswomen. A Premiership footballer may be sponsored by a sportswear company as much as £1 million per year. Add his wages of £800 000 a year and you soon see his take-home pay is quite good!

In pairs, discuss whether you think anyone is worth that amount of money. How do you feel when you read about top sportsmen and sportswomen earning £90 000 per week?

Many sports clubs rely on sponsorship for an income. Who sponsors your local football team?

Chapter 1   The leisure industry

Activity

▶ Find a television guide and work out how many hours are devoted to sport in one week on terrestrial, cable and satellite channels.

Did you know?

Facilities like football and cricket grounds offer spectators much more than an opportunity to watch a game. They have restaurants, souvenir and sportswear shops, conference suites, guided tours and even museums related to the club's history.

These additional facilities are aimed at providing spectators with a full day's entertainment, as well as encouraging them to spend more money. The main aim is to ensure spectators come back and bring along their families and friends. This is called repeat business and word-of-mouth advertising (see Unit 2).

Did you know?

Sport has great traditions. National and international events, like the ones shown below, boost its popularity.

- The FA Cup Final – probably the world's most famous football match.
- The Olympic Games – held every four years and moved around various venues throughout the world.
- The World Cup – football's premier competition.
- The Tour de France – known as the toughest bike race in the world.
- The Grand National – the world's greatest steeplechase held at Aintree racecourse, Liverpool.
- Wimbledon Lawn Tennis Championships – the world's top tennis tournament.
- Test match cricket – Australia playing England at Lord's for the Ashes.
- Rugby Union – the Six Nations' Cup.

Case study

The London Marathon

The first London Marathon took place in 1981. The race now attracts 33 000 runners of all abilities.

This is how Richard Brumby, aged 43, and a good club runner described his first marathon:

> There was great anticipation and excitement at the start. The atmosphere was incredible as more than 30 000 runners squeezed together and waited for the start gun.
>
> For the first ten miles I felt great as I was carried along by the cheering crowds. After this initial feeling I had to start concentrating on my running as I had another sixteen miles to go.
>
> Whenever I felt tired I looked round at all the sights and sounds of London in all its glory. I knew I was half way round when I crossed Tower Bridge.
>
> The second half of the race was a bit of a nightmare. I had to dig really deep into my energy reserves. Thank God, I had spent four months training for this. My legs felt like lead but I didn't care; I could see the finishing line. I felt so proud and relieved when I knew I'd done it.
>
> The words 'never again' sprung to mind, yet the following month I started making plans for next year's race. What a glutton for punishment!

1. Why do you think people like Richard Brumby put themselves through all that torture to run 26.2 miles?
2. What attractions does the London Marathon have for both runners and spectators alike?

The Olympic Games

Activity
1. What is the Olympic motto?
2. What was the name of the Frenchman who organised the first modern Olympics?
3. Who has won five Olympic gold medals?
4. How did Britain triumph in the Winter Olympics in 2002? What do you know about the sport of curling?

Many events at the 1900 Olympics were disorganised. Some sprints were run downhill. The discus and hammer were held in a city park where competitors kept hitting the trees. Swimming took place in a river with a strong current.

The Olympic Games have developed into a worldwide event incorporating summer and winter Games.

The Olympic motto is 'Citius, Altius, Fortius' which is Latin for 'Swifter, Higher, Stronger'. There is a second, longer, unofficial motto which describes what could be called the true Olympic spirit: 'The most important thing in the Olympic Games is not to win but to take part'. This might seem hard to believe nowadays in a world when winning seems to mean everything and coming second is often portrayed in the media as failure.

Talk about it
In your group, talk about the meaning of the unofficial Olympic motto. Do you agree with it?

Activity
Investigate the major controversies and incidents which took place at the following Olympic Games:

a Germany, 1936
b Mexico, 1968
c Munich (Germany), 1972
d Montreal (Canada), 1976
e Moscow (USSR), 1980
f Seoul (South Korea), 1988.

Talk about it
If an athlete sets a national or world record, he or she is automatically tested for banned substances. Use of banned substances can lead to penalties for athletes. In your group, discuss your views of athletes taking banned substances to improve performance.

What is the Olympic motto?

Chapter 1   The leisure industry

Talk about it

A 'Kick Racism Out of Football' campaign was recently launched in a bid to stop racist comments being hurled at footballers from different ethnic backgrounds during matches. The campaign had the backing of the football authorities and any spectator found guilty of this type of racism faced legal action and a ban from football grounds.

In your group discuss what role sport should play in overcoming racism.

Did you know?

Until recently, Yorkshire Cricket Club allowed only players born in Yorkshire to play for the club. This restricted playing opportunities for people from other parts of the UK and from other countries. Today, the doors at Yorkshire Cricket Club are open to talented cricketers from any part of the world.

Talk about it

Imagine your group has won £100 to spend on four arts and entertainment activities shown in Figure 1.3. In your group, decide where you would spend the money.

Activity

- Look at Figure 1.4 showing attendance at cultural events in the UK. What do the statistics tell you about the popularity of cultural events in 2001? Write down your answers.

Talk about it

In your group, do any of you go to the opera/ballet/theatre? What do you think attracts people to these activities and facilities?

Arts and entertainment

Arts and entertainment cover a wide range of leisure activities as shown in Figure 1.3.

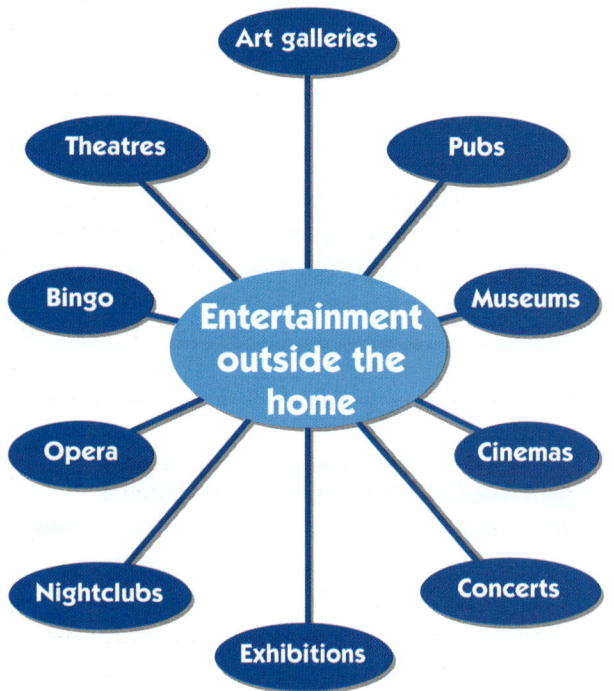

Figure 1.3 Entertainment outside the home

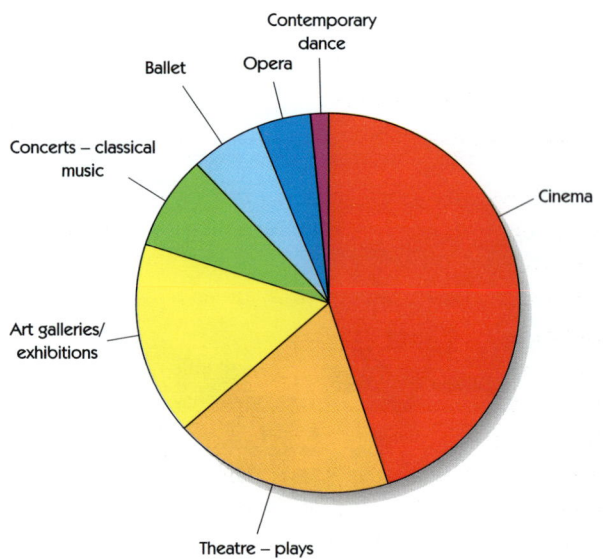

Figure 1.4 Attendance at cultural events, UK, 2001
Social Trends 29, ONS, 1999

Theatres

You can go to a theatre to see a play by Shakespeare or a clown being hit in the face with a custard pie. Theatre can make you laugh or cry, or frighten you. It can be acted, sung, or danced, or all three. Turn on the television tonight and you will probably find a play.

However, there is nothing to beat the excitement of an audience watching live performances on stage. Imagine you are watching these performers on television and then imagine them on a stage in front of you, only a few metres away.

Theatre is alive and exciting for everyone, from the audience to the actors on the stage to the many people behind the scenes.

Theatre does not just mean drama. Increasingly, theatres are used for a wide range of performing arts, such as concerts, cabaret and light entertainment.

Many theatres run clubs and workshops, as well as family membership schemes, designed to increase the interest of young people.

Activity

- Find out what's on at a local theatre. What range of productions does it offer?

- Find out as much as you can about the world of acting. How does a young performer start? Where do actors and actresses train? What types of production can they go into?

As well as the performance, theatres offer their customers other facilities such as food and drink, either through a coffee shop, bistro or theatre bar. A combined dinner and theatre ticket has become a popular way to spend an evening. This package is more usually offered by city theatres, which link up with a local hotel or restaurant. The ticket includes first and main courses served at the restaurant before the performance, then a break to attend the theatre performance, and then back to the restaurant to end the evening with dessert and coffee.

Some frequently asked questions about London theatres

Q Do I have to wear formal or informal clothes when I go to the theatre?

A It does not matter what you wear nowadays. You will not look out of place whether you wear a suit and tie, or jeans and a T-shirt.

Q Where can I get cheap tickets in London?

A The half-price ticket booth in Leicester Square sells top-price tickets for most shows at half price plus a small service fee. Nearly all theatres offer concessions to students, senior citizens and the unemployed, normally one hour before the performance.

Q How far in advance can I buy tickets?

A Usually two weeks in advance, except for really popular shows where two months may be needed. There is a possibility, if you are lucky, to buy tickets on the day.

Activity

- Find a copy of a national Sunday newspaper which gives a 'What's on' guide to the London theatres. In pairs, write down the name of six London theatres and make a note of what is being performed at each of them. Can you find out the ticket prices? What seems to be the most popular type of show?

- Recently, two long-running productions in London – 'Starlight Express' and 'Cats' – closed. Try to find out why this is.

Did you know?

There are 500 professional theatres in the UK, of which 96 are located in or around Greater London.

London has two National Theatre companies: the Royal Shakespeare Company (RSC) at the Barbican, and the Royal National Theatre on the South Bank.

Activity

- Find out which are the main theatres in Manchester, Birmingham and Bradford.

Did you know?

Making people laugh is a serious business. There are two basic types of gag or joke: those which are verbal, such as funny lines; and those which are physical, like falling flat on your face. There is often comedy in serious plays. This is because, as in real life, laughter keeps breaking in at serious moments.

Chapter 1   The leisure industry

Talk about it
Share your favourite joke with your group (keep it clean!).

Activity
▶ Try to make up a joke. How difficult did you find this?

Did you know?
Here are some common terms used in the world of theatre:

- understudy – actor or actress prepared to take over another performer's role in an emergency
- auditorium – the part of a theatre building where the audience sits
- props – any articles or objects used in a play, except for the scenery and costumes
- audition – a trial performance to judge an actor's or actress's skills and suitability for a role.

Activity
▶ 1. Find an example of a museum for each of the following categories: maritime, transport, film and photography, science.
2. What does the term 'listed building' mean?

Museums

Fact file
A **museum** is an institution housing collections of objects of artistic, historic or scientific interest, which have been preserved and displayed for the education and enjoyment of the public.

Museums appeal to people with a desire to understand the past and the present. Research has shown the most common reason for visiting museums was the chance to 'learn and find out about things'. The second most popular reason was to take advantage of 'facilities under cover protected from the weather'.

Talk about it
Museums are places where you can learn about the past. Imagine you were in charge of a popular museum. In your group, talk about how you could encourage learning to take place.

There are approximately 900 museums in the UK. More than half of these are housed in listed buildings, themselves a source of public interest. That interest extends to 110 million visits to museums each year.

Changing image
In recent years, many museums have tried to change their image from one of dark, dreary and unwelcoming places to one where visitors can learn about the past in a fun, exciting and entertaining way. Some have changed into living museums where actors and actresses play the roles of those who lived in the past to describe to visitors what life was like. Craftspeople have been invited into museums to show visitors processes that they would not normally have a chance to see. Other museums have introduced technology to bring history to life through animated displays.

To appeal directly to children, a number of museums have introduced a 'hands-on' policy which allows people to touch exhibits. The Science Museum in London, Jorvik in York, the new Royal Armouries Museum in Leeds, Tales of Robin Hood, Nottingham, and the Eureka! Children's Museum in Halifax are examples of a new kind of museum in action, while Ironbridge Gorge Museum, Beamish Museum, Wigan Pier and the National Maritime Museum in Liverpool are examples of museum sites which recreate historical times so that visitors can witness the sights, sounds and smells of times gone by.

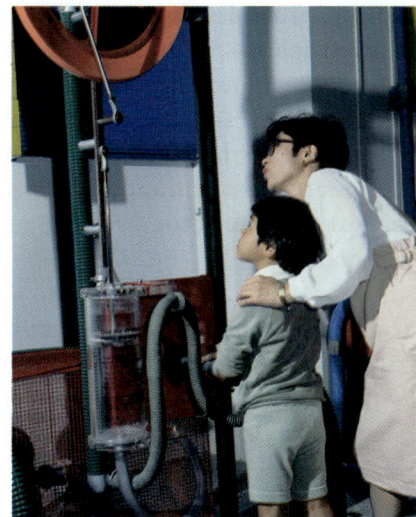

Hands-on exhibits are part of the modern museum experience

Activity

For any four of the following museums and galleries (British Museum, Science Museum, The Royal Armouries, National Railway Museum, The Tate Gallery and the National Gallery) find out:

a where the museum/gallery is
b what kind of admission fee is charged, if any
c what is exhibited there.

Working in museums

Case study

JORVIK

Many people in York work in facilities provided for tourists, for example the York Castle Museum, the National Railway Museum, the Yorkshire Museum of Farming and JORVIK, which has become one of the UK's most popular museums.

It is a new kind of museum, built on the site where archaeologists discovered the remains of the Viking City of York. A specially designed 'time-capsule' takes visitors on a journey through Jorvik, the name by which the Vikings knew York. The centre is a reconstruction of life in the Viking city.

An audio commentary is provided as the time-capsule carries its passengers back into the Viking Age, through streets, houses and workshops and past life-sized models of people as they were in AD 975.

Technology allows the noises and smells – both pleasant and unpleasant – of Viking York to be experienced. The centre allows visitors to experience at first hand, life as it once was, without the need for barriers or 'keep-off' signs. After the time-car journey, visitors can walk through a state-of-the-art gallery containing 800 of the finds discovered on site. Costumed 'Viking' staff complete the visitor experience.

1. Why do you think JORVIK is especially popular with foreign tourists?
2. JORVIK brings displays to life. How could you bring a pop music museum to life?

Art galleries

Fact file

An **art gallery** is a building or room for the public exhibition of works of art. In art galleries run by local authorities, works of art are usually exhibited (displayed) for public enjoyment or education; in privately run commercial art galleries, works are usually exhibited for sale.

The commercial art gallery plays an important role, both for collections of art and as the means by which living artists can sell their work and receive public recognition. Research has shown that attendance at art galleries tends to be class-based, with a lower proportion of people from unskilled, manual occupations attending than those from professional occupations.

London art galleries

The National Gallery in Trafalgar Square contains one of the finest collections of paintings in the world. Next door is the National Portrait Gallery, with a collection of more than 9000 portraits. The Tate Gallery, situated on the Embankment between Chelsea and Westminster, houses the largest collection of British paintings from the sixteenth century to the present day. In 1987 an extension opened to house the paintings bequeathed to the nation by the artist J M W Turner. There is also a new Tate Gallery of Modern Art – the Tate Modern – which is housed in the former Bankside Power Station in Southwark.

Activity

Find out how many people have visited the Tate Modern since it was opened. Do you think it is a popular visitor attraction?

Bingo halls

Bingo was at its most popular in the 1960s and 1970s but slumped in the 1980s due to the video 'revolution' and increased home entertainment.

Bingo is still popular in seaside towns. Try walking along the promenade in Blackpool or

Margate without being tempted in by a bingo 'caller'. Bingo attracts 3 million players each year, employing 24 000 people in 900 clubs and bringing in £96 million in revenue per year.

Many bingo halls were converted into nightclubs during the 1980s and there is now a campaign to bring bingo back to its previous popularity.

Nightclubs

> ### Case study
>
> **Rahul, newspaper reporter**
>
> Rahul was asked by his editor to report on the local club scene following claims by members of the public that the town's nightspots were becoming centres for violence and drugs.
>
> Rahul contacted the local police to ask if these claims were true. They said they had heard the rumours and so they had decided to take action. Below is Rahul's report which appeared in the local paper.
>
> #### Dogs on patrol
>
> Sniffer dogs are to be used in a local nightclub to scent out drugs. The dogs will be used at weekends at 'Hot Lights'. The club's owners will not give any warning of the dogs' use to increase the chances of catching the culprits. Staff will also be checked out by the dogs. Anyone found with drugs will be detained until the police arrive.
>
> Although there have been violent incidents at the club in the past, there have been no reported problems since last year. The club manager, Terry Downes, said, 'The area in front of the club was generally accepted to be a centre for trouble and we don't disagree that patrons were involved but we are confident in the steps we have taken.'
>
> Parents/carers are obviously concerned about your welfare when it comes to alcohol, drugs and violence. How do you feel about these issues?

Nightclubs are venues where people go to have a good time after a hard week at work. The atmosphere is lively, hot and loud and the dance floor is full of people enjoying themselves. People pay good money to go to clubs and in return they expect fun, good music and a good night out.

Not everyone has the opportunity to go to a club, or even wants to! Different cultures have different values; for example a strict Asian family may not allow their daughter to attend a club as this would not be part of their culture.

Countryside recreation

> ### Talk about it
>
> In your group, say if you would you prefer to live in the countryside or a town or city? Give your reasons.
>
> What are the advantages and disadvantages of:
>
> a living in the country
> b living in a town or city?

Some city dwellers escape to the countryside to get away from the noise, rush and hustle and bustle of the city. They find that the peace and quiet of the open spaces, the mountains, rivers and lakes, helps them relax. Similarly, some people who live in the countryside enjoy the noise of the city as a contrast to the peace and quiet of the country.

Many people are attracted to the dramatic scenery offered by the countryside – rugged landscapes, coastlines and picturesque dales – and places such as North Wales and the Scottish Highlands attract visitors in their millions.

Many people like to sit and enjoy the scenery whereas the more active take part in camping, sailing, potholing, hang-gliding or even fell running.

National and local government and voluntary sector organisations are all involved in countryside recreation provision such as picnic sites, allotments, open spaces, parks and gardens.

People are attracted to the countryside to enjoy the scenery and to take part in activities

The government recognises the importance of the countryside and has set up the Countryside Agency.

Activity
- Find the Countryside Agency website on the Internet and list its aims.

Cycling

One of the most popular ways of seeing the countryside is by bicycle and, as a result, the National Cycle Network was established. This is an ambitious scheme, funded by National Lottery contributions, to create 10 000 miles of cycle paths across the UK. It is promoted by the charity Sustrans, which stands for sustainable transport. Sustrans is dedicated to designing and building routes for cyclists and walkers. In June 2000 the first 5000 miles of the network were opened. The next 5000 miles are to be developed by 2005.

Activity
- Find the Sustrans website on the Internet and, using a map of the UK, see if you can trace the 5000 miles now opened. You might even find part of the network is near you and maybe you could organise a cycling event with your group!

Walking and rambling

Walking in the countryside has always been a popular pastime. There are many clubs for ramblers and walkers. The Ramblers' Association offers information about countryside walks and routes.

Heritage Coasts

Around 32 per cent of scenic English coastline is conserved as Heritage Coasts. These special coastlines are managed so that their natural beauty is protected and, where appropriate, accessibility for visitors is improved. The first Heritage Coast was the famous white chalk cliffs of Beachy Head in Sussex. Now much of our coastline, like the sheer cliffs of Flamborough Head with its huge seabird colony, is protected as part of our coastal heritage.

National Trails

Many stretches of beautiful coastline – and indeed our wider countryside – are easily accessible by a network of public footpaths and bridleways, some of the most challenging of which are designated as National Trails.

The Countryside Agency has designated 13 routes as **Long-distance Footpaths**, and pays for most of their upkeep and waymarking. Where possible the routes have used existing rights of way and the remaining sections have been established largely through negotiation with landowners.

Activity
- In 2001, an epidemic of foot-and-mouth disease in sheep and cattle virtually closed off the British countryside for months. What precautions were put in place to try to prevent the spread of the disease?
- What impacts did the foot-and-mouth outbreak have on tourism?

The foot-and-mouth epidemic of 2001 had an immediate and disastrous impact on both the rural community and the tourism industry. It is estimated that the outbreak cost the UK £1.6 billion. Thirty-four per cent of firms in the tourism industry said that, as a result, business was below normal. A report suggests that 80 per cent of accommodation providers were affected.

National Parks provide opportunities to enjoy the countryside

> ### Case study
> **Foot-and-mouth**
>
> This letter appeared in the *Mail on Sunday* in January 2002:
>
> > The foot-and-mouth epidemic may have been declared officially over this week but my farming business is still suffering terribly. We are swamped by bureaucracy. When an animal needs to be moved, we have to apply for a licence and wait 20 days. Then the lorry has to be disinfected both before and after, costing at least £20 a time.
> > Because so many animals have been slaughtered, there is a real shortage of replacement stock. In a typical year my farm turns over 2000 cattle. This year it will be 200. No compensation can allow for this.
>
> *Paul Turner, Mail on Sunday, 20 January 2002*
>
> How do you think the government can help farmers like Mr Turner?

The National Parks

The first ten National Parks were created between 1951 and 1957. They were defined as 'an extensive area of beautiful and relatively wild country'. Since then, the Norfolk Broads was designated as a National Park in 1998, and a further two areas – the New Forest and the South Downs – are seeking National Park status.

The National Parks have two purposes:

- 'to conserve and enhance the natural beauty, wildlife and cultural heritage of the National Parks
- to promote opportunities for the public understanding and enjoyment of the special qualities of the Parks'.

(Council for National Parks)

Services provided in National Parks include:

- information and interpretation services – information centres, leaflets, books
- a ranger or warden service
- facilities for improving access for visitors – footpaths, stiles, waymarking
- provision of car parks and picnic sites
- assistance to voluntary conservation and wildlife groups.

> ### Did you know?
> In 1998, two-thirds of the British population visited the countryside. Each visitor spent on average £7 per visit.

Areas of Outstanding Natural Beauty

The Countryside Agency is responsible for designating Areas of Outstanding Natural Beauty and advising the government on how they should be protected. These areas can be found by logging on to the Countryside Agency's website. A link to this website can be found at www.heinemann.co.uk/hotlinks.

> ### Activity
> Choose a National Park such as Snowdonia and describe its main features.
>
> Compare and contrast the Norfolk Broads and Dartmoor.

Park	Area (hectares)	Visitor days (millions)
Brecon Beacons	135 144	7
Dartmoor	95 570	4
Exmoor	69 280	1.4
Lake District	229 198	22
Northumberland	104 947	1.5
North Yorkshire Moors	143 603	8
Peak District	143 833	19
Pembrokeshire Coast	62 000	4.7
Snowdonia	214 159	10.5
Yorkshire Dales	176 809	9
The Broads	30 292	5.4

Visitors to the National Parks, 1999
Council for National Parks website

Camping and caravanning

The attractions of camping and caravanning include:

- more freedom to move from one area to another
- it is more economic than hotels (despite the initial outlay for the caravan)
- the open-air experience
- opportunities to meet fellow holidaymakers on caravan and camp sites.

Local bylaws prohibit camping on many commons and areas where the public have access rights.

Parks, open spaces and the countryside

Going for a walk is the most popular recreational activity. Fourteen per cent of urban areas are Open Green Space and 73 per cent of people live in urban areas.

- Approximately £1.5 billion is spent each year on the management of and maintenance of parks and open spaces.
- The National Park area in England is 9934 sq. km; and in Wales is 4098 sq. km.
- Total employment supported by visitor attractions to the countryside is estimated to amount to 354 000 jobs.
- Spending by all visitors to the countryside was estimated at £11 billion in 1998: 77 per cent from day visits, 22 per cent from UK tourists and 6 per cent from overseas tourists.

Backpacking

The activities of the backpacker are considered to be compatible with the idea of a National Park, as long as the backpacker:

- obtains permission (where possible) before setting up camp
- is as unobtrusive as possible
- stays in small groups
- avoids pitch marks left by other tents
- removes all litter
- disposes of excrement and waste water sensitively.

Backpackers should not:

- camp in enclosed moorland without permission
- stay on one site for more than two nights
- make unnecessary noise
- camp within 100 metres of a road
- camp within sight of a house or road
- camp in a reservoir catchment area
- camp on small common areas
- camp on areas heavily used for informal recreation.

Talk about it

In pairs, talk about the skills and qualities you think you would need to take up abseiling, rock climbing and orienteering. Are you the adventurous type?

Snapshot

Serge

Hi, I'm Serge and every weekend I go to Matlock, Derbyshire, to take part in my favourite activity – rock climbing. I started three years ago at school and I've been a regular climber with the local club since then. I am now able to lead climbs. This is a huge responsibility as not only have I got my own safety to think about, but also my colleagues below me.

The things I like about rock climbing are the challenges of the climb, the sense of achievement (and relief) when reaching the top and the friendship that goes with the sport.

My ambition is to progress to mountaineering, and eventually climb in the Alps or even the Himalayas.

The effect of leisure activities on the countryside

When tourism and the environment exist together without any harm being done, the countryside in particular and the environment in general can benefit. Canals, country parks and conservation areas have been developed to provide extra attractions for tourists.

Unfortunately, there are negative impacts. Much of the damage to the countryside is caused simply by the number of tourists. Pressure from tourism can damage the countryside by:

- creating litter
- increasing pollution
- disturbing wildlife
- reducing habitats
- altering landscapes.

Talk about it

In your group, discuss how you think we could reduce the negative impact of tourism in the countryside? Do you think we should take more measures to protect the countryside?

Home-based leisure

We saw earlier that entertainment takes place in cinemas and theatres. However, most of our entertainment today is of our own making and takes place in the home. Over the past 20 years home entertainment has expanded with the introduction of cable, satellite and digital television, as well as computers. As a result, watching television has become the most popular home-based leisure activity followed by playing computer games.

Home-based leisure activities include:

- watching television
- listening to music
- gardening
- cooking for pleasure
- reading
- playing computer games.

Home improvement (DIY) keeps many people occupied in their leisure time and is also big business. Advertising by home improvement superstores such as Texas Homecare, MFI and

Activity

People like to visit the countryside to enjoy the scenery, have picnics and take part in activities such as rambling or fell walking. Design a picnic area in the countryside which would prove attractive to visitors but would not have a negative impact on the area.

Tourism can have a negative impact on the countryside

B&Q, and television programmes on gardening and home improvements, have encouraged people to tackle all sorts of jobs around the house and garden.

Did you know?

The annual expenditure on home-based leisure is £40 billion. The number of UK households with access to the Internet in June 1997 was almost 1 million. As of November 1999, there were 7 million adults registered with access to the Internet. In 2002, one in two households had Internet access.

Talk about it

In your group, talk about the sort of things you might find on the Internet. Do you think too much time spent surfing the Net might lead to isolation, exclusion or even people looking too much into themselves?

Programme type	Viewers (%)
Children's	7
Documentaries and features	8
Drama	24
Films	11
Light entertainment	17
News	21
Sport	11
Other	1

Television viewing: by type of programme in the UK

Activity

▶ Using the statistics on television viewing (above), produce a pie chart showing the type of programmes we watch in this country.

People's choice of home-based leisure activities is affected by factors such as availability of a garden, housing conditions and standard of living. The use of leisure time will vary according to the home itself, family interests and possessions such as radio, television, computer or video. It also depends on the number of time-saving appliances like microwaves and washing machines which release members of the household from household chores, thus creating more leisure time.

Did you know?

Another home-based leisure activity involves our pets. For example, exercising the dog could be classed as both a leisure time activity (the enjoyment of walking) or a chore (it has to be done!).

Children's play activities

Young children love to play. In fact, it is their main leisure time activity. It helps develop their social and physical skills and is part of

How do you spend your leisure time at home?

growing up. Play also gives children the opportunity to use their imagination and develop their creative skills.

Play provision includes adventure playgrounds, activity centres, after-school clubs and youth clubs.

> **Talk about it**
>
> It has been said that without play, there would be no sports, no arts and no games. In pairs, say whether you think this is true? Give your reasons.

Play areas

Public play areas are built and maintained by local authorities. They are often located in parks or within sight of housing developments where they can be overlooked and supervised.

Through play children experiment and use every opportunity to touch, look, feel and listen, so play areas should offer opportunities for these sensory experiences. The following should be taken into account when play areas are built:

- safety
- supervision
- equipment which should be interesting and challenging to children in terms of size, shape and colour
- equipment which children would enjoy using.

It is not only the public sector that recognises the importance of play. In the private sector, some pubs have created both indoor and outdoor play areas where children can play in safety while parents/carers enjoy a drink and a meal. The play area is intended to encourage families to become regular users of the facility.

> **Activity**
>
> 1. Visit a play area and evaluate it in terms of safety, location and equipment. Talk to parents and children there and ask what they think of the play area, how often they use it and how far they have travelled to use it.
> 2. Design and draw a play area, taking the following into account:
>   - location
>   - type of equipment
>   - fencing
>   - toilet provision
>   - main roads
>   - far enough away from adult playing areas, e.g. cricket pitches
>   - seating for adults.
>
> You should say what age of children your play area is intended for.

Is there a children's play area in a park near you? Is it well maintained and safe?

> **Talk about it**
>
> In your group, discuss what parts of play develop creativity and socialisation in young children.

Holiday play schemes

Holiday play schemes are often run by local authorities and aim to provide worthwhile activities such as sports, day trips, nature walks and camping.

Snapshot

A day in the life of Shazia, a summer play scheme assistant

Before the children arrive, I talk to the other assistants to plan the day's activities. We then get the equipment out and wait for the children.

This is how the day goes:

9.00 am	Take names, addresses and telephone numbers just in case we need to contact parents/carers
9.10 am	The first activity is rounders. I enjoy taking the children for sports and organising them into teams
10.00–10.15 am	Breaktime – soft drinks to organise
10.15–11.30 am	Nature trail
11.30–12.00 noon	Pop quiz
12.00–1.00 pm	Lunch
1.00–3.00 pm	Trip to swimming pool
3.00–3.30 pm	Say goodbye to the children and clear up
3.30 pm	Exhausted!

Believe me, there's never a dull moment!

Visitor attractions

Talk about it

Why are some rides at theme parks called 'white knuckle rides'? Imagine you have been selected to test the world's biggest and fastest roller coaster ride that travels at 90 mph in complete darkness. In your group, describe how you would feel.

The UK's largest roller coaster

Activity

▶ Design a brochure for a holiday play scheme which shows the activities for the week.

Activity

▶ Write down the name of a well-known visitor attraction connected with each of the following:

a cultural heritage
b sport
c entertainment
d leisure shopping.

Talk about it

In your group, discuss what facilities/activities the following organisations could offer in terms of play:

a   a leisure centre
b   a fast-food outlet
c   a doctor's waiting room.

Fact file

A **visitor attraction** is a place that attracts tourists and offers enjoyment, amusement, entertainment and education.

Visitor attractions give tourists something to do; they are the reason why tourists visit a destination. When people go on holiday, day trips or short breaks, they first find their

Chapter 1   The leisure industry

accommodation and then they look for entertainment. Visitor attractions provide them with fun, interest and entertainment.

The English Tourism Council categorises visitor attractions into:

- historic buildings
- museums and galleries
- wildlife attractions
- gardens
- steam railways
- leisure parks.

The above are manufactured attractions. Natural visitor attractions include lakes, mountains, beaches, rivers, forests and hills.

Case study

Bluewater

Bluewater is Europe's largest and most innovative retail centre. Built on a disused chalk quarry in Kent, just one mile east of the M25, it opened on 16 March 1999. Bluewater undertook research to find out what shoppers wanted to make shopping a stress-free, enjoyable experience. The centre has a wide range of facilities to cater for all users, such as wider parking spaces, nappy changing facilities and feeding rooms for parents with small children and an adventure playground, rowing boats and a crèche for children. Hosts are available to provide information to shoppers about facilities and provide help with shopping.

The centre is made up of three distinctive malls: The Guild Hall, The Rose Gallery and The Thames Walk. Each mall has an associated leisure village: The Village, The Water Circus and The Wintergarden. Each of the areas has a different theme: gourmet food and lifestyle at the Village, entertainment and media at the Water Circus and the family at the Wintergarden.

1. Undertake some more research into the facilities that Bluewater has to offer. In groups make a list of the features that make Bluewater an attractive shopping environment.
2. What do you look for in a shopping centre of this type?

Activity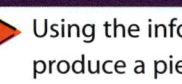

▶ Using the information below, produce a pie chart showing the percentage breakdown of visitors to United Kingdom visitor attractions in 2000.

Museums and galleries 23 per cent
Historic buildings 13 per cent
Wildlife attractions 6 per cent
Gardens 4 per cent
Leisure and country parks 27 per cent
Others 27 per cent

▶ Sixty per cent of all tourists from abroad visit London for the shopping and other attractions. Carry out some research and list some of the visitor attractions in London which act as a magnet to visitors.

Tourism is very important to the UK economy because of the income it generates. The British Tourist Authority estimates there were 400 million visits to visitor attractions in the UK in 2000.

Snapshot

David and Lena

David and Lena live in Brisbane. They come to the UK every four years to visit relatives and see the sights.

'We just love looking at your castles and stately homes. We haven't got anything like that back home, and we sure do like these Beefeaters at the Tower of London. We're moving on to Stratford to see Shakespeare's house and hopefully take in a play.

We usually spend a few days in Oxford to look round all the university buildings and then it's to Scotland to sample the delights of Edinburgh and the Highlands.

Next year we hope to do Europe for three months, spending six weeks in the UK. We just can't keep away!'

Think about it

What importance do you think tourism has for the UK economy? How did the terrorist attack on the World Trade Centre in New York on 11 September 2001 affect incoming tourism?

The case studies throughout this unit show the wide range of visitor attractions that the UK has to offer, including museums, historic sites, theme parks and shopping centres.

Activity

- In groups, carry out some research into London, Bristol or Chester Zoo. You need to find information about:

  a   admission charges
  b   public transport access from the nearest railway/tube station
  c   two other attractions close to the Zoo
  d   disabled facilities.

1. Who is most likely to visit this type of attraction?
2. Analyse the popularity of this type of attraction. (You may like to include wildlife parks as well).
3. Do you think the existence of zoos is justified when the public is concerned about maintaining animals in their natural habitat? (You may need to explore the types of research activity that can be carried out in zoos.)

Case study

Beaulieu

Fifty years ago, Beaulieu, located in the heart of the New Forest, first opened its doors to visitors. Today it is probably best known as being the home of the National Motor Museum. Even if you are not a fan of cars you will find something to enjoy. There is a range of attractions from a ride through motoring history to hands-on, interactive and multimedia displays. Visitors can see on display some of the world's most famous and glamorous vehicles.

As well as visiting the motor museum visitors can explore the delights of the Victorian Gardens, the fragrant Herb Garden and the surrounding less formal gardens and parkland.

Find out how Beaulieu is celebrating its fiftieth anniversary.

Case study

The Tower Of London

The Tower of London covers 900 years of British history. Guarded by the famous Yeoman Warders (Beefeaters), it has been a palace and a prison and has seen numerous executions including Lady Jane Grey and the ill-fated Anne Boleyn, whose ghost is said to still haunt the Tower. It is also famous for being the home of the Crown Jewels.

1. What ceremonies and traditions take place at the Tower of London?
2. The Yeoman Warders of the Tower of London are popular with tourists. Traditionally what is the role of a Yeoman Warder?

Case study

Meadowhall – leisure shopping

- Meadowhall is situated 3 miles (4.8 km) north east of Sheffield in the county of South Yorkshire (population 1.3 million), at the eastern end of the Lower Don Valley.
- The Lower Don Valley is an area approximately 2000 acres (about 800 hectares) stretching 3 miles (4.6 km) between Sheffield City Centre to the west, and the M1 motorway.
- Around 8.2 million people or 1 in 8 of the UK population live within an hour's drive of the site.
- Major towns and cities within this driving time include Leeds, Nottingham, Manchester, Hull, Leicester, Barnsley, Doncaster, Wakefield and Rotherham.
- The Centre occupies a level site extending 78.3 acres (31.6 hectares) immediately to the west of the M1 motorway. The site is bordered by an orbital ring road.
- The River Don flows in a clockwise direction around the northern site boundary and the riverside setting has been comprehensively landscaped to incorporate trees, walkways, cycling paths, seating and play areas.

Statistics

Since Meadowhall opened in 1990, the statistics have been impressive:

- Over 80 per cent of the multiple retailers at Meadowhall are in the 'Top Ten' of their company outlets, including 24 per cent which are the best performing outlet in the country.
- An average of 150 000 cars use Meadowhall each week.
- 20 per cent of customers use public transport.
- The average 'party' consists of 2.1 shoppers.
- The length of the average shopping trip is 2 hours and 17 minutes.

Attributes

Meadowhall offers an exceptional combination of all the attributes most commonly required of the local shopping environment. These are:

- location and catchment
- access and car parking
- size, design and layout
- leisure/catering
- customer service
- environment – clean, safe, secure.

Infrastructure

Motorway: The M1 motorway immediately adjoins the site, providing access from both northbound and southbound carriageways at Junction 34. A sophisticated computer-controlled traffic management system employing extensive CCTV coverage enhances road capacity and optimises traffic flow.

Car parking: 12 600 free car-parking spaces are provided. 350 of these parking spaces are specifically allocated for the disabled and parents with children.

Supertram: The Passenger Transport Interchange serves as a terminus for Sheffield's Supertram. A total of 88 trams per day, run every 10 minutes at peak times, linking Meadowhall with major city suburbs and the City Centre.

Coaches: The Meadowhall Coach Park provides parking for up to 200 coaches and is linked directly to the Meadowhall Centre by a footbridge.

Trains: Two stations accommodate Regional Railway trains, serving 240 routes nationwide every day. Intercity trains are also routed through the station.

All figures correct at time of publication – July 2002 (Meadowhall Centre Ltd)

What effect do out-of-town leisure shopping centres have on town centre shops?

Case study

Alton Towers

The park is open from 9.30 am each morning with rides running from 10 am. Closing times vary depending on the time of year. Visitors are advised to check in advance.

The magic gets stronger

At Alton Towers, there are world-class thrill rides and attractions, 200 acres of beautiful, mature gardens and loads for tiny tots or dotty aunties – so whether it's white knuckles or green acres you are after, there's something for everyone. In 2002, the thrills got better with the introduction of the unique flying rollercoaster, Air.

Relax and stay in a hotel with a difference. Opened in 1996, the Alton Towers hotel has 175 rooms set in beautiful private grounds. This is no ordinary hotel – it's filled with weird and wonderful surprises, from a 5-storey flying ship to eight unique themed suites, which include a chocolate room, a Coca Cola Fizzy suite and lifts like no others, the Alton Towers Hotel is the place to expect the unexpected.

Children love the magic of Alton Towers. They can discover a whole new world in Storybook Land. This enchanted area of charming surprises links Adventureland and Old Macdonald's Farm. Over in Cred Street, Barney the Dinosaur™ entertains young guests daily in his all-dancing, all-singing show.

More than a theme park

There's much more to Alton Towers than the themed attractions. With acres of gardens, punctuated with delightful unexpected surprises such as the Chinese Pagoda fountain, there's tranquillity alongside the thrills. And, of course, there are the Towers themselves. Still majestic, with origins dating back 1000 years, they cast an invisible aura around the park.

Visitors will find no shortage of great value restaurants and snack bars at the park. Whether you want a full three-course meal, fish and chips, a sandwich or just a soft drink, there's something to suit everybody's taste and pocket.

Some interesting facts

- A car on Nemesis travels 19 000 miles a season – enough to take it three quarters of the way around the world!
- Each assistant on the Grand Canyon Rapids walks 11 miles a day – the equivalent of walking from Lands End to John O'Groats over two-and-a-half times each season!
- Those who brave Nemesis experience greater G-Force than a NASA astronaut. Nemesis reaches a stomach-turning 4G, compared with the 3G experienced by an astronaut.
- Each Gondola on the Skyride travels 48 miles a day – enough miles in a season to get to Australia!

Alton Towers

1. Why is Alton Towers so successful?
2. Alton Towers is open between March and October. Find out what events are staged in the winter months.
3. What do people want from a day out at Alton Towers?

Case study
The Eden Project

The Eden Project is a living theatre of plants and people. In a giant crater in Cornwall the stories of the world are brought to life. In the huge covered conservatories, visitors can explore majestic rainforests, the Mediterranean, South Africa and California.

Eden is an international visitor attraction and a huge resource for education. Its main aim is to promote the understanding and responsible management of the vital relationship between plants, people and resources, leading to a sustainable future for all.

The conservatories that house the plants are called Biomes. The largest one is 200m long, 100m wide and 57m high. Even though it's the world's largest greenhouse it is hidden from view in a 60m crater the area of 35 football pitches.

The Eden Project is the only place in the world where, in a single day, you can visit a South American rainforest, Cameroon in West Africa, a Malaysian rainforest and the tropical Oceanic Islands. You can also meet plants that make chocolate and chewing gum, and plants that move.

The Eden Project

1. What makes the Eden Project unique?
2. How does it act as an education resource?
3. How can the Eden Project help the environment?
4. The following questions are part of a quiz organised for visitors to the Eden Project. See if you can answer them:
   a What fruit is thought to have been 'The golden apple' of mythology?
   b What were blackberries known as in the nineteenth century and why?
   c Which animals distribute grape seeds?

Case study
Las Vegas on the Golden Mile

Many new casinos are to open in seaside resorts in the UK following the government's relaxing of gambling laws.

In Blackpool, there are plans to develop a Las Vegas style gambling complex called Pharoah's Palace that would add new facilities to the town.

Other holiday centres including Bournemouth, Southend and Brighton are considering similar plans. This means that there may soon be over 200 casinos in the UK. At the moment there are 118.

These casinos will be allowed to offer live entertainment, alcohol on the gambling floor and games such as bingo and slot machines alongside traditional games such as roulette and cards.

In other planned changes, bingo halls will be able to offer rollover prizes and limits on prizes will be removed. Under-18s will be barred from using slot machines with a stake of more than 10p or a prize of more than £5.

1. What effects do you think these new regulations will have on resorts like Blackpool?
2. What does your group feel about gambling? You might like to discuss the positive and negative effects of gambling on individuals, on the establishments that run them and on society in general.

Activity

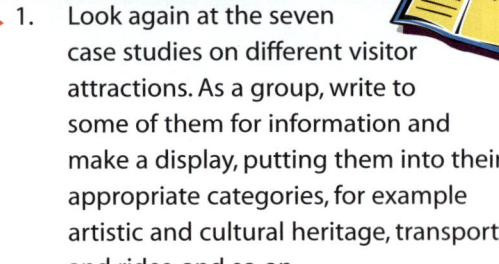

1. Look again at the seven case studies on different visitor attractions. As a group, write to some of them for information and make a display, putting them into their appropriate categories, for example artistic and cultural heritage, transport and rides, and so on.
2. Design and produce a leaflet which describes or 'sells' your area as a tourist attraction. Include illustrations to make the leaflet lively and interesting.
3. Find out and list the top ten tourist attractions in the UK.

Catering

Catering is linked with eating out, now classed as one of the most popular leisure activities in the UK. As a result, the catering industry has grown to meet this demand.

Catering is so much a part of modern life that it is estimated that up to a quarter of all food is now consumed away from home or taken into the home in a form in which it is ready to eat.

Fast-food outlets, bars and cafés, restaurants and pubs offer customers a wide choice of eating from quick snacks to à la carte meals. You can have your meal brought to you by a waiter or waitress or help yourself to a choice of dishes in a buffet.

Take-away services, in particular for Chinese and Indian meals and pizzas, have become increasingly popular. You can even have your meal delivered to your front door.

Probably the biggest growth in catering is in pub food. Many pubs now provide cooked meals, sandwiches and snacks. As families want to eat out together, pubs have introduced family rooms, play areas and children's menus to further attract this target market. What's more, pub food is popular as it is sometimes cheaper than restaurant food and yet can still be of a high quality.

Think about it

Fast food is quick and convenient, but is it good for us? Why do people like fast food and fast-food outlets so much?

Leisure facilities providing catering include the following:

- cinemas – confectionery, popcorn, hot dogs and drinks in the foyer
- leisure centres – vending machines and café
- theatres – bars and restaurants for interval drinks and a meal after the performance
- theme parks – fast-food outlets, restaurants, cafés, bars.

Activity

▶ Find out where members of your group like to eat out. Make a list and then classify the venues into four groups: pub food, fast food, ethnic and other restaurants. Which is the most popular?

▶ Write down the conclusions that you can draw from the eating out habits of the members of your group.

Eating out is a very popular leisure activity. It accounts for more than 30 per cent of our expenditure on food in the UK

Case study

Elizabeth, part-time waitress

Elizabeth is in Year 11. She has just started work as a part-time waitress in a small market town hotel. She works every Saturday from 7.00 am to 2.30 pm and 7.00 pm to 10.00 pm. Here she describes a typical day:

> Breakfast is served between 7.30 and 8.30 am. My first job is to make sure all the tables are set up and that everything is ready for the guests. 'Full English' is very popular around here and I can only dream of bacon sandwiches, as there's no time for me to grab a snack. After the rush of breakfast, it's time to prepare for the senior citizens' coffee morning, which starts at 10.00 am although they usually begin to arrive any time from 9.30 onwards. I enjoy the friendly banter with them but I have great difficulty getting rid of them (in the politest possible way of course). It's all very well to tell me about their vegetable patches and grandchildren, but I've got tables to set for lunch.
> My shift finishes at 2.30 pm and restarts at 7.00 pm. This is known as a split shift. Time flies by. As soon as one job is done, another needs doing. At the end of the day I am absolutely shattered. My feet are killing me and my mind is set on one thing only, a long, hot bath.
> I like the work as it pays for my social life and I work with some really great characters.

Jobs in catering are very hard work. The money isn't all that good either. As a result, there is a 'high turnover' of staff. What does this term mean? Why is catering such hard work?

Talk about it

Nearly everyone has had a bad experience eating out, for example the service has been terrible, the food has been inedible, and so on. In your group, share your worst experiences of eating out. What would you have done to improve the situation?

Meeting leisure needs in different areas

Think about it

How do you think the provision of leisure in a village differs from that in a town? Do people's leisure needs differ in these two areas?

Wherever you live there is usually a wide range of organisations and facilities which offer people the opportunity to take part in leisure activities of their choice. A village may have a tennis club, bowling green and a village hall which acts as both a sports and social facility. A town will probably have more leisure provision because of the number of people who live there. Cities have all the leisure facilities you can possibly think of to cater for residents, commuters and tourists.

Leisure provision in the three types of area identified above has changed over the past 20 years. Squash courts were being built everywhere 20 years ago as the sport reached its peak in popularity and participation. Leisure pools replaced rectangular swimming pools. Sunbeds and solariums were on offer to provide instant suntans. Skateboard parks were everywhere in the 1980s.

As always happens, fashions and trends change. Leisure provision now includes floodlit all-weather pitches for hockey, football and netball. Indoor tennis centres have sprung up and ten-pin bowling has become very popular.

A healthy lifestyle which includes looking good and feeling fit is being promoted in today's society. Hundreds of private fitness suites have opened across the UK which centre on the health and beauty market.

Ten-pin bowling has become very popular

Aromatherapy, complementary medicines and massages are now high on the list for people who want to improve how they look.

> **Talk about it**
> How does leisure provision vary in different parts of the UK? Why do you think this is?

How different parts of the leisure industry interrelate

The components, or parts, of the leisure industry that we have looked at are not standalone; they are often interrelated. For example:

- a leisure centre provides opportunities to take part in sport and physical recreation and, at the same time, it may have a bar and restaurant which therefore comes under catering
- mountaineering can be classed as both a sport and a countryside activity
- going to the theatre and then having a meal is a mixture of arts and entertainment and catering
- a theme park may have a children's playground which means there is a mixture of visitor attractions and children's play activities.

So, although the leisure industry is made up of different components, they are all more or less interrelated. Looking at them separately, as we have done, is the best way to show what makes up the whole of the leisure industry.

> **Talk about it**
> In your group, talk about how arts and entertainment may be interrelated to catering.

> **Case study**
>
> **Laura**
>
> Laura is 24 and leads a very full and active life. She loves going to aerobics classes with her friends because they have a good laugh at the Sports Centre and end up having a drink together.
>
> Laura's weekends are hectic. She will often drive to the Lake District on Saturdays to escape from the mad rush of the city, spend a couple of hours hiking and then have a pub lunch. She'll then drive home, put her feet up, watch a bit of television and fall asleep on the sofa.
>
> Laura spends Sundays with her niece and nephew aged 5 and 7. She takes them to the play park, treats them to a Happy Meal at McDonald's and then takes them to the cinema to watch a film.
>
> She looks forward to getting back to work on a Monday morning for a rest!
>
> Identify each of the components of the leisure industry that Laura takes part in and discuss their interrelationships.

Meeting people's leisure needs – leisure facilities

The term 'facilities' refers to equipment, buildings and structures and also features of the natural environment. The leisure industry has grown to meet people's leisure needs and is made up of a wide range of leisure facilities where people can relax and enjoy themselves.

Activity

▶ Choose three leisure facilities in your area and show how they meet the needs of the people who use them.

▶ Choose another leisure facility in your area and show how it could expand to accommodate additional activities. For example, a theatre may have a restaurant added to it.

Leisure centres

Did you know?

You can even get married in a leisure centre! Other non-sporting activities take place in leisure centres, for example children's birthday parties.

The first purpose-built sports and leisure centre in the UK was built in Harlow, Essex, in 1960. There are now more than 2000 leisure centres in the UK.

Taking part in leisure, sport and recreation activities is possible only if access to the necessary facilities is available. In the case of a game of squash, this requires a specific purpose-built facility, whereas sailing would need part of the environment – a lake or the sea (or possibly a reservoir – which, of course, will have been built).

Over the past 30 years there has been a change in the provision of leisure, sport and recreation facilities in the UK. There are now multi-screen cinema complexes, all-weather pitches, leisure pools with slides and flumes, and floodlit playing areas.

The first leisure centres were built in the centre of towns so they were easily accessible. This type of location, however, meant there was little or no room for expansion so they were limited in the activities they could provide.

The 1970s saw a new type of leisure centre develop as nearly every local authority built them with surrounding tracks and field areas for other traditional sports such as football, netball and tennis.

Activity

▶ In your group, write down the name of some of the leisure facilities in your local area and include them on a chart like the one shown below. You may want to use the following in your research: local directories such as Thomson's, Yellow Pages, family and friends, local newspapers, the Internet, your own knowledge.

Facility	Name
Cinemas	
Community centres	
Health and fitness centres	
Hotels	
Leisure centres	
Libraries	
Museums	
Nightclubs	
Parks	
Restaurants	
Swimming pools	
Theatres	
Travel agents	

One of Europe's largest indoor leisure centres is The Dome at Doncaster. It offers more than 50 sports and leisure activities such as squash, ice-skating, aerobics, indoor bowls, swimming, martial arts and badminton. It also has other facilities such as a bar, café, conference room and multi-purpose sports hall so that events such as concerts, weddings, antiques roadshows, exhibitions, business conferences and parties can take place.

Some leisure centres are attached to schools to ensure maximum usage. The school uses it during the day and the public use it after 4.00 pm and at weekends. This is called 'dual use'.

When planning a leisure centre programme, it is important to take into account the different needs of the various sections of the community. These groups include: the unemployed, the disabled, manual and clerical workers, senior citizens, clubs, young teenagers, toddlers and pre-school age children. A leisure centre should provide the widest possible range of facilities for the community, at the same time offering value for money.

There must be a balance when programming activities in a leisure centre. The programming mix should cater for the groups shown in Figure 1.5.

Figure 1.5 The programming mix of a leisure centre

The Dome is one of Europe's largest leisure centres

Snapshot

Shona, leisure centre supervisor

Shona is 22 years old and has been a leisure centre supervisor in Birmingham for two years. She left school at 16 and went to her local college where she gained a B in GCSE Leisure and Tourism. She became a lifeguard at the town's leisure centre and took additional qualifications in Customer Care, Lifesaving and First Aid. She became a recreation assistant at 19 and was promoted to her present position when she was 20. She aims to become an assistant manager in two years' time. She says: 'I've always wanted to work in a sports environment. One of my strong points is getting on with people, so for me this is the perfect job as I am in contact with the public and colleagues every day. My advice to young people is to 'concentrate on work which interests you, don't just do it for the money.'

Many leisure centres have swimming pools which not only fulfil the needs of the serious swimmer but also the fun swimmer.

Snapshot

Caribbean evening

One of Shona's jobs is to organise a Caribbean evening at the leisure centre's pool. This is how she did it.

> Stroll down to our Caribbean beach party this Saturday and sample the delights of:
> - a superb buffet of spicy chicken, rice, salad and barbecued spare ribs followed by fresh fruit salad with cream, iced melon and coconut surprise
> - a Caribbean steel band that will serenade you to the gentle beat of Jamaican love songs
> - our tropical wave machine which will lap warm water over you while you laze on our beach.
>
> Turn up in Bermuda shorts or swimwear depending on how the mood takes you.
>
> MIX IT ALL TOGETHER AND YOU HAVE THE PERFECT RECIPE FOR A NIGHT OF WARMTH, SWEET MUSIC AND FUN

Shona's customers say:

'It brings the Caribbean to the heart of Birmingham.'

'I could have swayed all night. The atmosphere was so romantic.'

'It was so real. I even rubbed on some suntan lotion.'

Activity

▶ Design and draw your own leisure pool. Give it an attractive name, for example Ocean Waves, and include the special features like slides and flumes which would make it popular. Remember people want fun, excitement and atmosphere.

Health clubs

The importance of having a healthy lifestyle has led to the rise of the health club. These usually contain a fitness suite which has all the latest hi-tech cardiovascular equipment such as rowing machines, exercise bikes and treadmills.

Some of the larger clubs have saunas, sunbeds and steam rooms (Turkish baths). Additional services include beauty therapy, with body massages, manicures and pedicures, eyelash and eyebrow treatments, aromatherapy and facial massage.

Many hotels, especially those belonging to national chains, also offer health clubs within the hotel itself. This additional attraction is aimed at increasing business by offering a wider variety of activities.

Most health clubs have up-to-date equipment and trained staff. The decor is usually quite luxurious and members are usually attracted by the bar and catering facilities.

Libraries

The 1850 Libraries Act permitted local councils to spend some of their money on creating and administering libraries. The 1964 Libraries and Museums Act stated that local councils should provide an efficient and free lending service to the public.

Libraries provide a huge source of information. Your local library will have a great deal of secondary information which will help towards your course. As well as books, they offer videos, CDs, cassettes and computers (so you can search the Internet for information).

There are approximately 2600 libraries in the country. They remain an important part of leisure – reading is still popular despite the competition from television, radio and computers.

Libraries have undergone an image change over the past 15 years. Lending systems are now largely computerised, and communal areas have been introduced where you can talk and read through the material you are researching. Libraries are now attractive and welcoming facilities which provide the perfect setting for you to do your GCSE coursework.

Activity

▶ In small groups, arrange a visit to your local library and find out what your library has to offer in addition to its book lending service. How often do you use your public library?

Talk about it

In your group, discuss what you think is the value of your local library to the community. Who do you think are its main users?

You can bring the magic of cinema to your own front room

Snapshot

Uptown Library users

Gideon
Gideon studies GCSE PE and is very interested in tennis. He needs information for a project about the past ten Wimbledon Lawn Tennis Championships so he goes to his local library to find the information.

Jackie
Jackie is 38 and works part time in her local library. She likes to help people with their research. She is doing an Open University degree and uses her library as a base for her studies.

Femi
Femi takes her three children to the library during half-term because it is Junior Book Week for 7–11-year olds and story time for the under-7s. During the week Femi's children can choose their own books, enter writing competitions and use a computer.

Video rental shops

Video recorders became popular in the early 1980s, enabling people to tape their favourite television programmes. Video rental shops appeared soon after and enabled people to rent their favourite films.

Since then, video rental shops such as Blockbusters, not only rent videos but also sell them. In addition, you can either rent or buy video games.

In fact, you can now bring the atmosphere of the cinema into your own front room. How? Picture this scene …

Stroll down to your local video rental shop and take out a film that everyone has been talking about. Pick up a plentiful supply of popcorn, soft drinks and sweets while you are there. Stroll back home, insert the video, put your feet up and watch the film. No queuing, or adverts, no car parking problems, no comments shouted from the audience, just a totally relaxing atmosphere in which you can concentrate on the film.

Activity

▶ What do video rental shops sell apart from videos?

Did you know?

The British Library in London is the national library of the UK and one of the world's greatest libraries. It houses 16 million books and has 2500 staff.

There is a downside to this. Hiring a video could lead to social isolation, that is staying at home on your own and not mixing with other people. Secondly, there is the danger that young people might watch unsuitable videos, for example a 10-year-old watching a film with an 18 certificate showing scenes of sex and violence.

Video shops are extremely popular. Another important point to note is that videos can now be hired from local corner shops. The extra competition for sales and the introduction of new technology could affect business in video rental shops.

DVD players have become the UK's fastest growing consumer entertainment product ever as they replace video recorders. The switch to DVD threatens to make many people's collections of video tapes obsolete, with VHS (the video system) seemingly heading the same way as vinyl records and turntables.

Talk about it

In your group, discuss whether you think videos portraying violent scenes influence the behaviour of those who watch them. Does violence on the screen lead to violence off the screen?

Cinemas and theatres

Cinemas

Figure 1.6 shows the trend in cinema admissions in the UK from 1984 to 2000. Cinema admissions more than doubled over this period to 137 million. This increase may be as a result of the development and expansion of multiplex cinemas. The increase in the number of PG films has also made cinema-going more accessible. The chart also shows that younger people (15–24 years) tend to go to the cinema the most, with a sharp increase in attendance by the over-45s between 1990 and 2000.

Activity

▶ Find out what's on at your local cinema over a two-week period and write down the films and the range of people the films are aimed at.

Why is cinema-going so popular nowadays? Write down your answers.

Theatres

The UK is one of the world's major centres for theatres. There is an enormous range of shows and plays to see with the larger productions being staged in the major cities. Many smaller theatre companies tour the country performing in more local venues such as sports halls and leisure centres.

Many of the world's most popular musicals are staged in London's West End. Although they are very expensive to stage, they attract large audiences and additional revenue from the sale of merchandise (e.g. tapes, CDs and t-shirts).

Pubs, restaurants and take-away restaurants

Pubs

The pub is the perfect place to meet friends, socialise, tell jokes, argue, play pool, listen to music, grab a sandwich and catch up with all the local gossip. It has a character all of its own.

No other country in the world can match the atmosphere of the UK pub. Tourists from overseas, especially Americans, usually head to a pub, as they have no places like this 'back home'. The log fire, the gentle hum of people talking and the general character of the pub make it unique. That's what makes it so attractive to tourists.

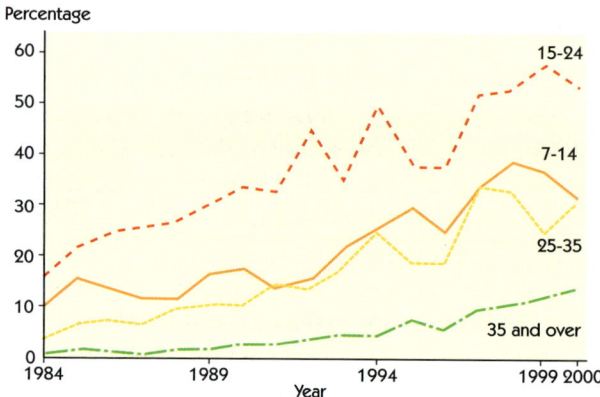

Figure 1.6 Cinema admissions by age, 1984–2000
Social Trends, No. 32, 2002

Nearly all pubs serve food. This attracts more customers, which, in turn, brings in more income. Promotions such as two meals for the price of one between certain times, 'happy hours' between 5.00 and 6.00 pm, or '£1 a pint until first goal scored' attract even more people.

The popularity of a pub depends on the welcome you receive, the decor, the cleanliness of the toilets and the general atmosphere.

Activity
▶ Wetherspoon's is the fastest growing company in the UK. It has created 10 000 new jobs over the past five years and plans to add another 30 0000 over the next ten years
(*Wetherspoon News Edition*, September 2001).

Find out more about this expanding pub chain by visiting the Wetherspoon website on the Internet.

Talk about it
In your group, discuss your thoughts on the 18 years age limit before you can go into a pub and be served alcohol.

Restaurants

If you enjoy eating out, there is a huge variety of restaurants to choose from, including fast food, à la carte, wine bars, bistros, family, hotel and ethnic (Chinese, Indian, Italian and so on). Such a choice has resulted in a lot of competition between restaurants to attract customers, so restaurants will try to tempt you in with the following:

- two meals for the price of one
- an extensive menu to offer a wider choice
- vegetarian meals
- children's menus
- reduced prices between 5.00 pm and 7.00 pm
- silver saver – discount for the over-55s
- an extensive wine list
- discounts for party bookings
- a free glass of wine with your meal.

There is a wide variety of restaurants to choose from

Did you know?
- The average weekly expenditure on eating out is £22.
- Eating out as a percentage of food expenditure in the UK is 33 per cent.
- The total amount spent on eating out in the UK is £16 billion per year.

Activity
▶ Why is eating out so popular? Write down your answers.

Take-away restaurants

These are also known as 'fast-food' restaurants. In the UK, fast food includes fish and chips, hot pies and pasties, burgers, kebabs, pizzas and soups. Drinks include milkshakes, fizzy drinks, tea, coffee and milk.

The advantage of take-away restaurants is that a broad range of snacks and meals is instantly available to the customer. Almost every town and city in the UK has a McDonald's, KFC, Burger King or Pizza Express.

Take-away restaurants are especially popular with teenagers and families, probably because value-for-money meals are available immediately with no washing up to worry about.

Being a rapidly expanding sector of the UK food industry, take-away restaurants have an impact beyond what was intended. For example, an increase in take-away food sales has meant an increase in the amount of packaging generated, which would not have existed had meals continued to be eaten in restaurants or in the home. This has negative environmental effects in terms of litter, yet employment benefits in terms of extra jobs in manufacturing the packaging.

Talk about it

There is growing concern about the quality of our diet, in particular the amount of highly processed foods containing high levels of refined sugars, saturated fats, salt and additives that we eat. Some people are worried that fresh, wholesome, home-cooked foods are being replaced by fast food.

In your group, discuss the advantages and disadvantages of take-away restaurants.

Community centres

These consist of facilities built for the local community where activities such as bingo, car boot sales, wedding receptions, youth clubs, discos, tea dances, community theatre and even blood donor sessions are held.

They are usually located in the middle of a residential area which enables easy access for the community. These centres are usually supported by the local authority and are run by a committee of volunteers.

Community centres are extremely valuable facilities for the local community in that they act as the focal point for organisations like clubs, societies and associations. In many places community centres seem to escape the threat of vandalism. This is possibly because the community places great value on the facility, takes good care to look after it and realises any damage or subsequent closure would be a great loss to the local area.

Wootton Community Centre

Wootton is a medium-sized village, with a mixed population, shops and a small industrial estate. It is a very lively community and the community centre is a true centre for the village. Its programme looks like this:

Monday
9.00 am–12.00 noon Playgroup
2.00–5.00 pm Whist and bridge club

Tuesday
9.00 am–12.00 noon Playgroup
3.30–5.30 pm After-school club
7.30–10.00 pm Panto rehearsal

Wednesday
12.00–2.00 pm Over-60s lunch club
6.00–10.00 pm Judo and aerobics classes

Thursday
10.00 am–12.00 noon Parent and toddler group
2.00–4.00 pm Women's Institute Meeting

Friday
9.00 am–12.00 noon Playgroup
3.30–5.30 pm After-school club

Activity

▶ In groups, find out if you have a community centre close to you. What activities does it offer? How much is charged for each activity?

Museums and art galleries

For information on museums and art galleries, turn back to pages 16–17.

Sports venues

Sports venues range from the playing fields where your local team plays to vast stadia such as Manchester United's Old Trafford.

Investigating leisure and tourism   Unit 1

Case study
Sports venues in two cities

Sheffield
In 1995 Sheffield was the first city to be designated National City of Sport by the Sports Council of Great Britain.

The opening of three major sports venues in the early 1990s – Don Valley International Stadium, Ponds Forge International Sports Centre and Sheffield Arena established the city as an important national centre for sports.

Sheffield Ski Village is the largest artificial ski-slope resort in Europe. Bramhall Lane and Hillsborough are home to Sheffield United and Sheffield Wednesday football teams.

Cardiff
Sports venues include the Cardiff Athletic Stadium, the National Ice Rink and the Millennium Stadium, costing over £100 million, which hosted the opening ceremony of the 1999 Rugby Union World Cup. Football and cricket are respectively played by Cardiff City at Ninian Park and Glamorgan Cricket Club at Sophia Gardens.

1. What is the nearest city to you? What major sports facilities does it have? (If you live near Cardiff or Sheffield, please choose another city!)
2. What sort of impacts do these facilities have on the city? Examples include increased employment, traffic congestion.

Activity

Match the sport with the venue:

Lords	Horse Racing
Old Trafford	Golf
Twickenham	Rowing
Silverstone	Tennis
The Crucible	Football
Aintree	Motor racing
St Andrews	Snooker
Wimbledon	Rugby
Crystal Palace	Cricket
Holme Pierrepoint	Athletics

Case study
Improving football's image

Sports venues, especially football grounds, have been modernised over the past 20 years so that spectators can now watch in comfort and safety.

During the 1970s and 1980s hooliganism, drunkenness and violence among football supporters began to bring the game into disrepute, and put people off going. Riots – before, during and after matches – and running battles in the streets between rival fans became commonplace.

It was essential for the football authorities to clean up the game on and off the field and to make life safer for spectators, especially after the fire at Valley Parade, Bradford, in 1985 and Hillsborough, Sheffield, in 1989 when over 90 Liverpool fans were killed by overcrowding in an area of the stadium.

As a result of the Taylor Report (1990), additional health and safety measures were introduced to football league grounds. More general improvements included all-seater stadia, big video screens for pre-match entertainment, facilities such as family stands to encourage women and children to attend, and to promote family participation, crèches and better catering arrangements.

Other changes included improved surveillance by closed-circuit television, stewards and police, and hospitality/executive boxes have been installed to bring in more money. These measures to improve facilities have gone a long way to clean up the image of the game and to encourage spectators to return to grounds.

1. Rugby League football places great emphasis on promoting matches as family days out. How do you think football clubs could encourage more families to attend matches?
2. Some football clubs have corporate hospitality suites. What are they and who uses them?
3. What sort of pre-match entertainment could football clubs put on for spectators?

Chapter 1   The leisure industry

Sunderland football club showed the greatest increase in supporters between the 1996/97 season and the 1997/98 season, when attendance rose from 21 000 to 35 000, an increase of two-thirds. This was, in part, due to a new stadium – the Stadium of Light – which can accommodate more people than the old one.

Activity

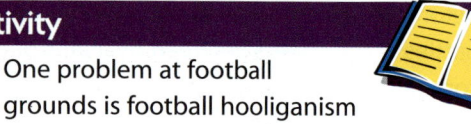

One problem at football grounds is football hooliganism which never seems to go away.

1. What do you think are the causes of football hooliganism?
2. What do you think could be done to stop it?

National sports venues

Sport England National Sports Centres are centres for sporting excellence, providing athletics with high quality sporting and residential facilities for both training and competition. Each centre provides a unique range of sports facilities, equipment and expertise. The centres also offer conference facilities. In England and Wales there are five national sports centres:

- Crystal Palace, London – athletics, swimming basketball.
- Lilleshall, Shropshire – cricket, football, gymnastics.
- Holme Pierrepont, Nottingham – rowing, sailing, canoeing.
- Bisham Abbey, Buckinghamshire – squash, football, tennis.
- Plas y Brenin, National Mountain Centre Snowdonia – mountaineering, rock climbing, canoeing and orienteering.

Case study

National Water Sports Centre Holme Pierrepont

The National Water Sports Centre Holme Pierrepont is one of the biggest centres of its kind in the world, with its 2000m regatta lake, canoe slalom course, water-ski lake and ski tows. Located near Nottingham on the River Trent, it is operated by Leisure Connection on behalf of Sport England.

As well as all the water-sports facilities, the Centre provides a multi-purpose sports hall, fitness training facilities, a sports medicine clinic, a lecture hall and function rooms.

It has been carefully landscaped so that environmental issues, such as waste, recycling and management of natural wildlife and plants, have been considered. Accommodation is provided for visitors within easy reach of all the facilities.

1. What range of water sports is available at Holme Pierrepont?
2. What Health and Safety procedures do you think visitors using the facilities have to follow? Relate these to one particular sport.

Activity

You are planning a residential weekend at The National Water Sports Centre Holme Pierrepont starting at 5.00 pm on Friday with a group of ten friends, one of whom is a wheelchair user.
In small groups design a programme of activities for the weekend, containing up to six activities. Include a wide range of the activities and facilities that the Centre has to offer.

Think about your transport arrangements to and from the Centre using public transport and your accommodation requirements.

There are a number of other sport venues of national importance:

- Hampden Park, Glasgow and the main premiership stadia e.g. Old Trafford, Anfield, Elland Road, St James' Park, Stadium of Light – football
- Murrayfield, Edinburgh, Twickenham, London, Lansdowne Road, Dublin and Millennium Stadium, Cardiff – rugby
- Lord's, London – cricket
- All England Lawn Tennis Club, Wimbledon – tennis.

Theme parks

Theme parks have become very popular since Walt Disney resurrected the amusement park industry in 1955 in the United States.

The bigger UK theme parks have been modelled on North American examples – the immensely popular DisneyWorld, Florida, possibly the most famous theme park in the world, and Disneyland in California.

The UK's first theme park was Thorpe Water Park at Chertsey, Surrey, its theme being maritime history. The UK's best known theme park is Alton Towers, Staffordshire. Other well known UK theme parks include: Chessington World of Adventures, Legoland and Camelot.

Theme parks as visitor attractions have developed from the idea of amusement parks with thrilling rides, such as roller coasters, or old or interesting exhibits to look at. The individual attractions in a theme park are now more numerous, more terrifying and involve more high technology than in traditional fairgrounds or amusement parks.

Think about it
A family ticket for one of the major theme parks can cost up to £70. Do you think this is value for money?

Case study
Legoland Windsor

Legoland Windsor is located to the west of London, two miles from the historic town of Windsor. It is easily reached by motorway (M25, M3 and M4) and is just half an hour from London by train. The theme park is set in 150 acres of parkland with over 50 rides and attractions. The park is divided into a number of different themed areas including the world-famous Miniland which contains around 32 million Lego bricks recreating scenes from Europe complete with real-life sound effects, trains, boats and traffic.

Miniland

New attractions include an interactive racing track modelled on the famous Le Mans circuit and new models of the London Eye and Buckingham Palace.

Visitors are provided with a number of facilities, such as cash dispensers, wheelchair hire, kennels and a well-equipped baby care centre to ensure that their visit is an enjoyable one. The first aid centre is staffed by qualified first aiders and managed by a qualified nurse.

1. Legoland is open from mid March to early November and from 21 December to 5 January. What events could it hold during the winter months when the park is closed?
2. What attractions does Legoland provide for the younger member of the family?
3. How does Legoland attract customers other than families?

Facilities that provide for home-based leisure

Video rental shops and take-away restaurants

Leisure activities that take place in the home are sometimes provided by facilities outside the home. For example, if there is nothing on television which appeals to you, the answer might be to rent a video and order a take-away.

The video can be rented from one of the many specialist video rental shops or even the local corner shop! You probably won't have very far to travel to get to one. Your choice of take-away may be Indian, Chinese, Italian, Mexican and probably a few more. You can order by phone and, if you prefer, have your take-away delivered.

> **Talk about it**
> In your group, how many of you regularly spend a night in like this? What are its attractions?

Bookshops and libraries

Reading books is the fourth most popular home-based leisure activity after watching television, listening to the radio and listening to music. On average, people spend four hours a week reading books at home.

The main source of books are bookshops and libraries. Nearly every high street in every town has a bookshop, which sells paperback fiction, best-selling autobiographies and student textbooks. These books are easily available and if the one you want is not in stock, the retailer will order it for you.

Joining a library is free, so there is easy access to a wide range of books. Again, if a book is not available, the librarian will search a database of other libraries within the area to see if it can be transferred to your library.

> **Activity**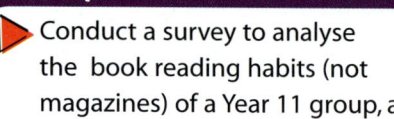
> ▶ Conduct a survey to analyse the book reading habits (not magazines) of a Year 11 group, a Year 9 group and a Year 7 group.

Shops selling computer games

Many people spend a considerable amount of time each week playing games on their home computer. This has led to the development of shops specialising in selling computer games. As technology advances rapidly, these shops are able to provide the most up-to-date games.

> **Activity**
> ▶ Find out the most popular computer games and work out how much time members of your group spend per week playing these games.

Products and services

Look back to page 3 to remind yourself of the definition of products and services.

> **Talk about it**
> In your group, discuss the range of products and services provided by the following leisure facilities:
> a   a hotel
> b   a theme park
> c   a cinema.

A theatre provides more than the actual stage production. It may have a bar and even a restaurant. It might even have a counter where soft drinks and confectionery are sold. The actual performances may include a range of productions such as pantomimes, plays, tribute bands, celebrity speakers, school productions and more.

Leisure facilities are now trying to attract more and more people by providing a range of products and services. A pub may provide drink, food, music, entertainment, a functions room, pool table and fruit machines. In other words, the more products and services a facility provides, the more people will be attracted to it.

Sports activities

Sports activities include swimming, badminton, squash, keep-fit, trampolining and many more. People take part in sports activities for a variety of reasons: to get fit and keep fit; to enjoy themselves; to socialise with friends; to feel part of a group; to win.

Lessons and classes for different age groups

Many people stop playing sport when they leave school. Some stop altogether, some take it up again later in life. One way of returning to sport or even learning a new one is to sign up for sports courses. This is especially the case in sports like swimming, yoga and badminton; non-contact activities which people can do at their own level without feeling under pressure.

> **Talk about it**
> In your group, discuss the types of classes leisure centres could put on for senior citizens?

Functions

Many leisure centres have multi-purpose sports halls that are suitable for both sport and social functions. This means they can put on functions like New Year's Eve dances, wedding receptions and even pop concerts.

Some people take up sport later in life

Food and drink

Many leisure facilities provide food and drink even though their main business activity may be something else, for example a leisure centre (sport), a hotel (accommodation), a cinema (films), a theatre (stage production). Food can range from quick snacks to a three-course meal.

> **Talk about it**
> In your group, talk about why leisure facilities provide food and drink for their customers.

> **Activity**
> ▶ What sort of food and drink do the following facilities provide:
> a theatres
> b hotels
> c cinemas?

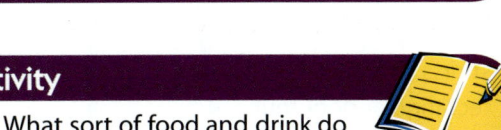

Special rates for members/groups

Leisure facilities try to attract as many people as possible. For example:

- cheaper rates for off-peak times and different user groups at a leisure centre
- activities for senior citizens and the unemployed may be charged at a lower rate
- family tickets may be sold at a theme park, offering reductions in order to encourage more families to spend a day there
- students may be entitled to discounts
- annual membership may entitle you to discounts or priority bookings.

Purchase and hire of equipment

Many leisure centres provide equipment like squash and badminton racquets. A deposit or a membership card is usually required. Some centres have their own sports shops where customers can buy a wide range of sports goods. This brings in more business and shows that the centre is trying to cover the whole range of products and services to satisfy its customers.

Case study

Downtown Leisure Centre – providing products and services for its customers

Situated in a small market town, the local authority-operated Downtown Leisure Centre serves a catchment area of 6000 people who live within two miles of the centre.

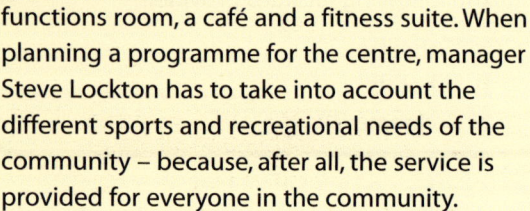

Facilities include a multi-purpose sports hall, a 25m rectangular pool, four squash courts, a functions room, a café and a fitness suite. When planning a programme for the centre, manager Steve Lockton has to take into account the different sports and recreational needs of the community – because, after all, the service is provided for everyone in the community.

The local authority has introduced concessionary rates to attract as many people as possible to use the facilities. For example, senior citizens and the unemployed may be charged a lower rate or there may even be free family tickets. Off-peak rates are lower than peak rates and a guaranteed block booking could mean cheaper rates.

Equipment hire is available, again at different rates or possibly free. For those users who may want to purchase sports equipment, items like squash balls, wristbands, racquet grips and shuttlecocks are sold at reception.

Downtown Leisure Centre provides something for everyone. It doesn't specialise in one sports activity, it provides a whole range. As a result, attendances have risen each year since it was opened three years ago.

1. What products and services does your local leisure centre provide?
2. What special rates does it have for members and groups?

Main factors influencing how people spend their leisure time

Activity

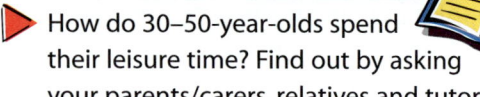
- How do 30–50-year-olds spend their leisure time? Find out by asking your parents/carers, relatives and tutors.
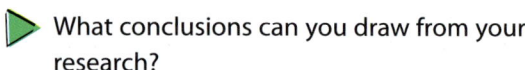
- What conclusions can you draw from your research?

Age group

Different age groups tend to have different leisure interests and needs. Young people aged 18–30 usually like to go to pubs and clubs – although that doesn't rule out anyone older enjoying the same things! As for holidays, young people may prefer fun-packed holidays where they can dance and party all night, every night. The holiday company Club 18–30 targets this market. Young people may also be attracted to adventure holidays, such as climbing in Snowdonia or trekking in the Himalayas.

In contrast, people over 55 often prefer to go out in groups, for example on day trips, or they may want to 'winter' in Spain. One organisation which specialises in holidays for the over-55s age group is Saga Holidays. It started in 1952 when the owner of a hotel wanted to attract guests during the low or off-peak season (winter) and found that the people who wanted to stay at this time were retired. Saga is now an international travel company offering all types of holidays for older people with varying levels of income.

Different age groups have different leisure needs. Some holiday brochures aim to attract particular age groups

Culture

Culture can be a difficult word to define. Very simply, it means the values and beliefs of society, or even our way of life. The UK culture is one brought about by our history and traditions. Our culture is based on hard work, which we probably inherited from the Victorian era when it was not uncommon to work a 60-hour week.

Our culture today includes watching television, on average 26 hours a week, usually glued to soaps and virtual reality programmes, for example Big Brother. Fast foods, new technology and improved travel have given us the opportunity to spend more time on our leisure activities. Whether this time is spent on leisure or work is open to question, for example do microwaves and dishwashers enable us to spend more time at home or do they give us more time to prepare for work?

Over the past 20 years we have seen a fitness boom in the UK – people have recognised the need to keep fit and healthy so many people believe in exercising three times a week, eating sensibly and cutting out smoking. As a result, private health clubs have developed, the National Health Service has vigorously promoted a healthy lifestyle and heavy drinkers and smokers are being constantly warned that excess in either habit 'can seriously damage their health'.

> **Talk about it**
> In your group, discuss the meaning of the term 'yob culture'. How does culture affect leisure activities in the UK?

The UK is a multi-ethnic society and with this comes traditions and beliefs from a variety of backgrounds and cultures. Different ethnic groups have different interests and needs which influence what people do in their leisure time. For example, many members of the Asian community like to watch Asian films at the cinema on a Saturday morning.

Certain beliefs and customs may restrict leisure activities. Strict Muslim women are not allowed to show their body in public so they have to find leisure centres which provide women-only swimming sessions where female lifeguards are on duty. These are usually available only in big cities so opportunities are restricted.

One of the more unfortunate aspects of UK culture is that we have a divorce rate of one in three, although this compares quite favourably with the USA where one in two marriages end in divorce. Divorce proceedings and maintenance payments can be expensive; for many families, divorce can mean a serious drop in income. All this can lead to a decrease in leisure activities from both a financial point of view, especially for single parents, and opportunity in terms of having the time, let alone the energy to take part in leisure time activities.

> **Activity**
> What sort of pressures does our culture place on young people?

Special needs

Groups who may have special needs include:

- people with disabilities
- parents with young children
- people who are unemployed
- ethnic minority groups.

The factors which influence how these groups enjoy their leisure time include accessibility to facilities, having enough money, language differences, cultural traditions and time.

People with disabilities can enjoy their leisure time as much as anyone else providing the following types of access are in place at leisure facilities:

- specially designated car parking bays close to the main entrance
- corridors and doors wide enough to give access to social areas, toilets and activity areas
- ramps and lifts.

Find out how your local leisure centre caters for people with special needs

Mothers or fathers with young children do not always have the time, money or even confidence to include leisure activities in their busy schedule. Providing for the family, paying for childminders and lack of transport could all restrict their opportunity for leisure. In some cases, the lack of opportunity to mix with other people can lead to a loss of self-confidence and a build-up of low self-esteem.

Unemployed people may also be unable to take part in the full range of leisure activities because of lack of money and transport.

Think about it

Think about what it would be like to be unemployed and how this might affect your participation in leisure activities.

An ethnic minority group may have political, cultural or racial differences from the larger population. Within the UK, ethnic minority groups might include Vietnamese, Ugandan, Asian, Afro-Caribbean and Polish people. Some of these groups may have difficulty taking part in leisure and recreation activities because of cultural traditions and because English may not be their first language.

Type of household

A family of four would probably have different leisure activities from a single person. A working couple with no children are likely to have more opportunity to take part in leisure activities than a couple with two children under the age of 5. Time, money, energy and the number of people involved are the main factors when it comes to taking part in leisure activities.

Case study

A hectic day

Steve and Emma have two daughters aged 6 and 3. Steve is a teacher and Emma works part time as a nurse at the local hospital. Below is a typical day:

7.00–8.00 am Rush hour! Feed and dress children. Get them ready for school and nursery.
8.00–8.30 am Take children to nursery/school and go to work.
3.30–5.00 pm Emma collects the children, takes them home, changes them for a friend's birthday party and drops them off. Goes to supermarket, then returns home to do household chores.
5.30–6.00 pm On his way home from work, Steve collects the children from the party.
6.00–8.00 pm Emma feeds, baths, reads to girls and puts them to bed. Steve cooks supper.
8.00–9.00 pm Supper time – time to catch up on the day's events!
9.00–9.30 pm Emma clears up while Steve does the ironing.
9.30 pm Crash out in front of the television. Read newspaper and magazines.
11.00 pm Crawl upstairs to bed – exhausted!

1. What opportunities are there for Steve and Emma for leisure activities during the week?
2. What types of leisure facilities tend to target families like Steve and Emma's?

Talk about it

In your group, describe a typical day in your household.

Gender

Men and women have different needs and interests when it comes to how they enjoy their leisure time. Women tend to prefer aerobics to playing rugby. In general, women don't usually take part in contact sports. An activity like aerobics serves two purposes for women – to help them look and feel good. Men, in general, are not as concerned about their waist size and physique as women.

Equal opportunities in sport have enabled women to take part in activities that were previously the domain of men, for example in athletics the pole vault and triple jump. Women jockeys race alongside men and there are women's football leagues.

Think about it

Do women have the same opportunities as men to take part in leisure time activities?

Social group

This is sometimes referred to as socio-economic grouping. It is a way of categorising people under the headings of marital status, education, jobs and income. In general, people who have similar incomes and similar jobs have similar leisure interests.

The most widely used method of grouping people when researching lifestyles and leisure activities based on income and occupation is shown in the chart below.

It is assumed that the people in each category have similar amounts of disposable income and buying habits. It is also assumed that people in social grouping A have the highest level of disposable income.

However, there are some problems with this type of classification system. For example, some people in C1 and C2 may have a higher disposable income than those in A and B, who might decide to pay for private education for their children or private health care for all the family.

Talk about it

In your group, discuss the leisure time activities that you think people in groupings A and D take part in.

How much of a part does money play when deciding which leisure activities to do?

Other factors affecting choice of leisure activities

The availability of local facilities

Most towns today have a leisure centre which usually has a swimming pool. Others have restaurants, a theatre and possibly a cinema. These facilities give people a range of opportunities where they can enjoy their leisure time.

Facilities can be provided by the local authority, for example leisure centres, parks

Grouping	Social status	Occupation	Products and services
A	Upper middle class	Lawyers, chief executives	Expensive holidays, exclusive golf club
B	Middle class	Doctors, teachers	All-inclusive holidays
C1	Lower middle class	Supervisors	Fly/drive holidays
C2	Skilled working class	Plumbers, electricians	Package holidays
D	Working class	Semi-skilled, unskilled labourers, cleaners	Cheaper package holidays
E	Unskilled, pensioners, widows	Casual workers	Coach holidays, day trips

Social status and leisure activities Registrar-General's Social Classification

and libraries, and by the private sector, for example, cinemas, pubs and restaurants, where the aim is to make a profit.

It can be a different story in villages and in the countryside where the only leisure facility may be the village pub, which obviously has restrictions for under-18s. The nearest facility could be the local secondary school whose sports centre is open to the public as well as the students, but that could be several miles away. Choice may be restricted in these areas by lack of facilities. Private or public transport is essential to reach the nearest facility.

Talk about it

In your group, discuss the type of leisure activities that would be available to people who live in an area where there aren't many leisure facilities.

What do you think it would be like to live in an isolated part of the countryside?

The availability of transport

Nowadays, many households have one, possibly two cars. This allows people to travel to the leisure facilities of their choice. This is especially so when it comes to travelling to the countryside where people may be attracted to the dramatic scenery of North Wales, the Lake District or the Scottish Highlands.

Those people who do not have their own transport have to rely on public transport such as buses and trains. This adds extra cost and could restrict the time spent on leisure activities because of the actual travel involved.

There is also the problem of the reliability and frequency of the public transport available. In the countryside, buses may run only once an hour and the last bus back home on Saturday night might be at 9 o'clock! Trains are subject to cancellation and delay.

Talk about it

In your group, discuss the quality of public transport in your area

Activity

▶ Running a car or motorcycle costs money. Find out the running costs per week of an average saloon car.

People's interests

It may sound strange but some people deliberately restrict their leisure time interests. They choose to spend much of their time working and class their work as a leisure time interest. Not surprisingly, these people are described as 'workaholics'; they may work from 7.00 am until 9.00 pm six days a week so don't have much time for anything else.

On the other hand, some people can't wait to finish work and readily dive into their favourite activity whether it be fishing, aerobics, photography, travel or football. In fact, some people have a great passion for their chosen hobby and put everything into it so that work acts as a means of supporting the hobby.

The type of interest you have depends upon the time available and the money you may need to spend on it.

Other people try to develop perhaps two or three leisure activities and strike a balance between work, home and hobbies.

Activity

▶ Find out how many hours a week the following people work:

a   teachers
b   publicans
c   builders.

Fashion

Fashion, in this context, refers to trends, that is what is popular at the moment. Not so long ago line dancing, skateboarding and aerobics were all the rage.

Times change and with that change comes new fads or 'crazes'. There is certainly a trend for people to follow a healthy lifestyle by taking up more exercise. This has developed over the past 20 years. Types of keep-fit have included

The latest fitness trend is 'spinning'

aqua splash, circuit training, aerobics, jogging and even marathon running. At the time of writing, the latest trend in keep-fit is 'spinning' in which people exercise as a group, usually in a semi-circle on 'static bicycles', with the instructor changing the tempo of the effort.

> **Talk about it**
>
> In your group, list the latest fashions or trends in leisure. How long do you think they will last?

The influence of family and friends

Many leisure activities are carried out by the family group, for example watching television or eating out. When it comes to sport, there is a tendency for sporting interests to be passed on from parents to children whether it be football, ice-skating or horse riding.

Friends also have an influence on which leisure activities we choose to do. For example, a group of friends may play in the same football or netball team. Another group may decide to go to the cinema every Saturday afternoon or just meet in town and walk round the shops.

Many leisure activities are geared towards groups or teams so there is a type of peer pressure to take part in similar leisure activities as friends.

> **Think about it**
>
> Are your leisure activities influenced by your friends and family?

The amount of disposable income

This is the money left over after all bills, rent and taxes have been paid, in other words, the amount that you can spend how you choose.

People on a low income such as the unemployed, casual workers and many pensioners have a limited amount of disposable income which obviously restricts their leisure activities. In the same way, students often have similar financial restrictions, even if they are able to find part-time work.

The more disposable income people have, the more they can spend on holidays abroad, going to restaurants and taking part in relatively expensive hobbies like skiing, gliding and ballooning.

> **Think about it**
>
> Congratulations! You have just won £5 million on the National Lottery. How would this change your leisure activities?

Employment opportunities in the leisure industry

> **Talk about it**
>
> In your group, discuss the qualities you need to work in the leisure industry.

> **Activity**
>
> ▶ Look up a job in the leisure industry that you would like to do and say why you might be good at it.

If you are interested in a career in the leisure industry there are a number of ways to begin your search for paid employment or voluntary positions. Many vacancies are advertised in local and national newspapers. The following magazines, which may be found in your local library, also advertise vacancies in this industry:

- *Health and Fitness*
- *Leisure Week*
- *Leisure Opportunities*
- *Leisure Management*.

You will need to know about the range of jobs in the leisure industry. Below are some specific ones that you will need to know about.

Leisure assistant

Leisure assistants in leisure centres carry out a range of duties including setting up equipment, answering enquiries from the public, both face to face and over the phone, collecting tickets, cleaning changing rooms and working in reception.

Career progression involves studying for additional qualifications, taking a genuine interest in people and showing drive, enthusiasm and initiative. Many Directors of local government leisure departments started on the bottom rung of the ladder and reached their present position by the age of 35.

Your career route in a leisure centre might look something like this:

leisure centre assistant/lifeguard→ supervisor→assistant manager→manager

and it could take you as little as ten years.

Don't expect to get anywhere without hard work. Be prepared to work shifts and weekends. Be prepared to learn from other, more experienced staff. What's more, don't expect things to happen in your career. You have to make them happen.

Fitness instructor

Fitness instructors teach many activities such as step aerobics, keep-fit and circuit training. They may work for an organisation like the local authority in a leisure centre or they may work for themselves. This is called being self-employed. If so, they build up their own work, book the appropriate facilities and carry out their work with a number of different employers. Fitness instructors may teach individuals – in this case, they are known as personal trainers – or groups.

Awards and qualifications are essential and include: RSA/Sport England Basic Certificate in the Teaching of Exercise to Music or the Physical Education Association's Certificate in Exercise and Health Studies.

Snapshot

Bernadette, fitness instructor

Bernadette teaches aerobics, keep-fit and exercise to music as well as helping individuals with their own fitness programmes.

She took a course run by the Physical Education Association of Great Britain and started working two hours a week in her local leisure centre. As her experience and popularity increased, so did her workload. She now runs 15 different classes and has built up a client bank of ten people who want personalised fitness training programmes.

Bernadette says:

> *I am on the go all the time. You need to be fit, enthusiastic and hard working to be successful. You can never show how tired you feel.*
> *One thing I have had to learn to do is to manage my finances properly because being self-employed, I am responsible for paying my own tax and National Insurance. I'm not sure how long I want to continue. There must be some sort of lifespan to this job. All I am interested in at the moment is to continue building up my business and possibly expanding it so I can employ my own staff.*

Lifeguard

The first priority for a lifeguard is to ensure the safety of swimmers in and around the pool. To do this, you must be capable of rescuing people who get into difficulties in the water. Lifeguards must also hold relevant, up-to-date qualifications like the National Pool Lifeguard Award. A knowledge and qualification in first aid is also desirable.

A lifeguard needs to be physically fit, be able to work as a member of a team and to deal with the public. You are expected to work evenings and weekends as leisure centres and pools are usually open seven days a week from 8.00 am to 11.00 pm. You should be able to attend training sessions as part of your duties.

A lifeguard's main duty involves overseeing the safety of all bathers. Other tasks include cleaning, checking equipment, reporting any maintenance requirements and recording all incidents in the appropriate book.

Becoming a lifeguard is the first step on the career ladder in leisure centre management.

Ground staff

Sports clubs, leisure centres, golf clubs, parks and open spaces present job opportunities for ground staff. The work involves grass cutting, maintaining greens on golf courses and ensuring that all surfaces are well looked after and maintained.

A knowledge of irrigation techniques, turf technology and soil fertilisers is required, although this knowledge can be acquired through training. It is possible to start this type of career without any formal qualifications.

To progress to senior or head groundsman (or woman), you would need appropriate qualifications and experience in soil care, turf maintenance and ground construction work. Obviously, you would have to like working outdoors in all weathers. There are lots of opportunities for progression and, who knows, one day you may be responsible for looking after the Centre Court at Wimbledon!

A lifeguard has responsibility for the safety of bathers

You need to enjoy the outdoor life to be a park ranger

Park ranger

Again, this is mainly outdoor work and involves looking after an area of countryside to make sure the environment isn't damaged in any way, either naturally or by the public.

You may find you can get a park ranger's job locally, but usually you will have to move away from your home area.

Duties include constant maintenance and tending of natural resources such as forests, ponds, walks and coastal pathways. Park rangers also have to deal with the public, giving them information, help and advice, and sometimes may be expected to do some administration and office duties such as writing reports.

You should be over 18, hold a clean driving licence, a GCSE in Leisure and Tourism, have good communication skills and be prepared to work long, unsociable hours.

Restaurant manager

The restaurant manager has responsibility for the entire restaurant and works closely with the head chef dealing with matters like menus, prices and budgets for departments. The restaurant manager supervises the maintenance, staffing and quality of service within the restaurant.

A good knowledge of customer care skills, sales and marketing and finance are the main ingredients that make a good restaurant manager.

To become a restaurant manager, you would probably start off as a waiter or waitress, gain extensive knowledge of wines and spirits and work in a variety of restaurants, both at home and abroad. In fact, a second language would be useful. Qualifications are essential if you wish to progress to becoming a highly paid restaurant manager in a top London hotel.

Did you know?

Sport and physical recreation provide over 400 000 paid jobs.

Check your knowledge

1. In your own words, write down a definition of leisure time.
2. Give two examples of facilities in the arts and entertainment component of the leisure industry. What activities take place in these facilities?
3. Crystal Palace offers participation in which component of the leisure industry?
4. In which component of the leisure industry would you put a Sea Life Centre?
5. Describe two products and services offered to visitors at an attraction like the Tower of London?
6. Name and describe two jobs in sport and physical recreation.
7. Name and describe two jobs in catering.
8. What type of activities does a summer play scheme provide?
9. What is the best location for a theme park?
10. How can leisure facilities be designed to cater for everyone, including people with disabilities?
11. How could you make museums more attractive to primary school children?
12. What type of sports activities would you do in Snowdonia?

Chapter 2: The travel and tourism industry

This chapter examines travel and tourism in some detail. It looks at the different parts of the industry, types of holidays and the four main methods of travel used by people to get to their destinations. The chapter also looks at a variety of tourism destinations ranging from seaside resorts to places in the countryside. Finally, the range of employment opportunities available in the travel and tourism industry are covered.

What you will learn

- What are travel and tourism?
- What makes up the travel and tourism industry?
- Types of holiday
- Travel
- UK tourist destinations
- The social, economic and environmental impact of tourism
- Employment opportunities in travel and tourism

Activities

1. In 15 words or less, explain the meaning of travel.
2. In 10 words or less, explain the meaning of tourism.

What are travel and tourism?

Fact file

Travel is concerned with how people get to their chosen destination and how they travel around the area they are visiting.

Tourism is 'the temporary, short term movement of people to destinations outside the places where they normally live and work and the activities they take part in during their stay at these destinations' (Tourism Society, 1976).

Travel is the key factor in the development of tourism.

Tourism is a broad area to define, but it usually covers temporary travel away from home or work. An essential part of tourism is the traveller's intention to return home afterwards.

The USA still generates the greatest number of overseas tourists to the UK despite the events of 11 September 2001. The UK economy benefits from the money spent by overseas tourists.

Fact file

Incoming tourism – those visitors who come from overseas to visit the UK and spend their holidays here.

Domestic tourism – people from the UK who spend their holidays or go on day trips within the UK.

Outgoing tourism – people who spend their holidays (and their money) overseas.

When people from the UK go abroad for their holidays, the money they spend benefits the economies of the countries they visit such as the USA, Spain, France and Greece.

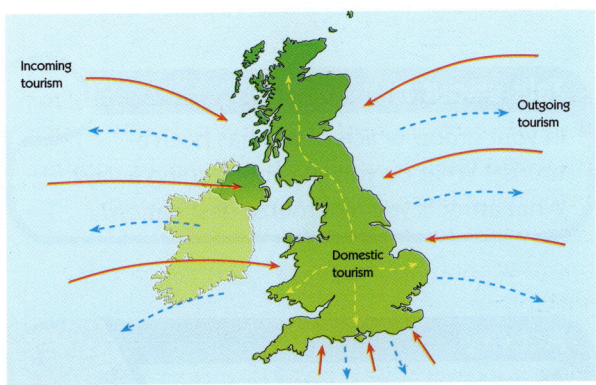

Tourism is the temporary movement of people away from home for leisure purposes

Did you know?

Tourists are people who are:
- away from home
- are on visits which are short term
- are travelling for leisure or business.

The development of the travel and tourism industry was not really possible until after the establishment of the railways in the nineteenth century.

It was in 1841 that the 'grandfather' of travel, Thomas Cook, organised an excursion by rail for people travelling from Leicester to Loughborough for a meeting. Ten years later, Cook was organising the travel arrangements of workers to the Great Exhibition in London, and by 1855, he started the Grand Tour of Europe for rich tourists.

The travel and tourism industry is now one of the world's biggest industries and it is likely to continue to grow and develop.

Activity

- Find out about Thomas Cook.
- What influence did Thomas Cook have on the travel and tourism industry?

In 2000, total tourism spending in the UK was estimated to be £52 billion, comprising £23 billion spent on domestic tourism day visits, £16 billion spent on domestic holidays of one night or more, £13 billion spent by overseas visitors while in the UK.

Talk about it

In your group, which of you has been a tourist? What do you like about going away? What attracts you to a tourist destination?

Activity

- What are the essential features of a popular tourist destination?

The ever-increasing economic importance of tourism has now gained the attention of most countries of the world. Tourism was given little political relevance as recently as ten years ago. Now most countries, developed and less developed, have some sort of tourism policy. Many countries devote considerable amounts of money to tourism promotion. 'Tourism is one of the most important economic, social, cultural and political phenomena of the twenty-first century' (World Tourism Organisation).

Talk about it

In your group, talk about how you think the events of 11 September 2001 affected the world tourism industry? What have been the knock-on effects?

The purpose of visits

An essential part of tourism is the traveller's intention to return home afterwards. The purpose of a visit might be any of the reasons given below.

A holiday

Examples might be:
- two weeks in Majorca soaking up the sun
- one week in Skegness enjoying the delights of the seaside
- three weeks trekking in the Himalayas
- a four-week cruise in the Caribbean.

Talk about it

In your group, say where you would like to go on holiday, and why.

Sightseeing

This involves seeing the sights of a location and taking in the atmosphere, such as:
- a weekend break, e.g. in London taking in all the sights like the Houses of Parliament and St Paul's Cathedral
- a day trip, e.g. to the Lake District taking in the lakes and mountains.

Visiting an attraction

There are thousands of places that a tourist might visit in the UK. They range from seaside funfairs to art galleries and museums, historic country houses to theme parks and shopping malls. Just about the only thing they have in common is that people want to visit them. They have an entertainment value which can cover the excitement of a ride on Oblivion at Alton Towers or, in contrast, the cultural and educational experience of a walk round an art gallery.

Activity
▶ Find out about the Trafford Centre in Manchester and explain its attractions.

The Trafford Centre

▶ Compare and contrast Meadowhall, Sheffield and the Trafford Centre, Manchester.

Visiting friends or relatives (VFR)

This type of visit (in terms of tourism) is usually associated with travelling away from home for at least a day. Examples include:

- a family reunion in Blackpool 140 miles away
- staying at a penfriend's house in France
- an American father visiting his daughter at Cambridge University.

This type of tourism accounted for around 25 per cent of all holidays taken by UK residents in 2001. Perhaps its popularity is due to the fact that this type of tourist usually enjoys free accommodation thanks to the friends or relatives. The money saved on accommodation will be spent on eating out, visiting leisure facilities and travelling around the area. This type of tourism is more popular nowadays as a result of Britain becoming a more multicultural society.

Case study
Buckingham Palace

Buckingham Palace is one of London's most famous tourist attractions. As the official residence of the Queen it flies Her Majesty's personal standard when she is in residence.

Visitors may tour the State Rooms, which include the Throne Room, the Picture Gallery and the State Dining Room. The extended tour includes the garden.

1. Find out when Buckingham Palace opened its doors to the public as a tourist attraction.
2. Why do you think the Queen allowed her residence to become a visitor attraction with guided tours and the sale of souvenirs?

Going to a sports event as a spectator or to take part

Imagine going to the Olympic Games, one of the world's biggest sporting events. As a tourist, you would stay in a hotel, use restaurants, buy souvenirs and go sightseeing, as well as enjoying the Games themselves.

Other major events like the Tour de France, the World Cup Finals, Wimbledon, Test Match cricket, all attract tourists who not only spend their money at the event site but also in the surrounding area. This boosts the economy of the area by bringing in money and also creating jobs.

The Tour de France cycle race attracts competitors and spectators from around the world. On what sorts of things might spectators spend their money?

Exhibitions and trade fairs

- A tourist development officer from Lincoln visits the UK travel trade fair in Manchester.
- An architect travels to attend the Ideal Home exhibition at the NEC, Birmingham.

Conferences and conventions

- The Institute of Leisure and Amenity Management's annual conference, Leisure 2000, in Bournemouth.
- The Conservative Party holding its annual conference in Blackpool.

Did you know?

- Tourism provides 1.7 million jobs (7 per cent of the UK's workforce).
- Tourism creates one in five of all new jobs.
- Over 200 000 businesses, mainly small independent ones, hotels and guest houses, restaurants, holiday homes, caravans and camping parks are responsible for the bulk of tourism services.
- In 2000, the UK welcomed 26.2 million overseas visitors.

As well as travelling to watch sports events, many people travel and take part. This could range from a local rugby club going on tour to Wales for Easter weekend to a running club staying overnight in London in preparation for the London Marathon.

As a spectator, you might go to Trent Bridge to watch England play Australia in a one-day cricket international or enjoy a day out at Holme Pierrepont National Watersports Centre.

Activity

> In pairs, contact the English Tourism Council and the British Tourist Authority and find out their main roles and responsibilities.

Business tourism

Tourism is not solely a recreational concern. Many people travel both within the UK and internationally for business purposes.

Business meetings

- A British sportswear manufacturer flies to India to meet suppliers and negotiate prices.
- A Marketing Director flies to Saudi Arabia to meet potential clients and set up new products.
- A local politician travels by train from London to Leeds and back again the same day to meet constituents.

Activity

> Which features in your area could be classed as tourist attractions?

Talk about it

In your group, discuss how you would promote tourism in your area.

Snapshot

Students invade Ibiza

George, Ravi, Ben and Ziad had just completed their A-levels. Now for the fun! The plane landed at 2.00 pm so it was down to the beach and seek out the sun. The lads had worked hard for their exams and had managed to save up for this holiday through their part-time jobs in a fast-food outlet and the local cake factory.

For two glorious weeks they were going to enjoy themselves, and enjoy themselves they did.

Social activities and nightlife started at 11.30 pm and finished at 6.30 am, just in time for breakfast.

The clubs held upwards of 3000 young people, all out to have a good time. Daytime was spent sleeping, sun bathing, sleeping, playing cards and sleeping.

Food consisted of beans on toast, pizza and corn beef sandwiches.

After two weeks of constant fun, romance and enjoyment, the lads arrived back in England, needing another holiday to recover from the last one!

What makes up the travel and tourism industry?

The travel and tourism industry industry is vast, and in the same way that we divided the leisure industry into its key components, or parts, we can divide the travel and tourism industry into seven key components as shown in Figure 1.7.

Figure 1.7 The main components of the travel and tourism industry

Travel agents

You have only to look along the high street to see the number of travel agents there are nowadays. Obviously, they are all in competition with each other. This is shown by their window displays:

The main aims of travel agents are:

- to sell holidays and associated products like insurance, car hire, currency exchange
- to provide information
- to advise clients.

They provide the following services:

- plan travel itineraries
- work out costings
- issue tickets
- keep accounts
- book airport car parking spaces.

Much of the information provided by travel agents to clients is delivered through the medium of brochures. Specific data on travel and accommodation arrangements are checked through computer reservations systems. Travel consultants who have been on educational visits to some destinations can also draw on personal experience. Some travel agents will lend clients videos which feature popular resorts.

Travel agents sell their products and services in much the same way as any high street shop in that they advertise what they sell and supply customers with what they want. However, there is one essential difference – travel agents do not charge their customers for their service. They are paid commission by the companies whose products they sell. In other words, they act as agents for the industry's suppliers or 'principals' as they are known.

These consist of tour operators, airlines, rail companies, hotels, ferry companies and car hire companies.

Retail travel agents

Retail travel agents tend to sell a wide range of popular summer sun and winter holidays such as two weeks in Gran Canaria or a week's skiing in Andorra. They also deal with long-haul flights, that is those beyond Europe such as Australia, the USA and the Far East.

Business travel agents

Business travel agents specialise in arranging transport and accommodation for business people who want to see suppliers, attend conferences, develop new business, and so on. They arrange flights, transfers and accommodation in much the same way as retail travel agents do for holidaymakers. Some large companies like Boots the Chemists, whose business travel requirements are high, have a travel agent on site. This is known as an 'in plant' travel agency.

> **Talk about it**
>
> In pairs, list the skills and qualities you think you would need to work in a travel agents.

Multiples and independents

The retail travel industry in the UK is dominated by national multiples which have agencies throughout the country, for example Lunn Poly and Thomas Cook.

There are also many independent travel agents which do not form part of a national chain. They usually consist of one retail unit although they can still be classed as independents if they have up to six branches.

Travel agents sell a wide range of holidays. What other services do they provide?

Independent travel agents are not usually found on the high street but in an office above another retail outlet. They tend to provide a local service in the suburbs or villages. Independents are vulnerable to take-overs by national multiples.

Another type of travel agent is the regional 'miniple' which enjoys close connections with business and leisure travellers in its region. It sometimes starts out as a one-shop family business and develops over time.

> **Activity**
>
> ▶ Find one business travel agency and one independent travel agency in your area and compare the products and services they offer.

Currency exchange

One of the services provided by travel agents is currency exchange. This is offered because at some stage where overseas travel is involved, sterling will have to be exchanged for another currency. The main means of exchanging currency include:

- changing sterling for foreign currency or traveller's cheques
- changing sterling for a travel agent's own traveller's cheques – some travel agents, particularly business travel agents, deal in traveller's cheques, while some of the larger ones, such as Thomas Cook and American Express, issue their own cheques
- Eurocheques which allow the holder to pay for items or draw cash in European currencies.

Despite some fears within the travel industry about travel agents going out of business because holidays can now be booked on the Internet, travel agents are still very much in evidence on the high street. Perhaps people still like to book their holiday through travel agents because of the personal service they offer. What's more, any complaints about the holiday can be dealt with face to face.

Case study

The euro

On 1 January 2002, some 300 million Europeans had a new currency – the euro.

It has been adopted by 12 countries that now have the same currency. The UK, Sweden and Denmark are members of the European Union but have decided not to replace their currency with the euro at the moment.

In countries that have adopted the euro (e.g. Spain and France) their previous currencies (peseta and franc) are no longer legal. They now use euros instead. It's the biggest currency change the world has ever known.

This will make it easier for people travelling to the European Union countries. They will now be able to understand how much they are paying for things. If a cup of coffee cost 6 euros in one country and 3 euros in another, it's simple to work out which has the cheaper coffee.

Travel agents are in the business of advising clients about currency exchange, so having the euro makes it easier for them.

1. How much is a euro worth today against the pound?
2. Find out which 12 countries have adopted the euro.
3. Visit three travel agents and find out how they recommend you travel with euros if you are taking traveller's cheques.
4. Why do you think that travel agents might welcome the euro?
5. What is the symbol for the euro and what denominations does it come in?

Location of travel agents

The main role of travel agents is to sell products from a convenient location. In the past, many were located near to travel terminals at pier heads, docks or railway stations. However, they are now usually located in major centres in towns and cities, where they can be easily found and used.

Ground-floor premises in a busy street with convenient nearby parking make an ideal location. The window can be used to display brochures, posters and publicity about all destinations. The street window can paint a picture of a world full of glamour and excitement waiting to be explored.

Tour operators

When you go into a travel agent to book a holiday you are usually given a selection of brochures to look through. These brochures are produced by organisations known as tour operators that provide holidays for customers.

A tour operator puts together holiday packages which consist of:

- travel – road, sea, air, rail
- accommodation – hotels, guesthouses, self-catering
- travel services – transfers, car hire, excursions.

Tour operators organise package holidays to a range of different domestic and international destinations. Most tour operators are wholesalers in that they produce a package holiday and then negotiate the product with the travel agent which then sells on the product to its clients.

There are two types of tour operator:

- Wholesale operators put together and operate tours only through retail travel agents.
- Direct sell operators do not make their products available through travel agents but sell the package direct to the public.

Some tour operators specialise in domestic tourism, that is organising tours within the UK for UK residents. Incoming tour operators specialise in tours for overseas visitors in the

UK. In both cases, money is spent in this country which therefore helps the economy.

Examples of well-known tour operators include Thomas Cook and American Express, both of which operate worldwide.

A tour operator needs to take the following into account when budgeting the costings of a holiday package:

- marketing of brochures
- employment and training of staff, e.g. holiday reps
- market research – which principals and clients to sell to
- reservations – maintaining booking systems.

Of course, some people like to arrange all their own travel and accommodation which is not part of any package. These are known as independent travellers who like the freedom and control to make their own itineraries.

Talk about it
In your group, discuss the advantages of travelling independently.

Tourist information and guiding services

Organisations providing tourist information

Tourism is big business. It is good for the economy and provides jobs for about 1.7 million people. It brings new jobs to areas hit by the decline of other industries – on average, for £30 000 spent on tourism, one job is created.

The English Tourism Council
The English Tourism Council is funded by the Department for Culture, Media and Sport. It aims to:

- improve standards in accommodation and service quality to meet the increasing demands of tourists
- provide forecasts, research and guidance to foresee future trends
- make a positive contribution to the social, economic and environmental well-being of national life.

British Tourist Authority
This was established in 1969 with the aim of promoting the UK to overseas visitors. It does this by having sales offices in many countries abroad including, for example, Germany, Australia, France, Saudi Arabia and the USA. These offices distribute promotional leaflets and brochures about the UK to overseas visitors. In addition, they liaise with overseas travel agents and tour operators by organising seminars, exhibitions and travel trade shows.

The British Tourist Authority also promotes the UK by sponsoring stand space at the world's largest tourism exhibitions, e.g. the World Travel Market which attracts visitors and trade representatives from all over the world.

National, regional and area tourist boards and tourist information centres
Information for tourists is provided by national, regional and area tourist boards and local tourist information centres (TICs). Their job is to market and monitor the quality and development of the particular tourism area they serve.

There are four national tourist boards, one for each of the individual countries that make up the UK – England, Wales, Scotland and Northern Ireland. Their main job is to encourage tourists to visit their respective countries and to improve tourist facilities. They are funded by central government.

To help the national tourist boards in promoting each country, there are a number of regional and area tourist boards which concentrate their efforts on small, specific regions or areas within each individual country. Regional tourist boards receive funding from the English Tourism Council. They oversee local tourist information centres and coordinate the promotion and development of tourism in their own region.

Local tourist information centres tell visitors about accommodation, car hire, visitor attractions, restaurants and transport. They also provide maps of the town and region they serve. They are mainly funded by local authorities which sometimes own and manage tourist attractions themselves, for example theatres and museums. Local authorities usually have a tourism section within their leisure services department.

What skills and qualities do you think a tour guide should have? Discuss this in your group

Guiding services

You may have been on a guided tour, perhaps of a castle or stately home, the aim of which is to make the tour as informative and interesting as possible.

Some of the best guided tours can be made on open-top buses around cities like London, York and Bath. The tour guide gives a running commentary which usually includes interesting stories about people and places on the route.

Some tour guides are volunteers who have a special interest in the history of a place. Others are retired people who have a vast wealth of knowledge about an area and who have the time to pass on their knowledge and enthusiasm to tourists.

Activity
- Using your research skills, gather information about the Blue Badge Guide scheme.

Online travel services

More and more people are now booking their holidays, flights and accommodation on the Internet.

Travel companies like Itavia and Cyberes are able to buy air seats in bulk and so can afford to charge fares at a cheaper rate than tour operators and travel agents. Most of the bookings they receive are made via the Internet.

Hotels can be booked on the Internet by individuals logging on to needahotel.com.

These companies advertise their website addresses in newspapers and magazines or they can be found by using search engines such as Yahoo! or Ask Jeeves.

As a result of online bookings, some travel agents have seen their business decline. Although many people still prefer the face-to-face contact when booking through a travel agent, more and more people are using the Internet. Trends suggest this will continue to increase, especially for independent travellers who prefer to make their own travel arrangements.

Talk about it
In your group, discuss the advantages and disadvantages of using online services for making holiday arrangements.

How can travel agents overcome the competition from Internet bookings?

Accommodation and catering

The hotel and catering industry provides accommodation, food and drink for those who are away from home.

Did you know?
Accommodation and catering employs 20 per cent of the UK tourism workforce and brings in money to both the national and local economy.

Overseas visitors spend one-third of their 'holiday' money on accommodation and catering.

There is a wide range of facilities in accommodation and catering:

Accommodation can be divided into two basic categories:

- serviced accommodation – where meals are provided, e.g. hotels, guesthouses
- self-catering – e.g. cottages, chalets and some hotels.

Tourists decide for themselves the type of accommodation they want. When it comes to eating arrangements, they can choose the following options:

- full board, known as the American plan – three meals are provided
- half-board, known as the Modified American plan – includes breakfast plus midday or evening meal
- bed and breakfast, known as the Continental plan.

Location affects the type of accommodation available

Location affects the type of accommodation available. For example, in a city there is likely to be a wide range of hotels including luxury five-star hotels. These may be part of an international chain, for example Holiday Inn. In a small town or rural area there will more likely be guesthouses and farmhouses offering bed and breakfast. In a seaside resort rows upon rows of guesthouses, usually offering family accommodation, along the promenade are more common.

64 Investigating leisure and tourism   Unit 1

Hotels can be placed under several headings according to their location:

- city centre hotels
- beach hotels
- resort hotels
- country house hotels.

Each serves a different type of client.

Grading schemes

These help tourists distinguish different types of accommodation. The best known are the English Tourism Council, AA and RAC ratings which offer a clear guide to the type and quality of accommodation. Properties are visited annually by trained, impartial assessors so that guests can be confident that their accommodation has been thoroughly checked and rated for quality. This is how the scheme works:

- Hotels and self-catering accommodation are all given ratings between one and five stars – the more stars awarded, the higher the quality and the greater the range of facilities and level of service provided.
- Holiday, touring and camping parks inspected by the English Tourism Council are also given ratings between one and five stars, while those inspected by the AA are given ratings between one and five pennants (flags). In each case, the number awarded is based on the quality of service, cleanliness, environment and facilities provided.
- Guest accommodation covers a wide variety of serviced accommodation, including guesthouses, bed and breakfast, inns and farmhouses. Establishments are rated between one and five diamonds, with the same minimum requirement for services and facilities applying to all guest accommodation. The more diamonds awarded, the higher the overall quality in areas such as cleanliness, service and hospitality.

Catering

Tourists 'eating out' want a wide choice of catering outlets to choose from. A family of four may want to go to McDonald's, a young couple may want a romantic candlelit dinner in a bistro, whereas a group of men might want a few pints in the local pub, followed by a curry.

The standard of catering in hotels can sometimes make or break a holiday. That's why some people like to play safe and choose self-catering.

Talk about it

In your group, discuss who would stay in the following types of accommodation:

a   a country house hotel
b   a Blackpool guesthouse
c   a city centre hotel.

Activity

▶ Compare the prices and facilities of a local 4-star hotel with a bed and breakfast.

Attractions

These can be divided into two types:

- natural attractions, e.g. the Lake District, the National Parks, Niagara Falls, the Grand Canyon, the Giant's Causeway
- man-made attractions, e.g. Alton Towers, the Albert Dock, Liverpool, Disneyland Paris, the Leaning Tower of Pisa, Hadrian's Wall, Stonehenge.

The reason why many people make trips is to see attractions. For example, tourists go to Blackpool to see the Tower, to stroll along the 'prom', to visit the Pleasure Beach and to see the 'lights' (the illuminations) which are promoted as the 'greatest free show on Earth'.

Theatres, museums, country parks and historic buildings are all classed as attractions. They provide some type of entertainment for visitors. The more attractions an area has, the more tourists will visit the area. This will benefit the local economy.

Case study

Stonehenge

Stonehenge is a 5000-year-old World Heritage site surrounded by intrigue and mystery. It is a prehistoric ceremonial centre – a reminder of our past – located in the south of England near Salisbury and is a site of international importance. For its time it was an amazing feat of engineering. It is surrounded by the remains of ceremonial and domestic structures, some of which date back beyond the origins of the monument itself. Even to this day the purpose of Stonehenge is unclear. Its orientation to sunrise and sunset remains one of its most amazing and intriguing features.

1. How would you get to Stonehenge by road and rail from where you live?
2. Stonehenge is shrouded in mystery. In what way could you use this feature to attract more people to it?

Activity

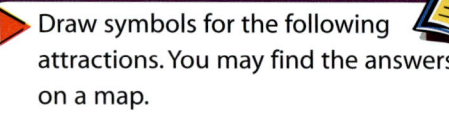

Draw symbols for the following attractions. You may find the answers on a map.

- abbey or cathedral
- aquarium
- camp site
- caravan site
- castle
- country park
- golf course
- historic house
- information centre
- nature reserve
- picnic site
- wildlife park
- zoo.

A big sporting event could also be classed as an attraction. The London Marathon attracts 25 000 runners and thousands of spectators, many of whom want overnight accommodation. Other sporting events which attract thousands of visitors are:

- the Olympic Games
- the Tour de France
- the FA Cup Final.

A National Code of Practice ensures visitor attractions have agreed to provide a high standard of customer service, cleanliness, courtesy and maintenance. They must also deal promptly with enquiries and provide proper access for people with disabilities.

Transportation

Rapid and efficient transport systems by road, rail, air and sea have given tourists the chance to travel far and wide and gain a greater knowledge of the world.

Choice of transport depends on:

- price
- destination
- time – how much is available
- reason – visiting friends or relatives, business or leisure
- departure points – how easy it is to get there.

Transport is a capital-intensive industry. Airlines, railways and shipping companies need to invest large amounts of money in buildings, planes, trains or ships and equipment in order to provide modern, efficient services to passengers.

The increase in travel, particularly by car, has raised a number of issues like congestion and pollution, especially in cities, on motorway routes and in the countryside.

The busiest weekend of the year in England is the one when schools break up for the summer holidays. Traffic jams form on the M55 into Blackpool, the A17 to Skegness and the M5 into Cornwall. People set off at 3.00 am to try to avoid the chaos.

The government has invested heavily in road and motorway systems to try to ease traffic congestion, and it is constantly urging people to use public transport and not their own cars.

New developments such as the Channel Tunnel have made travel easier and faster. Heathrow, situated to the west of London on the M4, is one of the busiest airports in the world and long-haul flights are now available from Manchester and Birmingham.

In order to satisfy the demands of their customers and stay one step ahead of the competition, airlines, shipping and railway companies have to keep investing in buildings, staff and equipment.

Activity
- Trace a map of the UK and mark on it the main air and sea ports.

Types of holiday

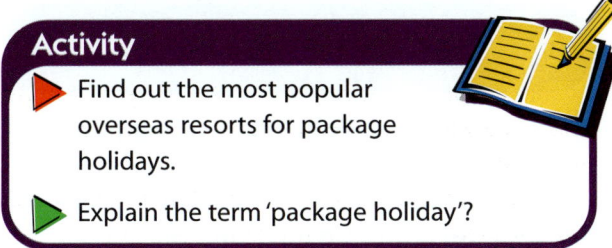

The main types of holidays

Package holidays

Activity
- Find out the most popular overseas resorts for package holidays.
- Explain the term 'package holiday'?

Package holidays are sometimes referred to as inclusive tours (Its) or package tours.

The package holiday is a total tourism product. It usually consists of transport to the destination and accommodation and sometimes includes other services such as entertainment and recreational activities like excursions or golf course fees for golfing holidays.

The overseas package holiday was first organised by Thomas Cook. His tours were usually journeys in which the tourist took in several destinations not just one.

Package holidays, as we know them today, started in the 1950s, but their popularity increased in the following four decades so that in the 1990s around 15 million people from the UK each year went on an overseas package holiday.

Two important factors led to the growth in popularity of the package holiday:

- New technology in aircraft development meant shorter flight times so allowing international destinations to become realistic as holiday resorts for UK travellers.
- Although some people had the time and money to travel overseas, they were reluctant to do so on their own. The organised package holiday, which took away any worries travellers had, gave them the necessary sense of security for their holiday plans.

Package holidays are put together by tour operators and sold by travel agents, although some tour operators will allow travellers to book direct with them. Several tour operators offer all-inclusive packages which means that meals, drinks, sports and entertainment are included in the price of the holiday. These packages are becoming increasingly popular as more and more people are finding it so much more convenient to have everything provided for them.

Independent holidays

Some people prefer to make their own travel arrangements rather than book package holidays. These people are known as independent travellers as they like the freedom and control to organise their own itineraries.

The increase in package holidays since the mid-1970s has been matched by a growth in independent travel holidays. This shows that an increasing number of people like the greater flexibility in travel arrangements that independent travel can offer.

> **Talk about it**
> How do independent travellers plan their holidays?

Domestic holidays

Domestic holidays are taken by people from the UK and may involve short breaks or even day trips within the UK.

There are still many people who take their annual holidays in the UK. These holidays may be their main holiday or a second or even a third holiday. Short breaks are very popular and this market continues to grow.

An example of a domestic holiday is a family from London spending a week in St Ives, Cornwall. In fact, the West Country is the most popular destination for UK domestic holidays – 25 per cent of all domestic holidays lasting longer than four nights are spent in this region.

Many people are unaware that domestic holidays can be booked through travel agents whom they assume take only overseas bookings. In fact, UK holidays are a valuable source of earnings for travel agents as commission levels are usually well above those of overseas operators.

> **Talk about it**
> In your group, say why you think some UK holidaymakers prefer to spend their holidays in the UK rather than abroad.

> **Activity**
> Find some holiday brochures advertising holidays in the UK. Identify three different types of holiday.

Inbound and outbound holidays

Inbound tourism

Inbound holidays are taken by visitors who come from overseas to visit the UK and spend their holidays here. The USA still generates the greatest number of overseas visitors to the UK despite the events of 11 September 2001.

An example of an incoming holiday is a French couple flying from Paris to Heathrow airport or a Dutch family arriving by ferry at Harwich. Incoming tourism is sometimes known as inbound tourism.

> **Think about it**
> What makes the UK attractive to overseas visitors?

> **Activity**
> List the top five overseas countries that provide the most visitors to the UK.

Outbound tourism

This type of holiday includes those people from the UK who spend their holidays (and their money) overseas. This means that economies in the USA, Spain, France and Italy, for example, all benefit from UK outgoing tourism.

An example of an outbound holiday would be a group of students from Leeds flying to Gran Canaria for a two-week holiday.

The number of outbound holidays taken by UK residents has increased steadily in recent years, rising from 15 million per year in the 1980s to 28 million per year in the 1990s. Consequently, this had led to a decrease in domestic tourism.

Holidays involving short-haul and long-haul flights

Short-haul flights usually take less than five hours and destinations include Greece, Spain, Germany and Scandinavia. Package holidays to Europe involve short-haul flights. Short-haul destinations have been the traditional market for overseas holidays and while this type of holiday still makes up the major part of the market, long-haul destinations began to catch up by the mid-1990s. This trend is likely to continue as long-haul travel becomes less expensive and travellers have more personal disposable income available to spend on holidays.

However, the world political situation could well mean that people would feel safer travelling short-haul rather than long-haul.

The long-haul holiday market over the past five years is the fastest growing segment of the holiday market.

Long-haul destinations are considered to take at least five hours by air to reach and so are those beyond Europe, for example the USA, the Far East, Australia and the Caribbean. New long-haul destinations include West Africa (the Gambia), Goa and the Dominican Republic. Travellers can choose to do whatever they want including snorkelling, deep-sea fishing, going on safari, celebrating a wedding, honeymoon or anniversary in a far-off, romantic location.

People were first tempted away from the Mediterranean resorts by the creation of DisneyWorld in Florida. Holidaymakers began to want something new and exciting and were prepared to spend 12 hours on a plane to achieve their goal.

From this, cruise companies introduced packages whereby the traveller could fly to Miami and then cruise around the Caribbean, which is now the cruise capital of the world.

Two of the most popular long-haul destinations are Thailand and Hong Kong which, with their cheap prices, fine service and a touch of the exotic, prove extremely attractive to UK holidaymakers.

Activity
> Which long-haul destination would appeal to you? Describe the attractions of one long-haul destination.

Talk about it
> In your group, consider why short-haul destinations like Spain and Greece are so popular with UK holidaymakers?

Special interest holidays

Some people prefer to combine their holiday with their interests, for example sport. Specialist tour operators work out programmes for their clients which can be as active or relaxing as the client wants. For example, Neilson Active Holidays offers packages which include sailing, diving, cycling windsurfing and mountain biking.

Another popular sports holiday is golf. The Algarve in Portugal is a regular haunt of many amateur golfers. Of course, another type of sports holiday is skiing, with the French, Austrian and Swiss resorts being the main destinations.

Activity
> Visit a local travel agent and gather as much information as you can about special interest holidays.

Cultural holidays

Many people travel with the purpose of seeking artistic and cultural inspiration. Their holidays include visiting art galleries in Italy, wine tasting and food appreciation in France, visiting gardens in Jersey or even South Africa. There is even a tour of the battlefields of France for those interested in war history.

Specialist tour operators have sprung up to offer hang-gliding trips in Wales or train spotting excursions in India.

Short-break holidays

People who can't spare the time to take a longer holiday, or who may not be able to afford two weeks abroad, can take a short break. This type of holiday can also be in addition to the main holiday.

Short breaks have become increasingly popular. The Channel Tunnel and cheaper air and ferry prices have opened up continental Europe for the traveller who perhaps wants to spend the weekend in France or Belgium.

Short-break holidays are not just restricted to destinations like Paris, Amsterdam or Dublin. Weekend breaks to New York for Christmas shopping or Boston for sightseeing have developed.

In the UK, City Breaks to London offer a mini-package holiday which includes transport, accommodation, theatre tickets and sightseeing tours.

Paris is a popular short-break destination

Weekends are, of course, the most popular time to travel. Thomas Cook Holidays describes and promotes its city breaks in the following way:

> You could be enjoying a Guinness in Dublin, or riding a gondola in Venice, eating swordfish in Lisbon, or shopping in Macy's in New York; exploring a live volcano near Reykjavik, or watching the opera in Verona; riding a camel in Cairo, or scouting the art treasures of Florence …

Activity

- Find one city break destination (apart from London) and describe the attractions it offers. You may find some useful information on the website link at www.heinemann.co.uk/hotlinks.

Travel

Transport

Transport is a capital-intensive industry. Airlines, railways and shipping companies need to invest large amounts of money in buildings, planes, trains or ships and equipment in order to provide modern, efficient services to their customers. Governments also need to provide money to build roads and motorways for car owners and coach operators. Tourism has developed as an industry as a result of the improvements made in transport technology.

Without transport, there would be no travel or tourism. Its importance can be summed up in three ways:

- Transport provides the means of travel to a destination from the tourist's place of origin and return.
- Once tourists have arrived, it provides the means of travelling around a destination, for example the use of a taxi or bus to visit a major attraction such as the Tower of London or Edinburgh Castle.
- Transport can be a major feature of the tourist trip, for example a train journey on the Orient Express. It may also be an integral part of the holiday experience, such as a fly-cruise package tour, a flight on Concorde or a cruise on the *QE2*.

Methods of travel

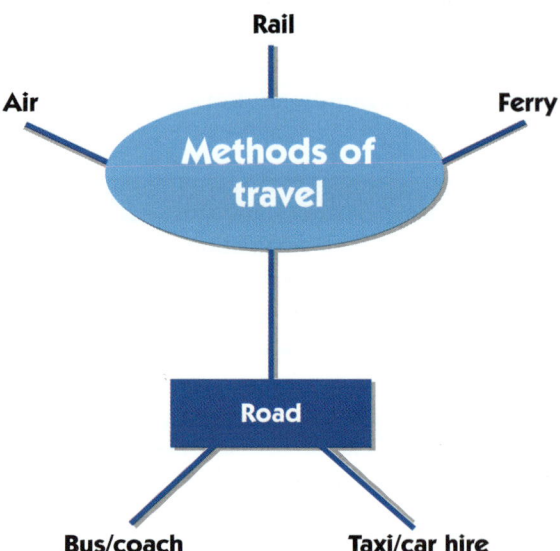

The main methods of travel

Talk about it

In your group, say what your favourite method of travel is. How do you think travel 100 years ago was different from today's?

Air travel

Travelling by air has become very popular in recent times because it is quick and has become more affordable now that airlines are competing more for passengers. Many overseas visitors arrive by plane and the UK has a number of airports which make it easy for tourists to visit different parts of the country. These include London Heathrow, London Gatwick, Stansted, Birmingham, Manchester, Leeds/Bradford, Newcastle, Bristol, Glasgow and East Midlands.

By far the largest number of overseas trips, both outward and inward to the UK, are by air. International passenger statistics suggest that around 85 per cent of all holidaymakers prefer to fly to their overseas destinations.

Since the events of 11 September 2001, however, the number of people travelling by plane, especially to the USA, has fallen. This has had a knock-on effect on the airlines in terms of profits and job losses.

Air travel has the advantage of coming up against no natural barriers. The only things which prevent aeroplanes taking the shortest route between two points are adverse weather conditions, air traffic congestion and countries which restrict flights across their country for political reasons.

Air transport can be divided into three main areas:

- Scheduled air services – scheduled flights which regularly operate specific domestic or international routes according to published timetables or schedules which are fixed in advance.
- Charter flights – services organised to meet travel needs at specific times, are not fixed to a specific timetable and can be altered or cancelled if passenger numbers fall off. Most charter flights are usually organised by tour operators for the purpose of transporting holidaymakers, and for this reason, the majority of the flights are organised in the summer to holiday destinations such as the Mediterranean. If a tour operator cannot sell enough seats on a particular flight, it can seek to combine those passengers on another flight to the same destination. This is known as consolidation.
- Air taxi services – these are generally offered by small private charter companies, who carry upwards of 18 passengers to specific destinations. Being small, these aircraft can often utilise the runways of small as well as large airports. As such, they are of particular interest to business executives in that, for example, they allow passengers to fly out to a meeting in a specific location and fly back the same day.

Figure 1.8 Locations of UK airports

Activity

- Figure 1.8 shows the airports in the UK. Name as many as you can.
- Name three different airlines that use the airport nearest to where you live. Find out how the airport has developed over the last ten years.

Travelling by air

Advantages
- speed.

Disadvantages
- limited departure/arrival point
- transfer time needed to city/final destination
- luggage restricted.

Rail travel

Trains play an important part in moving people between and within countries. Trains are particularly used for domestic tourism – leisure and business. They are a quick and convenient way of travelling between cities, and in the UK, for example, 17 per cent of all business travel uses trains. The majority of people who travel first class on trains are people who are travelling around the country for business purposes.

Most trains offer passengers a choice of facilities and services: sleeping accommodation, restaurant cars, serving snacks and meals, bars and telephones. Most train services offer different classes or grades of travel, according to the price paid for the ticket.

A major growth area in train travel has been the re-emergence of private steam railways. In the UK there are 45 such lines in operation. Locomotives, both full size and narrow gauge, have been lovingly restored by voluntary labour and attract visitors to take nostalgic rail journeys in locations like Ffestiniog in Wales, the Severn Valley and Minehead in Somerset.

Travelling by rail

Advantages
- fast, particularly over long distances
- normally 'walk on', no need to book (although at some peak times you have to)
- choice of joining points
- catering on many trains, although not cheap
- least impact on the environment.

Disadvantages
- restricted to rail routes – some cross-country journeys take a long time
- restricted to timetable service – you can't go wherever and whenever you want
- luggage limited to what you can carry
- cost – despite special offers, still more expensive than road journeys
- standing room only on busy trains, sometimes for long journeys.

The Channel Tunnel

The UK is now linked to mainland or continental Europe via the Channel Tunnel. This has had important outcomes for the travel industry:

- The Channel Tunnel takes 40 per cent of cross-Channel passengers.
- 5000 people are employed to staff the tunnel.
- Thousands of other jobs have been created in engineering, transport and, not least, tourism.

Activity

1. Find out some statistics about the Channel Tunnel, for example length, journey time, etc.
2. Find out some information about Eurostar.

Steam railways have become popular visitor attractions

Ferry travel

It doesn't take a genius to work out that as the UK is an island it is obviously surrounded by water. In fact, you cannot find any place in the UK that is further than about 80 miles from the sea (in a straight line). Ferries are a popular way of travelling, especially for European visitors who want to visit the UK.

The UK is linked by regular ferry services to all European countries with North Sea coasts and with Ireland. These ferry services are usually used by passengers in combination with some form of local transport, for example coach, train or car which carries them to the ferry ports from their places of origin, and on to their final destination after the sea crossing.

Despite the opening of the Channel Tunnel, ferries remain a popular means of holiday travel to continental Europe.

The success of ferry companies depends on being able to get cars and passengers on and off ferries rapidly. This again reinforces the need for good transport links; in this case, between port and the road system leading out of it. Demand varies seasonally, peaking in the holiday months of July and August. Day trips to France, often involving shopping in French hypermarkets, have been a recent growth area, boosting low-season demand. However, all ferries, including services operated by hovercraft and hydrofoils, can be seriously affected by adverse weather conditions. Delays and cancellations are always a risk in winter.

Ferry services form a vital link with Ireland, and with smaller islands like the Isle of Wight, the Isle of Man the Hebrides and the Shetlands.

Activity

1. Make a list of as many different ferry companies as you can find.
2. Collect some information about hovercrafts.

Travelling by ferry

Advantages
- sometimes the only transport form available (e.g. Isle of Wight)
- vehicle ferries can take private cars.

Disadvantages
- the timetable can be restricting
- some services are passenger ferries only and cannot take vehicles.

Activity

- There are major ferry ports dotted around the coastline of the UK. Try to name the ports shown in Figure 1.9, using ferry brochures and an atlas.
- Find out where your nearest ferry port is and identify the destinations of the ferries from it. How can tourists get to this port? If you live in a port town, choose another example.

Road

Lots of people travel by road whether it is by bus, taxi or car. Long distance journeys can be made by motorway so that travelling time is reduced. Another point about motorway travel is that many attractions in the UK are close to the motorway network e.g. the Lake District.

Obviously motorways cannot serve every route and direction that tourists and travellers need to take. This is where 'A' and 'B' roads come into it. They cover the country to form an intricate network of routes. 'A' roads with low numbers (e.g. A1, A2 and A3) radiate mostly from London, whereas roads with higher numbers, such as the A10 and A20 connect with the A1 and A2. The motorways form the basis of a good inter-connecting road system along with the major trunk roads.

Figure 1.9 Ferry ports in the UK

Activity

1. Which motorway connects Liverpool and Hull?
2. Which motorway circles London?
3. Which motorway takes you from London to the West Country and Wales?

▶ Where and what is 'spaghetti junction'?

Did you know?

London Transport has estimated that over 20 per cent of all passengers on its famous red London buses are tourists.

Bus/coaches

Coach operators offer a wide choice of tourism services by way of:

- private hire service
- express trunk routes for domestic and international travel
- tours and excursions
- transfers from, for example, airports to tourist destinations.

Although not particularly popular with business travellers, this form of travel is sought after by the young and the elderly since it offers one of the most convenient (local pick-up and direct delivery right to the resort) and cheapest means of travel. New express coaches seek to attract other users by providing a much wider range of services, including such extras as on-board toilets, reclining seats, telephone, video, as well as snack bar refreshments, even stewards/stewardesses.

Local bus services, too, are often used by visitors in large towns and cities.

Taxi/car hire

Taxis provide an important service to leisure and business tourists. Many of the customers of taxi companies in cities are visitors who use taxis as a fast and convenient way of moving around unfamiliar streets.

In the UK alone, car rental generates £600 million a year. Within the UK the majority of car hire rentals are for business people or for overseas tourists. Travel agents regard car hire as an important add-on to a sale. For example, when they book a rail, air or coach inclusive holiday for the customer they can also make a car rental booking. The customer may not have considered hiring a car at his or her destination.

Some of the major car rental companies are Avis, Budget, Dollar Rent a Car and Hertz.

Travel by car

The increase in private ownership of the motor car was part of the reason for the decline of the railway system in many countries. Today, the car is the most popular means of transport by far for tourists. In the USA, journeys by car account for 85 per cent of all holiday travel.

The car offers people greater freedom in terms of where they go, the route they follow and where they stop on the way.

Travelling by bus/coach

Advantages
- goes straight into town/city
- choice of 'joining' points
- overall cost relatively low
- all passengers must have a seat, no standing
- many services have catering and on-board toilets.

Disadvantages
- restricted to service routes
- restricted to timetable service
- luggage limited to what you can carry
- seat can be guaranteed only by booking
- slower than rail/air.

Travelling by car

Advantages
- highly flexible – you decide where and when you travel
- large amounts of luggage easily carried
- door to door
- cost per mile is low
- you can hire one if you don't own one.

Disadvantages
- high initial cost in buying, licensing and insuring, even though the cost per mile is low
- parking can sometimes be a problem
- traffic congestion can cause delays.

Alongside the growth in car ownership was an increase in the purchase of camping gear and caravans. Services like roadside catering, car hire and motels have also flourished.

The UK offers a wide range of tourist destinations

Coastal areas

Seaside towns

Seaside towns were at their most popular during the 1930s, 1940s and 1950s. The type of holidaymaker who spent perhaps one or two weeks in places like Scarborough, Blackpool or Margate was one who travelled by train, stayed in a guesthouse, was content to stroll along the prom and perhaps paddle in the sea and play bingo in the amusement arcades.

Blackpool attracted the cotton mill workers from Bury, Manchester, and Bolton, whereas Skegness on the east coast was a haven for miners from Yorkshire and Nottinghamshire.

The 1980s saw a drop in popularity of these resorts as low priced overseas package holidays to Spain became available to more people. Seaside towns in the UK couldn't compete with the sunshine of the Costa del Sol and so they went about bringing what was essentially a 1950s product into the twenty-first century.

Publicity officers from these seaside towns realised that the days of knotted handkerchiefs and 'Kiss Me Quick' hats were long gone. New markets such as families and young people were targeted. All-year-round entertainment was developed and holiday camps became fully modernised family entertainment centres. This had to happen otherwise the seaside resorts would have died. Now they are aggressively marketing the attractions and benefits of UK seaside resorts and encouraging visitors to spend their money at home rather than abroad.

Case study

Torquay

Torquay is one of the most stylish resorts in the UK. Its elegant Victorian terraces, white villas and famous seven hills provide the backdrop to popular modern facilities such as the Riviera Centre and a busy shopping mall.

Torquay's waterfront is the focus of life in the town. Here you will find the palm-lined promenade, a lively harbour and an international marina. Within minutes of the town centre there are beautiful beaches which are easily accessible by foot, by car or by bus. The high standards of water quality and beach facilities mean that many carry coveted awards, including no fewer than three European Blue Flags – more than any other resort in the UK.

Back on dry land, Torquay has as wide a range of cosmopolitan restaurants as most big cities, plus a host of specialist local seafood, eating houses unique to the area. For evening entertainment you can choose from a range of theatres offering musicals, concerts and comedy.

1. What is meant by 'cosmopolitan' restaurants? Give some examples.
2. What are European Blue Flags?
3. What makes Torquay so attractive?

Heritage Coasts

Around 32 per cent of scenic English coastline is conserved (preserved) as Heritage Coast. Forty-four Heritage Coasts have been designated in England and Wales.

They were set up because of concerns that increasing numbers of visitors were harming key sites around the coast. These special coastlines are managed so that their natural beauty is protected and, where appropriate, the accessibility for visitors is improved. A coordinated plan was designed to create a system of footpaths, clean up the seawater and remove litter.

The first Heritage Coast was the famous white chalk cliffs of Beachy Head in Sussex. Now much of our coastline, like the sheer cliffs of Flamborough Head, with its huge seabird colony, is protected as part of our coastal heritage.

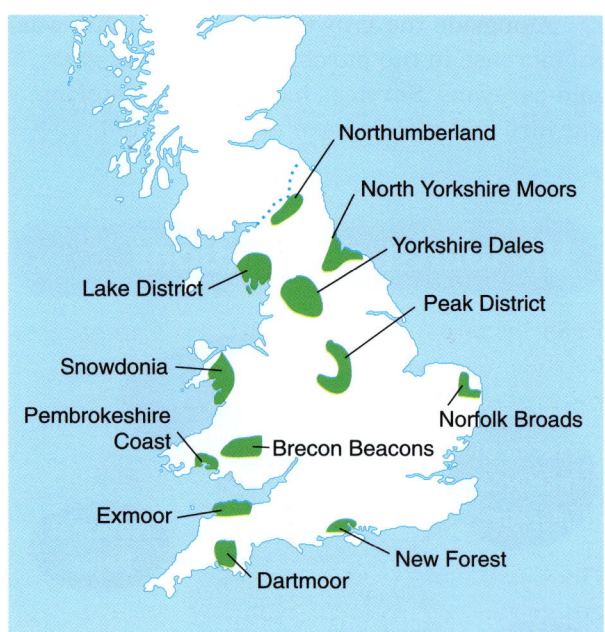

The National Parks of England and Wales

Activity

1. Find five other areas designated as Heritage Coast. What steps can we take to protect our coastline?
2. Choose two seaside resorts and find out where they are located, what they offer visitors and describe the main transport routes to them.

The National Parks

The idea of the National Parks was first suggested in 1931. In 1945 they were defined as 'extensive areas of beautiful and relatively wild countryside'. The 1949 National Parks and Access to the Countryside Act stated that within these parks, priority should be given to conservation and public access while at the same time agricultural use was to continue. The Act also stated that:

- the characteristic landscape should be strictly preserved
- access and facilities for public open-air enjoyment should be provided
- wildlife and buildings and places of architectural and historic interest should be suitably protected.

Services provided in the National Parks include:

- information and interpretation services – information centres, leaflets, books
- a ranger or warden service
- facilities for improving access for visitors – footpaths, stiles, waymarking
- provision of car parks and picnic sites
- assistance to voluntary conservation and wildlife groups.

Activity

- What is the importance of the National Parks?
- The New Forest and the South Downs are seeking to become designated as National Parks. What benefits might National Park status bring to both areas? (Follow the link on the Heinemann website (www.heinemann.co.uk/hotlinks) to the Council for National Parks website to help you.)

Threats to the National Parks

The legal protections given to our National Parks do not make them sacred. There continues to be change within the parks and some of these changes are threatening the concept of a National Park. The natural beauty can be affected and the scope they provide for open air recreation restricted.

The main threats are:

- changes in agricultural practice
- military use – live firing and road building
- quarrying and mineral extraction
- urban encroachment – housing developments
- planting trees that are not native to the UK
- new roads.

Refer back to the chart in Chapter 1 on page 21 for the size and numbers of visitors to the National Parks.

Areas of Outstanding Natural Beauty

The Countryside Agency is responsible for designating Areas of Outstanding Natural Beauty and advising the government on how they should be protected.

There are over 40 Areas of Outstanding Natural Beauty in England and Wales which are deliberately protected from any type of development for the benefit of the public. They vary in size and include features like forests, mountains and lakes.

The 1949 National Parks and Access to the Countryside Act gave the National Parks Commission power to preserve and protect these designated areas, although they can also be popular destinations for tourists.

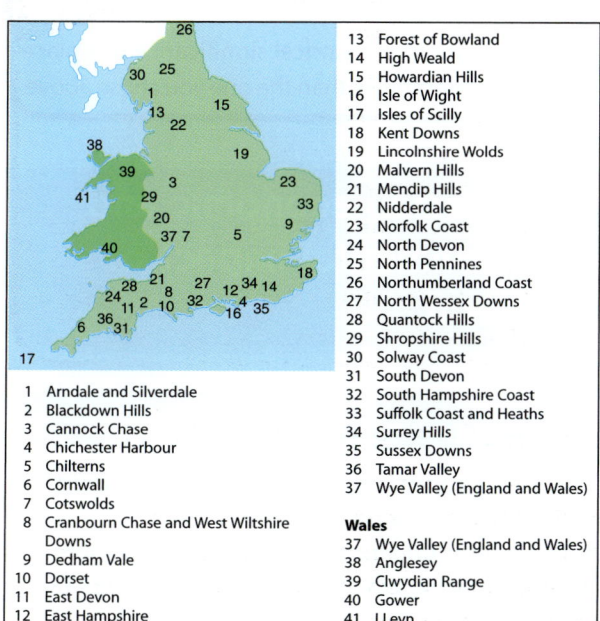

1 Arndale and Silverdale
2 Blackdown Hills
3 Cannock Chase
4 Chichester Harbour
5 Chilterns
6 Cornwall
7 Cotswolds
8 Cranbourn Chase and West Wiltshire Downs
9 Dedham Vale
10 Dorset
11 East Devon
12 East Hampshire
13 Forest of Bowland
14 High Weald
15 Howardian Hills
16 Isle of Wight
17 Isles of Scilly
18 Kent Downs
19 Lincolnshire Wolds
20 Malvern Hills
21 Mendip Hills
22 Nidderdale
23 Norfolk Coast
24 North Devon
25 North Pennines
26 Northumberland Coast
27 North Wessex Downs
28 Quantock Hills
29 Shropshire Hills
30 Solway Coast
31 South Devon
32 South Hampshire Coast
33 Suffolk Coast and Heaths
34 Surrey Hills
35 Sussex Downs
36 Tamar Valley
37 Wye Valley (England and Wales)

Wales
37 Wye Valley (England and Wales)
38 Anglesey
39 Clwydian Range
40 Gower
41 LLeyn

The Areas of Outstanding Natural Beauty in England and Wales

Towns and cities

Not everyone wants to take beach holidays in the UK, probably because the climate is so unpredictable. The alternative, apart from going abroad, is to explore the many individual towns and cities which have become tourist centres.

Attractions in such places include:

- historical buildings
- shopping centres
- cathedrals and churches
- trips and excursions
- monuments
- art galleries and museums.

Activity

 1. On a map of the UK, locate the following towns and cities:

   a Edinburgh
   b York
   c Oxford
   d Cambridge
   e Stratford-upon-Avon.

2. For each of the towns listed above, find out the following information:

   a the best way of accessing the city/town by three different means of travel
   b three attractions in the towns
   c a brief history of the town or city.

   Present your findings to the group.

 1. For one of the towns listed above, find out what types of visitor are most attracted to it and analyse why.

2. Carry out a full investigation of one attraction in the town. Find out what the purpose of the attraction is and analyse the type of visitor who might visit it.

3. How does your chosen attraction relate to the history of the town or city?

Some towns and cities are tourist centres in their own right, such as Stratford-upon-Avon, with its connection to Shakespeare, and York, with its museums and Minster. Other towns have developed into tourist centres because of their position close to or within a tourist area. Keswick, for example, is a tourist centre for visitors to the Lake District, as is Whitby which is close to the North York Moors.

Activity

Name the attractions in the following towns and cities:

a	Bath	f	Coventry
b	Berwick-upon-Tweed	g	Inverness
		h	Ross-on-Wye
c	Buxton	i	Stirling
d	Caernarfon	j	Tunbridge Wells.
e	Cambridge		

Compare your answers with those on page 86.

Some towns and cities become popular tourist destinations because they host international or local sports events. They experience an influx of tourists during the event.

Activity

Find out what major international sports and events take place at these sporting venues:

a	Aintree	g	Elland Road
b	Wimbledon	h	Headingley
c	Lords	i	Hampden Park
d	Twickenham	j	Crystal Palace
e	Don Valley	k	Lansdowne Road
f	Millennium stadium	l	Holme Pierrepont.

Theme parks

As we saw earlier in the unit, theme parks have grown enormously over the past 20 years. They provide a range of attractions on one site, catering for families and young people and offering an all-inclusive admission price for an unlimited number of rides. Others do not have an admission fee, for example Blackpool Pleasure Beach, which attracts 9 million visitors a year, but visitors are charged for individual rides. Similar examples include the Palace Pier, Brighton, Pleasureland Southport and Laserbowl, London.

Activity

- Trace a map of the UK and mark on it the location of as many theme parks as you can find.
- Describe the accessibility by road of two of the parks.

Places of historical interest

This category includes stately homes, castles and abbeys, cathedrals and churches, industrial monuments such as windmills and mines – in fact, anything which has historical significance, for example Stonehenge. These places attract both UK and overseas visitors.

The majority of these historical attractions are owned by private individuals, public companies and charitable trusts.

Did you know?

Sixty per cent of all incoming tourists visit London for its historical attractions.

Activity

- Choose one place of historical interest in the UK, explain why it attracts visitors and identify the road and rail transport routes to it.
- Describe the historical significance of a place of interest other than the one you chose above.

The social, economic and environmental impact of tourism

Sustainable tourism

Sustainable tourism seeks to tackle the long term environmental and social issues surrounding uncontrolled tourism development. In other words, governments worldwide need to try to balance conservation and the needs of local people against the tourist's desire for access to an area of great scenic beauty.

Case study

The Lake District

Visitors like to see picture-postcard views

The Lake District attracts around 16 million visitors each year and so tourism has come to play a major part in the economy of the area. However, tourism presents a number of challenges for the area.

As more and more cars join our roads, the pressures increase on areas like the Lake District. Millions of visitors a year – as well as local people – come to walk, climb, sail or just look. This means that even more care and expense has to be put into keeping the area as beautiful as everyone expects. Visitors like to see traditional dry-stone walls, grassy green fells, natural rock falls and picture-postcard cottages.

On the other hand, visitors bring in much needed income to support a multi-million pound local tourism industry. An estimated 24 000 people are employed as a direct result of tourism spending in Cumbria. A further 19 000 are employed indirectly as a large amount of the money from tourism goes back to the local economy.

It seems likely in the not-too-distant future that action will need to be taken to reduce the amount of traffic to ease congestion and pollution. For example, some passes may soon be made accessible to residents only. Coaches may be restricted to certain roads, and speed limits reduced.

Even where car parking facilities are provided the very process of finding land for car parks can be difficult. Fells are under pressure from the constant trampling of visitors' feet and footpaths especially are put under intense pressure during the main visitor season between Easter and October.

Repairing footpaths is expensive and slow work – but it is vital if the most popular paths are not to become ugly areas of wasteland.

What can you suggest to allow tourism in the Lake District to continue to develop but at the same time protect the environment?

Case study

The London Eye

British Airways London Eye is the world's highest observation wheel and offers passengers amazing views of London. A 'flight' on The Eye is 30 minutes long, taking visitors 450 feet above the Thames in 32 high-tech fully enclosed capsules. The London Eye gives visitors the opportunity to see London from a unique viewpoint.

Facts and figures

Diameter	135 metres
Weight	2100 tonnes
Weight of a single capsule	9.3 tonnes
Time to revolve	30 minutes
Viewing distance	25 miles

Benefits

As the most popular paid-for tourist attraction in the UK, the London Eye plays a major role in the tourism industry and economy of London.

The London eye has attracted a large number of overseas visitors and has played a key role in the regeneration and transformation of the South Bank in terms of jobs and attracting new business.

The number of people employed directly by The London Eye varies from 200–370 depending on the season, with a further 873 jobs being created across the whole of London from new bars, shops and restaurants.

1. What type of jobs do you think the London Eye has created?
2. Lambeth Council have extended planning permission for The Eye by 25 years. Why do you think they have done this?

Did you know?

An organisation called BTCV enables volunteers to take part in activities such as coastal conservation, dry-stone walling, fencing, hedge laying and improving access, both in the UK and overseas.

Taking part in BTCV International Conservation can qualify you for the residential project of the Duke of Edinburgh Gold Award.

Activity

▶ Log on to the BTCV website (a link to which can be found at www.heinemann.co.uk/hotlinks) and find out how you can help play an active part in countryside conservation.

The negative impact of tourism

When tourism and the environment exist together without any harm being done, the countryside in particular and the environment in general can benefit. Canals, country parks and conservation areas have been developed to provide extra attractions for tourists.

Unfortunately, there are negative impacts (effects) of tourism on the countryside. Much of the damage to the countryside as a result of tourism is caused simply by the volume of tourists visiting these attractions.

The money and impetus which tourism brings to an area can help to restore and maintain the countryside, but the pressure that it brings is often harmful. Pressure from tourism can damage the countryside by:

- causing physical erosion
- creating litter
- increasing pollution
- increasing congestion
- disturbing wildlife
- reducing habitats
- altering landscapes
- encouraging inappropriate development.

Tourists inevitably travel in numbers to natural and man-made attractions in the countryside.

The social impacts of tourism

The beneficial effects of tourism include:

- creation of jobs
- rebirth of traditional cultural activities
- regeneration of regions
- more health and leisure opportunities
- increased social life for the local population.

Most man-made attractions such as Alton Towers are designed and built to handle the pressure. But often the infrastructure and approaches to such attractions cannot cope, and a popular attraction on a public holiday can cause major traffic jams which lead to noise, pollution and frayed tempers!

Natural attractions in the countryside can often suffer problems because of increasing tourism. In areas where visitors leave their cars and continue on foot, the damage to grass or heather can lead to erosion. Some areas like sand dunes and peat bogs are fragile and particularly vulnerable. The pressure not only damages wildlife habitats but also disturbs and endangers wildlife itself.

Case study

Blackpool

Today, Blackpool attracts millions of visitors per year, generating £435 million – more than all the Greek Islands and mainland Greece combined! There are 3500 hotels, guesthouses and holiday flats, containing 120 000 holiday beds – more than the whole of Portugal!

Blackpool has lots of attractions and activities for holidaymakers. However, it must be remembered that local people also use these facilities. The people who work in the tourism industry in Blackpool – hoteliers, traders, publicans, deckchair attendants, tram conductors – come face to face with holidaymakers every day. They have a chance to meet and get to know people. In fact, some holidaymakers return to the same hotel every year because they have got to know the owners and know they will be well looked after.

Local people not involved in the industry also get the chance to meet tourists in their local pubs, leisure centres or restaurants. Local people are often friendly towards tourists because it is in their nature to be so and also because they know tourists are good for the town.

There are many positive social effects of tourism for people in Blackpool. The tourists benefit from the facilities and activities provided for them, but the locals have the same opportunity to use these facilities where they have the chance of meeting new people or learning new sports or hobbies. Senior citizens can benefit from the public transport system built up around tourism, students benefit from getting summer jobs, e.g. hiring out deckchairs or working on the trams, and local businesses benefit from tourist money.

Blackpool does get busy – very busy. It gets overcrowded and the tourists tend to stare into people's windows. This can make life difficult for local people who want to go about doing their everyday things. The roads get blocked with the increased volume of traffic, which can increase journey times to work, and the trams, buses and trains can be full of tourists. There are obviously no special seats for local people.

The increase in visitors can lead to more crime – whether from rowdy or drunken holidaymakers causing damage or locals committing theft. Unfortunately, this is inevitable wherever there is a massive influx of visitors determined to enjoy themselves.

Most jobs in Blackpool are geared towards the tourism industry and this has spread to the surrounding villages, which are now doing a roaring trade in B&Bs and afternoon teas. This 'modern' tourist industry has tended to take over traditional jobs.

Positive economic impacts

Thousands and thousands of holidaymakers bring in millions and millions of pounds. Money is spent on food and drink, accommodation, tourist attractions, souvenirs, taxis, entertainment and presents. As a result, local businesses are booming, money for tourism is invested in new facilities which everyone can use and improved services can be provided by the local council – all because of the money brought in from holidaymakers.

Job creation is another 'plus' – whether it is a summer job in a café, a permanent job on the Pleasure Beach or a waiter in a restaurant, there are many job opportunities as a result of

Case study continued

tourism. However, jobs are also created in the supply of goods and products necessary to run the hotels, for example butchers, dry cleaning for hotel laundries and factories for souvenirs. People in local shops, newsagents, bookmakers or clothes shops all gain extra income from tourism, and jobs created in these areas are as a result of the money brought in.

Blackpool is booming. It has a reputation as the UK's number one fun spot. It attracts political party conferences, business conventions, international superstars and millions of tourists. It is famous and known throughout the country as one of the most popular seaside resorts.

The image it creates is one of vibrancy, life, energy and activity. These are all very positive images. Old, derelict sites like the airfield (now Stanley Park) have been developed, in the case of the airfield into a magnificent zoo, an exclusive hotel and an international standard golf course. The old open air swimming pool is now the Sandcastle leisure pool, where a 'tropical temperature awaits the castaways who land on Blackpool's treasure island, the water is warm so you don't mind a soaking as you soar down swirling slides and frantic flumes'.

Tourism has transformed Blackpool. Its party-time image is aimed at entertaining everyone – families, 18–30s and senior citizens. It has managed to keep up with the times to stay as the number one seaside resort in the UK.

Negative economic impacts
However, there are also some negative impacts:

- Prices tend to rise in tourist areas such as Blackpool for goods, services and houses – including increased local taxes and higher business rates.
- Seasonal work – Blackpool isn't open as a resort all year round so tourist jobs tend to available only from April to November.
- As long as the economy is stable, people will be able to visit Blackpool. However, external factors such as increases in taxation, interest rate rises or an economic recession would mean that people have less disposable income to spend on places like Blackpool.
- Loss of local services – shops which may previously have served the local community are now geared towards tourism, selling gifts and souvenirs or afternoon teas, rather than vegetables or groceries.
- Jobs in tourist areas are notoriously low paid, which means those employed have to cope in a relatively expensive area.

Positive environmental impacts
- Derelict areas have been cleaned up and regenerated.
- Old buildings, especially disused barns in rural areas, have been converted into restaurants and accommodation.
- Blackpool town centre has been pedestrianised, some areas covered in, and decorated with flowers. Good signposting and one-way systems have made traffic flow easier.

Negative environmental impacts
- Traffic congestion occurs along the promenade and en route to Blackpool on the M55.
- Problem of litter along the promenade, beach and town centre.
- Increased air and noise pollution.
- Pollution in the sea – caused by increased demands for water, particularly sewage systems in the 'high' season.

Reducing the negative impacts
- Managing visitors and monitoring the number of tourists, good signposting; peak and off-peak prices throughout the year.
- Managing traffic – the M55; public transport, trams and park and ride.
- Legislation – codes of conduct and customer charters.
- Education – to reduce negative impacts of leisure and tourism.

1. Why is Blackpool so popular?
2. Would you like to live there? Give your reasons.

Reducing negative impacts

One of the most straightforward ways of controlling visitors to an attraction in the countryside and preventing congestion and overcrowding is to provide clearly defined routes around the site by using signposting and waymarked walks.

In the countryside, the provision of footpaths – which may or may not be fenced – can encourage tourists to keep away from easily damaged areas. Highway authorities are legally required to erect a signpost at every point where a footpath, bridleway or byway meet, and may give a destination and distance.

With so many tourists visiting beautiful countryside areas, it has become necessary to try to control the impact of people and traffic on the environment. One initiative is to try to persuade people to use public transport instead of their own cars. More and more information is now becoming available which can give ideas about the many places you can reach by public transport.

Some of the busiest roads in the National Parks are closed to traffic at peak times. This is aimed at encouraging hikers and cyclists to enjoy the countryside in complete safety and explore areas away from noise and traffic pollution.

Another initiative which many local authorities have introduced is the provision of cycleways in countryside areas. Obviously, bicycles do not cause pollution and it gives cyclists the opportunity to take in the beauty of the scenery.

One useful way of controlling visitor flow is the siting of car parks. Most people are reluctant to walk more than 500 metres or so from their car. At a countryside property, siting a car park where you wish to concentrate visitors, or further away from where you do not want them, can be a useful way of controlling visitor flow.

Activity
> Which organisations would be able to give advice about getting to the countryside by public transport?

Talk about it
In your group, discuss how you could reduce the negative impacts of tourism on the countryside.

Employment opportunities in travel and tourism

The travel and tourism industry is the biggest growth industry in the UK, employing around 2 million people and contributing a vast amount of wealth to the UK economy.

The industry offers a wide range of jobs and, like in any occupation, there are rewards for people who show enthusiasm, determination and the ability to work hard.

Jobs in the travel and tourism industry often involve close contact with the customer. It is possible to develop customer service skills, but if you don't positively enjoy working with the public you are probably unsuited to a career in travel and tourism.

People can often be very demanding – good communication skills and a friendly manner will count for little if you are unable to show patience and tolerance when confronted by angry clients.

In most travel and tourism work you will also have to work closely with your fellow employees – teamwork and cooperation are very important.

Signposts are a legal requirement

> **Talk about it**
>
> In your group, discuss what you think it would be like to work in the travel and tourism industry.

> **Talk about it**
>
> In your group, discuss the skills and qualities you would need to be a travel consultant.

Did you think working in travel and tourism would be glamorous and exciting? Well, it is, *but* it is a job like any other, not a paid-for holiday even if the work means being based in a country where it's warm all year round. Ask people who work in the industry about the worst parts of their jobs and they will probably say the long and unsocial working hours.

Much of the work involves tasks such as taking bookings, sending out information, organising and cashing up at the end of the day. Accuracy is essential. Would you want to deal with a holidaymaker who's been booked into the wrong hotel or put on a wrong flight?

That is the reality of the work. Do not be put off! People who work in travel and tourism usually point to the variety of the work, the enjoyment they get from meeting and helping people and the satisfaction they gain from providing a first-class service.

> **Activity**
>
> ▶ In pairs, list as many jobs as you can think of in the travel and tourism industry. Share your answers with the rest of the group. As a group, you should be able to think of at least 30 jobs!

Below are some jobs in the travel and tourism industry that you need to know about.

Travel consultant

A travel consultant's main tasks are to arrange transport and accommodation for clients and sell all-inclusive holidays. The job also includes arranging day trips, walking holidays and even booking theatre tickets.

Travel consultants must enjoy working directly with the public. They must like helping and advising them, and be happy working in what is effectively a selling environment. Since travel agencies are open six days a week, they must be prepared to work a number of Saturdays and Sundays.

Conference organiser

A conference organiser is responsible for the daily administration of conferences and other functions such as wedding receptions, exhibitions and business meetings.

You must have good administrative skills, be able to communicate well with people, manage staff and be a good sales person.

The job involves long and unsocial hours, but the prospects into management in either a hotel or for specialist conferences are good.

Organising a conference may start months or even years ahead in order to plan the programme, decide the venue and invite the speakers.

During the run-up to the event the conference organiser will send out promotional literature, take bookings from delegates, arrange hotel accommodation, book coaches, organise equipment and book temporary staff.

A conference organiser is someone who may have had experience in the travel industry or worked part time at conferences. It is a demanding job with deadlines to be met, responsibilities before, during and after the conference, and a host of different organisations to please.

Coach driver

This job involves a lot of personal contact with customers. The coach driver is responsible for safe travel, keeping to a timetable and helping passengers with their luggage.

Shearings, a company based in Wigan, Greater Manchester, organises coach holidays to a variety of European destinations and throughout the UK. In common with other coach holiday operators, its policy is to have driver-couriers, so coach companies have to be satisfied that they employ drivers who can relate well to customers.

What qualities do you think air cabin crew need?

Air cabin crew

When considering job opportunities in air travel, most people immediately think of the air steward or stewardess, or cabin crew as they are known. Many people see these staff as airbound waiters or waitresses, which is not the case. Air cabin crew need to be able to handle any kind of emergency and initiate the appropriate safety procedures straight away. First aid skills, social skills and initiative are all qualities required by cabin staff.

Tour guide

A tour guide's key quality is probably his or her personality. You need to be flexible, have a genuine interest in people, a thirst for knowledge, patience and tolerance to cope with awkward visitors or situations and good organisational skills. As a tour guide, you cannot afford to lose people or miss deadlines.

Resort representative

Once a holiday has been chosen and booked, it becomes the responsibility of the resort representative to make sure that clients enjoy their holiday.

This is an extremely demanding job. So what sort of person makes a good rep? A friendly personality with a sense of responsibility is as important as academic qualifications. Good communication skills, both verbal and written, are important. Most companies expect applicants to have GCSEs in English and maths plus evidence of language ability, if only at beginner level.

Children's reps, who run activities for young holidaymakers, normally have nursery nursing, teaching or similar experience.

Keeping up to date with employment opportunities

It is important to keep up to date with employment in the industry as the article below shows.

Travel giant wields axe

Travel giant Thomas Cook is shedding 1500 UK jobs and forcing staff to take pay cuts of up to 15 per cent.

Stunned employees at the German-owned company now face an uncertain future.

The decision to cut 1500 jobs in the UK out of 2600 across Europe suggests bosses have been keen to limit the pain in their own country.

Any suggestion that workers here have been victimised to save jobs in Germany will fuel anger throughout the company's UK operation. Half of the job losses in the UK will be compulsory as the company aims to save more than £140 million.

UK executives have agreed to cut their pay by 15 per cent and the firm is asking staff who earn more than £10 000 to accept cuts of between 3 and 10 per cent.

The cuts and job losses have been blamed on the September 11 terror attacks in the US which, Thomas Cook claims, have affected bookings.

However, the TSSA union attacked the pay cut demand. A spokeswoman said: 'People working in the retail shops don't earn much in the first place. Agreeing to take a pay cut does not guarantee jobs will be safe in the future.'

Daily Mail, November 2001

Check your knowledge

1. You and your family are going to France for a week. What sort of tourism is this?
2. What does the term 'business tourism' mean?
3. What products and services do travel agents provide apart from selling holidays?
4. In which component of the travel and tourism industry would you put Eurostar?
5. What are the advantages of booking a holiday 'online'?
6. Explain what a package holiday is.
7. Describe three products and services offered to tourists at an airport like Heathrow.
8. What are long-haul flights?
9. Explain the links between leisure and tourism in the following situations:
    a A football team from Preston, Lancashire, who need to stay overnight in Newark, Nottinghamshire, in order to play in a football tournament the following day.
    b A group of students from Leeds who are organising a travel and tourism exhibition in the local community centre.
10. What are the positive and negative impacts of increased tourism in an area like the Lake District?
11. How can careful management of the Lake District reduce the negative impacts?
12. What skills and qualities would you need to be a travel consultant?
13. Name and describe three jobs in the transportation component of the travel and tourism industry.
14. Which holiday company specialises in holidays for people aged 50 and over?
15. Give an example of domestic tourism.
16. What are the attractions of an area like the Lake District?
17. What are the advantages and disadvantages of air travel?

Answers to Activities on page 78

a   Roman baths, eighteenth-century spa town, museums
b   Northumbria Coast and Holy Island
c   Peak District, Chatsworth House
d   Castle
e   University, museums
f   Cathedral
g   Loch Ness
h   Wye Valley
i   Castle
j   Eighteenth-century spa town

Chapter 3: Links between leisure & tourism

What you will learn
- How leisure and tourism are linked

Although the leisure and tourism industries are generally considered separately, there are many links between the two, for example accommodation and catering, attractions, and transportation. Both industries are dependent on each other for customers. Here are some examples:

- A visit to a theme park is both a leisure activity which involves travel (getting to the park) and tourism (a day out).
- A trip to Cardiff to watch the FA Cup Final involves leisure (sports spectating) and tourism (travelling away from home).
- Visiting friends and relatives involves tourism (overnight stay or longer) and going to the cinema with them involves leisure.
- Going to Greece for a two-week holiday involves both travel and tourism; windsurfing while you are there is a leisure activity.

The following case studies will help you to understand how leisure and tourism are often linked.

Case study

Japan here we come

Tariq, Dev, Vickram and Bal have been football supporters for as long as they can remember. They had seen Manchester United in cup finals at Wembley and Cardiff. Now they were going to follow the England team to the World Cup Finals in Japan and South Korea. Their dream was to see David Beckham lift the cup for England, preferably having beaten Brazil in the final.

Much planning had gone into the trip – raising the money and organising passports and visas were just some of the things that they had to do.

The lads also decided to book their flights and accommodation online in order to find the best deal. This took quite a long time because the team was playing each match in a different city.

As well as watching the football, they also wanted to make the most of this trip of a lifetime by taking in as many visitor attractions in Japan and South Korea as possible.

This is what their planning looked like:

- Check air fares and accommodation online and shop around to get the best deal.
- Go to travel agents to find out about insurance, visas, currency and health information.
- Write to Japanese and South Korean embassies to get information on culture and attractions.
- Check flight times, costs and transfers to hotel.

With three months to go everything was falling nicely into place. It was all systems go. The lads could talk of nothing else but their amazing future journey.

1. What links can you identify between leisure and tourism?
2. Why would the lads need to find out about culture?
3. How else could they have gone about booking their trip?

Case study

Thrills and spills at Alton Towers

The Ross family decided to go to Alton Towers for the weekend. James Ross, dad, had been lucky enough to get five numbers on the National Lottery and had scooped £1200, so a weekend away seemed a great idea.

James phoned Alton Towers and booked a family room for himself and his wife, Pam, 12-year-old son, Jack, and 8-year-old daughter, Zara.

They drove down from Halifax starting out at 7.00 am and stopped off at Uttoxeter for a big breakfast at McDonald's. They checked into the hotel at 11.00 am, dumped their bags and headed off for Nemesis. Three hours later, after testing most of the white knuckle rides, they had a KFC take-away and sat in the gardens enjoying the views and talking excitedly about the great time they were having.

More rides in the afternoon, then back to the hotel to watch television and generally chill out.

Dinner in the restaurant was at 8.00 pm and consisted of soup, scampi and chips followed by lashings of ice cream. At the end of the day they were all whacked.

The following day was a repeat of day one with more rides, more food and more fun.

The journey back was long but was broken by an eat-as-much-as-you-like deal at a Chinese take-away.

The money had all but gone but it was worth it. It's not every day you can say you have spent two full days at Alton Towers without leaving the park!

1. What links can you identify between leisure and tourism?
2. Identify the different types of catering the Ross family enjoyed.
3. How else could they have travelled to Alton Towers?

Case study

Happy anniversary!

Anne and Jim Wood had paid off the mortgage, got the kids off their hands and even managed to save a bit of money.

They planned their 25th wedding anniversary to be something special; a luxury weekend in London taking in the sights, a show and staying in a five-star hotel. After all, it wasn't every marriage nowadays that lasted 25 years.

Friends took the Woods to the railway station. They caught the 9.15 am train from Grantham to London King's Cross, arriving at  11.20 am. As they had decided to 'splash out', they took a taxi to the Carlton Hotel on Park Lane and checked in for the night.

After settling in, they visited the London Eye and enjoyed the magnificent views of London it gave them. A guided tour on an open-top bus took in Trafalgar Square, the City and Pall Mall. The courier was brilliant, telling them stories about all the famous places they saw.

Back to the hotel to shower and change, and they were then ready for a night on the town. First stop by taxi was a restaurant on the King's Road, Chelsea, followed by a trip to The Sands Casino where they had a flutter on the roulette wheel.

Having won £75, then lost £50, they headed off to a nightclub with the attitude that they still felt young enough to dance the night away.

By 3.00 am they decided enough was enough. Time had taken its toll and so the Woods admitted defeat gracefully. After all, tomorrow was another day; more sightseeing, a show at the Palladium in the afternoon, followed by shopping in Harrods. If nothing else, the Woods were certainly young at heart.

1. What links can you identify between leisure and tourism?
2. Imagine you were on a school trip to London. How would you like to spend the day? Show the links between leisure and tourism on your day out.

Everything you need to know about leisure and tourism facilities in any area can be provided by the local tourist information centre. Here they will tell you about how transport providers like coach operators can take you to see places of interest for both the leisure market and tourists. In fact, there are over 560 tourist information centres in England. If you are in a town or city which is new to you and want to know what to see, where to eat and perhaps where to stay, it is very likely that you will head straight for the tourist information centre. They can also give you information about other parts of the UK. They provide information to tourists about accommodation, car hire, entertainment and leisure facilities in a particular locality.

Many local authorities have their own leisure departments which usually include a tourism section. They fund local tourist information centres and promote leisure and tourism in their area.

Check your knowledge

1. Give three examples of a link between leisure and tourism in your area.
2. What type of information do tourist information centres give about leisure and tourist facilities?
3. What sort of skills and qualities would you need to work in a tourist information centre?
4. Where would be an ideal location for a tourist information centre in York?
5. How can tour operators and accommodation providers work together to promote and encourage business? What benefits would this have?

Snapshot

Kirsty

Kirsty is manager of a very busy tourist information centre in York. The centre has three full-time and three part-time staff who assist over 5 million visitors a year.

Today, they have had their usual range of enquiries from the UK, the USA, Japan, France and Germany asking for anything from bus timetables to the way to visitor attractions.

Kirsty says: 'We keep information on theatres, buses, trains, day trips, sports events, local clubs and societies. You could book theatre seats, join the Youth Hostel Association or one of the motoring organisations here. Oh yes, we also sell stamps and phone cards.'

And the job itself? Kirsty goes on to say: 'You really have to like meeting people. You must be able to work under pressure because it gets very hectic when people are waiting.'

Unit 1 Assessment

After each question there are helpful tips which might help you answer the questions better.

1   a   Rufford Country Park is situated in the heart of Nottinghamshire. Many people spend some of their leisure time there.

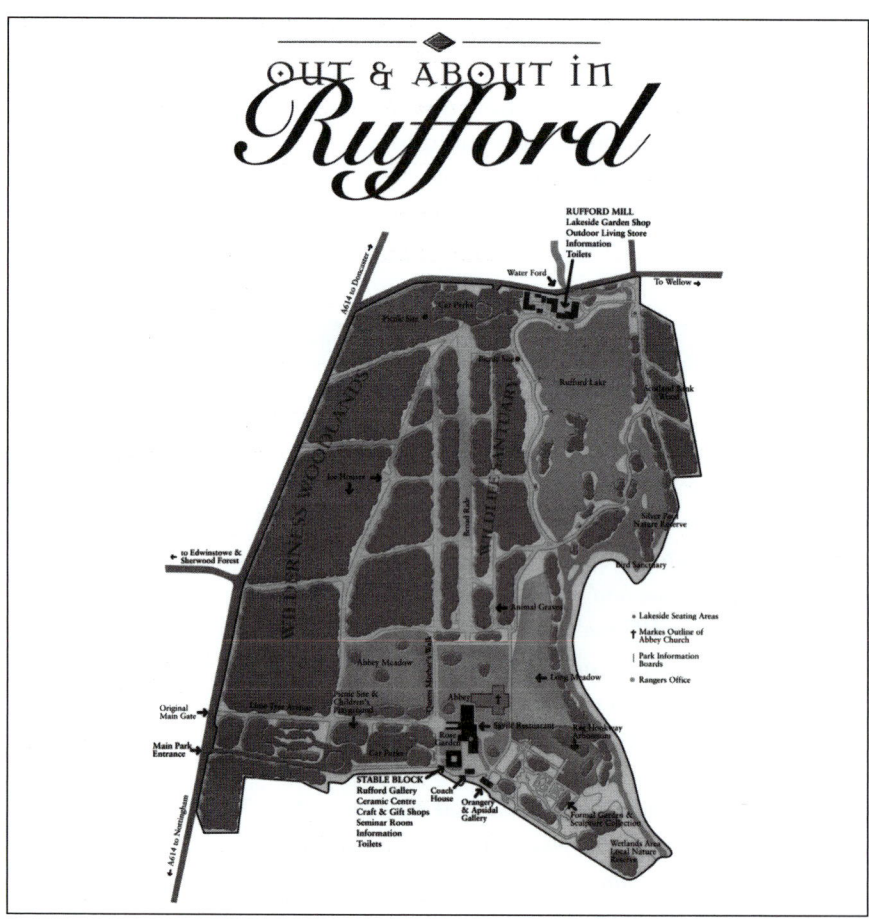

Identify four leisure activities that people can enjoy at Rufford Park.

i   _____ 1

ii _____ 1

iii _____ 1

iv _____ 1

Think of leisure activities particularly associated with the countryside.

b Give three reasons why people enjoy traditional outdoor activities.

i _____ 1

ii _____ 1

iii _____ 1

First of all, identify some outdoor activities (not football). This will give a better idea of of why people enjoy them.

c Explain two ways in which leisure facilities like Rufford Park attempt to increase their visitor numbers.

i _____ 2

ii _____ 2

Imagine the park would close if they don't increase visitor numbers.

d Name two types of customer that Rufford Park aims to attract.

i _____ 2

ii _____ 3

Think of individuals and groups.

e Give two types of job that are available at Rufford Park.

i _____ 1

ii _____ 1

Think of jobs that involve dealing with the public and selling goods.

f What sort of leisure activities can people do in the countryside? Why is the UK countryside so popular with tourists?

(9 marks)

Imagine you are having a day out in the countryside. What would you do there? What would attract you to it?

2 a Give three reasons why outbound tourists leave the UK.

i _____ 1

ii _____ 1

iii _____ 1

Think about sunshine, work and family.

b Most airlines claim that their passengers will always receive the best possible service.

Give two examples of what this service might involve.

i _____ 1

ii _____ 1

What do you look for from staff when you are a customer?

c Many people start their holidays from the UK's busiest airport, Heathrow.

Give three ways that people could travel from Newcastle to Heathrow.

i _____ 1

ii _____ 1

iii _____ 1

Don't necessarily think of the route – think of how you would get there.

Choose the most suitable method of making this journey for a couple with no children.

Method _____ because _____

Think of convenience and time.

d Explain why the UK is so popular with overseas visitors.

(9 marks)

Why do visitors come to the UK? Is it for the weather? Think about attractions and history.

e Tourism can sometimes damage the countryside. Explain how this can happen and suggest how this environmental damage can be minimised. **(6 marks)**

What causes environmental damage? Think of the ways it can be reduced.

3 a Lincoln is an important location for tourism.

Identify two of Lincoln's major attractions.

i _____ 1

ii _____ 1

Study the information carefully.

Give two reasons why part of Lincoln is now a traffic-free zone.

i _____ 1

ii _____ 1

Imagine you are shopping there.

b Lincoln has a river flowing through its built-up area.

Name two leisure activities that local people or tourists might use this river for.

Think about what you can do in or on a river.

i _____ 1

ii _____ 1

c   Study the details of Lincoln's sports centres. Identify two ways they attract the 18–21 age group.

SPORTS CENTRES

CITY SPORTS CENTRE
SKELLINGTHORPE RD   683946

Early morning swimming (7-8am) Tuesday and Thursday; adults-only Monday, Tuesday, Friday and Sunday evenings. Sports hall, fitness room, two squash courts, six tennis courts, two floodlit netball courts, floodlit outdoor multi-use games area with synthetic turf. Student discounts. Racket hire available, and licensed bar (evenings).

YARBOROUGH LEISURE CENTRE
RISEHOLME RD   524228

Swimming pool open weekdays, early morning swim-fit 6.30-8.30am; evenings, 6.30-9.40pm; weekends, 10am-4.40pm. Sports hall, full-size synthetic turf pitch, athletics track, outdoor pitches, sauna, sunbeds, 1500m cycle track, three squash courts.
Student discounts. Licensed bar (evenings) and cafe.

BIRCHWOOD COMMUNITY & LEISURE CENTRE
BIRCHWOOD AVE   685166

Sports hall, two squash courts, games room and floodlit outdoor multi-use games area (synthetic turf).

NTH KESTEVEN SPORTS CENTRE
MOOR LANE, OFF NEWARK RD
NTH HYKEHAM   883311

Only centre offering daytime swimming, Tuesday 10.30-11.30am. Pool also open 7-9am Tuesday, Wednesday, Friday, Sunday - centre not open Monday, Thursday. Squash, tennis, badminton, racket ball, health suite/gym, aerobics, step and spinning classes. Student discounts.

Lincoln City Council also runs six other community centres with a sports programme, as well as 22 football pitches, two rugby pitches, two grass cricket and two artificial wickets, one putting green, five grass and 14 hard tennis courts, and a free 12-hole golf course at South Common. It also provides all the latest fitness facilities at the Meridian Gym, based at Lincoln City FC's Sincil Bank ground. For bookings and details, telephone DELTA on Lincoln 873502 or 873468. For North Kesteven Sports Centre, telephone Lincoln 883311 or North Kesteven District Council on 01529 414155.

SPORTS ON CAMPUS

DMU CAYTHORPE CAMPUS - includes indoor swimming pool, snooker room, various pitches, tennis courts, sports hall. Details on 01400 272521

DMU RISEHOLME CAMPUS - includes swimming, canoeing, clay pigeon shooting and golf. Details on 522252

i _____ 1

ii _____ 1

Imagine you are 18. What sort of activities would attract you to one of the sports centres?

d Choose a leisure facility in your area that you know. Explain how the products and services offered by this facility meet the needs of different types of customers.

Name and location of chosen leisure facility:
_____

Explanation: _____

Think of the different users – individuals and groups – and say why they are attracted. **(6 marks)**

e Leisure facilities change according to trends. Over the past 20 years the UK has seen many changes in the provision of leisure facilities. Choose an area you know and describe the new leisure facilities that are available there.

Name of chosen area: _____

Types of leisure facilities: _____

Think about sport, lifestyles, health, new technology. **(9 marks)**

4 a Choose one city which is an important tourist destination in the UK. State four economic impacts of tourism in that city.

Name of city: _____

i _____ 1

ii _____ 1

iii _____ 1

iv _____ 1

Economic impacts are linked with money and investment.

b Choose one job in leisure and tourism and describe in detail the duties involved.

Choose a job in leisure and tourism that you want to do and use that as an example.

(10 marks)

c Choose a coastal resort you have studied and describe its attractions and the type of visitors who go there.

Imagine yourself at the seaside. Look around you. Who and what can you see?

(11 marks)

Unit 2: Marketing in leisure and tourism

Marketing involves finding out about people's wants and needs and developing effective ways of meeting them in order to make a financial or social profit. This may sound complicated, but don't worry. Simple explanations backed up by examples are given throughout the unit.

The basic principle of marketing for any leisure and tourism organisation is getting the right product to the right people in the right place at the right price using the right promotion at the right time.

The leisure and tourism industries are highly competitive and customers are becoming more demanding in what they want. This means that organisations which fail to market their products and services effectively may not succeed.

This unit will help you to understand the importance of marketing. It introduces you to the four key aspects of marketing that leisure and tourism organisations use:

- target marketing
- market research
- the marketing mix
- SWOT analysis.

You will investigate the marketing activities of leisure and tourism organisations and look in detail at the marketing activities of one organisation. Part of your work will include producing an item of promotional material for your chosen organisation.

This unit builds on the introductory work you completed in Unit 1 Investigating leisure and tourism and links with Unit 3 Customer service in leisure and tourism.

You will be expected to show your understanding of marketing in leisure and tourism organisations and that you can put the theory of marketing into practice.

Assessment

Unit 2 is assessed through portfolio work. You will find more details about this at the end of the unit.

What you will learn

Chapter 1 What is marketing?
Chapter 2 Target marketing
Chapter 3 Market research
Chapter 4 The marketing mix
Chapter 5 SWOT analysis
Chapter 6 Promotional campaigns

Chapter 1: What is marketing?

Whatever the type of leisure and tourism organisation and its reason for providing products and services, the basic principle underpinning marketing is the same – getting the right product to the right people in the right place at the right price using the right promotion. This chapter explains the principles of marketing.

What you will learn

- Principles of marketing
- Generating income and making a profit
- Informing customers
- Ensuring customer satisfaction
- Promoting products
- Influencing product development
- Influencing customer choice

Activity

 In pairs, write down your ideas about what you think marketing is all about.

Principles of marketing

If you asked someone in the street, 'What is marketing?', you might receive the following replies:

- I haven't a clue!
- Is it where you see offers in supermarkets like buy two and get one free?
- Isn't it something to do with advertising and selling?
- All that junk mail we receive about double glazing and bank loans.
- Something to do with all those adverts on television.

Apart from the first reply, the others certainly form part of the answer. However, it is incorrect to say marketing is another name for selling, advertising or junk mail.

Fact file

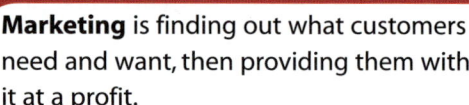

Marketing is finding out what customers need and want, then providing them with it at a profit.

The profit referred to in the definition of marketing above can either be financial, which is self-explanatory, or social, which will be explained later.

Marketing puts the consumer or customer at the centre of the organisation's decision-making. It is all about attracting customers and keeping them. After all, if there are no customers, there will be no organisation. So, marketing is getting the right product to the right customer at the right price, in the right place at the right time. That is the theory; an example of the practice is shown in Figure 2.1.

Activity

 Try to answer the questions below.

Product: A two-week summer holiday in Playa del Ingles, Gran Canaria.

Who would be the right customer?
What would be the right price?
Where would it be promoted?
When would be the right time?

Compare your answers with those on page 98.

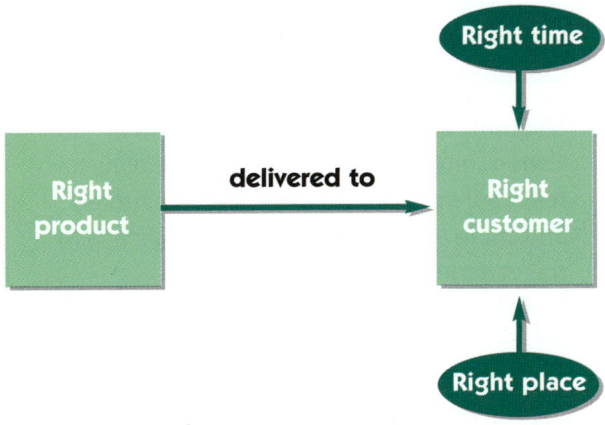

Figure 2.1 The principles of marketing

Marketing is just as important in the public and voluntary sectors as it is in the private sector as they all have customers. Since customers are at the centre of all marketing activities, it is vital that everyone in an organisation should know that marketing is their responsibility.

One of the main aims of marketing is to generate income and make a profit. These aims are related to the customer, the product and the way the product is sold. Leisure and tourism organisations market themselves in the same way, as can be seen in Figure 2.2.

Figure 2.2 The aims of marketing

Generating income and making a profit

Activity

> What is the formula for working out profit?

One of the main aims of marketing is to attract customers and keep them. Customers spend money on products and services like food and drink, theatre tickets and swimming lessons.

By finding out what customers want, charging them the right price and promoting the product (such as swimming lessons) to create awareness means that people will be attracted to the leisure centre, and spend their money. Hopefully, they will return and tell their friends about it.

Making a profit

Case study

Paul, gym owner

Paul opened his gym three years ago. After working as a deputy manager of a local authority leisure centre for five years, he decided to 'take the plunge' and start his own business.

At first, Paul had a 12-station multi-gym and five sets of 'free' weights. As membership increased, he was able to invest in two treadmills, five rowing machines and five exercise bikes. Next year he plans to add a health suite comprising a sauna, steamroom and sunbeds.

The profit Paul makes looks like this:

Profit = Income generated from subscriptions and fees − Overheads (rent, wages, fuel bills, equipment, etc.).

Paul receives £32 550 from annual subscriptions, £51 795 from fees and £28 275 from catering. He has to pay £5650 rent per year for the premises, £30 000 on staff wages, £8765 on heating and electricity and £15 000 on equipment. How much profit does he make per year?

When leisure and tourism organisations have met the expense of all the running costs, any money left over is classed as profit. Profit enables future investment and survival of the organisation. Effective marketing can lead to customers spending their money and so creating profit.

Marketing campaigns are aimed at attracting customers and that is why many organisations have a marketing budget or even a marketing department to ensure this happens.

Generating social profit

Not all organisations aim to make financial profit from their operation. This is particularly true in the public and voluntary sectors where the main aim may be to provide a community service. However, these organisations still market their products and services.

Answers to Activity on page 96

The right customer – young people, probably aged 18–25 years, who want lots of nightlife and fun in the sun.

The right price – people expect to pay a certain price for a holiday; in this case, probably around £350 depending on the type of accommodation and whether it was half-board or self-catering. Value for money would be a key factor in the buying process.

The right place – the most obvious place for the holiday to be promoted would be a travel agent but teletext and the Internet are being used more and more to advertise holidays.

The right time – a holiday may be taken in August but booked a year in advance, although many people take a chance on late holidays in the hope of getting a reduced price holiday bargain.

Case study

Shamuna, community centre manager

Shamuna has been manager of Cadmon Community Centre for five years. She aims to make sure the centre breaks even financially and, more importantly, to provide a service to the community.

The centre is located in the heart of a council estate in a large town and the idea is to provide activities for the local residents. The people who use the centre come from all walks of life: single parents, senior citizens and anyone else who wants to get out of the house and mix with other people.

Shamuna sees her main task as going out into the community, finding out what sort of activities people want and then providing them. To her, that's what marketing is all about.

Shamuna says:

> In this area the best type of advertising is by word of mouth because it is a very close-knit community. Other types of promotion include posters which are displayed in the health centre, library, doctor's surgery, and dentist's waiting room.
> It's a bit of a struggle to reach our financial targets but we try to make up for it by the amount of social profit we generate – by providing the type of activities the community wants.

1. How else could Shamuna advertise what's on at the centre?
2. What role do community centres play within a local community?

Talk about it

In your group, discuss how a local authority leisure centre can generate social profit. Which voluntary organisations provide a social profit?

Informing customers

Organisations need to let people know exactly what they are offering in terms of location, activities, prices and facilities.

This information could be included in brochures, leaflets, and newspaper advertisements. Probably one of the most understated forms of informing customers is by staff spreading the word about the facility and using their knowledge and expertise to answer customer enquiries.

Talk about it

In your group, discuss what part staff can play in informing customers in the following facilities:

a   a cinema
b   a restaurant
c   a hotel.

Ensuring customer satisfaction

Satisfied customers tell their friends and return for more. Marketing helps keep customers happy by:

- finding out what they like
- giving them what they want
- asking them for their ideas
- showing an interest in them.

Meeting customers' needs

This is another way of keeping customers happy. Here are some examples:

- Providing disabled people with facilities such as ramps, wider car parking spaces and lifts to give them full access to public buildings.
- Senior citizens on a coach trip want an interesting and knowledgeable courier.
- Young children want interesting, colourful and challenging play equipment in play areas, while their parents/carers want seating, toilets and a location which is safe for their children.

Fact file

Some customers keep going back to the same facility because they enjoy going there. This is called **repeat business**.

Think about it

How can leisure and tourism facilities meet the needs of the following groups: the unemployed, sports clubs, families?

Marketing research helps determine what people need and want (see Chapter 3).

Promoting products

Promotion of products plays a major part in marketing. We are overwhelmed nowadays with so much promotion. It is all around us and can include:

- travel agents promoting special holiday offers on television
- holiday programmes showing the delights of the Caribbean
- brochures advertising 'what's on' at the local theatre
- advertisements in local newspapers for coaching courses
- posters displaying activities at the community centre.

Products are promoted in a variety of ways

This type of promotion aims to attract customers to facilities and encourage them to spend their money on the products and services on offer.

Products and services in the leisure and tourism industries need to be marketed if organisations are to survive. The types of products and services which are marketed are:

- holidays – marketed by travel agents
- sports activities – marketed by sports centres
- concerts and shows – marketed by theatres
- films – marketed by cinemas
- meals and menus – marketed by restaurants
- day trips to the coast – marketed by coach operators.

If organisations fail to keep up with present trends, it is likely that they will go out of business. The leisure and tourism industries are constantly changing, so new products have to be developed to meet the demand. The chart below shows some of the changes over the past 40 years.

New products and services have to be marketed so that customers can choose what they want.

Activity

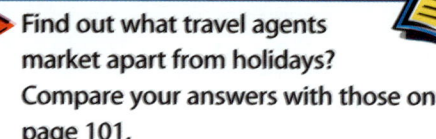

▶ Find out what travel agents market apart from holidays? Compare your answers with those on page 101.

▶ Write a short report describing how a hotel might market its weekend breaks?

Talk about it

Alton Towers introduces new rides and facilities like its hotel to retain its customers (or guests as they are called). In your group, discuss how the following organisations and facilities have developed their products and services to keep up to date and hold on to their customers:

a   Butlin's holiday camps
b   professional football clubs
c   cinemas.

Compare your answers with those on page 101.

Influencing product development

Market research shows what customers want. The result of market research should be analysed and changes should be made to the product or service if it is found that existing products or services do not match customers' needs and wants.

Influencing customer choice

This can be done by marketing campaigns which show activities that will benefit customers. For example, keep-fit and healthy lifestyle classes help you lose weight, get you fit and make you feel good. With promises like that, you would be only too happy to join!

	1960s	2000+
Holidays	Foreign holidays for the minority of people	Overseas package holidays popular with the mass market
Car ownership	One-car family	Two- or even three-car family
Popular sports activities	Cricket and football	Hang-gliding, jet skiing, windsurfing, parachuting
Home entertainment	Black and white television, radio	Computers, videos, CDs, home improvements, exercise at home
Outings	Day trips to the countryside or walk to see a friend	Trips to theme parks, multi-screen cinemas, indoor shopping, leisure pools
Eating out	A rare treat	Fast-food outlets, pubs with family rooms, family restaurants with play areas

Changes in the leisure and tourism industries over the last 40 years

Check your knowledge

1. Write down your own definition of marketing.
2. Think about the following product and answer the questions:
   Product: A day trip to the seaside to sit on a deckchair, have forty winks, enjoy watching the world go by, buy some fish and chips …'
   a Who would be the right customer?
   b What would be the right price?
   c Where would the trip be promoted?
   d When would be the right time for the trip?
3. What does the term 'social profit' mean?
4. What are the main aims of marketing?
5. What is the formula for working out profit?
6. How can a youth club generate social profit?
7. How could a local museum promote a forthcoming exhibition?
8. What is repeat business?
9. What new products and services can a theatre develop in order to keep up to date and retain customers?
10. How have pubs developed their products and services so that they can attract a wide range of customers?

Answers to Activity on page 100

Car hire, insurance, foreign exchange, concert tickets, tours, accommodation.

Answers to Talk about it on page 100

a Butlin's changed its image from holiday camps to indoor and outdoor family entertainment centres with modern facilities. Its cafés became restaurants, chalets were converted into well-appointed apartments and even the name changed, for example Butlin's at Skegness became Funcoastworld, making it sound more attractive.

b Football grounds – all seater stadia, souvenir shops, museums, guided tours, improved catering.

c Cinemas – multiplex, luxury seats, located near fast-food outlets.

Chapter 2 Target marketing

Target marketing is a tool that helps an organisation ensure it is offering the right goods and services to different groups of customers. In other words, target marketing is concerned with matching the right products with the right people.

This chapter looks at how leisure and tourism organisations divide the market into smaller sections, or segments, to enable them to target their customers effectively.

What you will learn
Marketing segments
How markets are segmented

Fact file
The **market** for a product or service is the total number of existing and potential customers who may want to use or buy the product or service.

Activity
- In pairs, think about three different television advertisements that are aimed at particular customers. What features of the advertisements made you identify these particular customers? Think of two or three and then discuss these with your group.
- Identify one particular customer group and create an advertisement for any product that would appeal to that group. How did you decide what to include in your advertisement to make it appeal to that particular group? Discuss this in your group and with your tutor.

Marketing segments

The activity above asked you to create an advertisement aimed at a particular group of people. In carrying out this activity, you would have used some of the marketing tools that organisations employ when they start to market their products.

It is important for leisure and tourism organisations to recognise that different groups of customers, known as **market segments**, have different needs.

A target market consists of:

- existing customers – those who have bought in the past and will continue to do so
- potential customers – those who may buy in the future and may become regular customers.

Target marketing is aimed at both groups.

The chart below shows how a product is matched to a target group.

Product	Target market
Saga Holidays	Senior citizens with money to spend
Youth clubs	12–16-year-olds
Club Med holidays	18–30-year-olds
Swimming clubs – 5.00–7.30 pm	School-age children
Bargain holidays in July to end August	Families with school-age children
'Bums and tums' 10.30 am	Mums with children at school
Long winter breaks in Spain	Senior citizens with money to spend

Matching the product to the target group

Activity
1. How do television advertisements target potential or existing customers?
2. Who would be the target market for:
   a   a week at Butlin's Funcoastworld, Skegness
   b   a day at Alton Towers
   c   a game of bowls.

> **Did you know?**
> Many organisations, including banks, building societies and mail order firms, keep an eye on your details so they can target you with particular products to 'meet your needs'.

It is important to get the right product to the right people, but how do we know who the right people are? The answer is to divide the market into smaller sections, or market segments. This enables organisations specifically to serve these segments so the customers are given what they want. This way, both the organisation and the customer benefit.

Different market segments have different needs. For example, if we say that all people who take part in sport are a market, we can then divide this market into segments according to their needs.

Different age groups will have different sports needs, for example men aged 16–35 might want to play football whereas senior citizens might want to play bowls.

A hotel's general product may be accommodation for the whole market – the people who want to stay there. However, it may offer different types of accommodation for particular market segments, for example:

- family rooms for families
- conference facilities for business people
- the honeymoon suite for newlyweds.

> **Think about it**
> How can a theme park cater for different market segments?
> Why is it important that leisure and tourism organisations target particular market segments?

How markets are segmented

Organisations need to know who their customers are and what they want. Advertising and promotion can be targeted more effectively if market segments are recognised. There are five basic ways of segmenting the market, by:

- age
- gender
- social group
- lifestyle
- ethnicity.

These methods enable organisations to build up profiles of their customers.

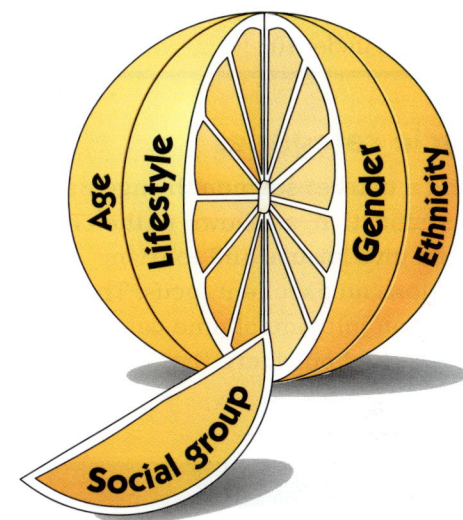

Market segments

> **Fact file**
> A **market segment** is a group of people in a market, which may be based on age, gender, socio-economic grouping or geography.

Age

Different age groups tend to have different leisure interests and needs. Senior citizens usually prefer to go out in groups, for example day trips, or they may want to 'winter' in a warmer climate such as Spain.

One organisation which specialises in holidays for the over-50s is Saga Holidays. It was established in 1952 by the owner of a hotel who wanted to attract guests during the low season and found the target market was retired people. Saga is now an international travel company offering all types of holidays for older people with varying levels of disposable income. It even has its own magazine – just like your age group!

In contrast, people aged 18–30 years tend to prefer fun-packed holidays where they can dance and party all night and every night. Club 18–30 targets this market. This age group also enjoys adventure-type holidays such as climbing in Snowdonia or trekking in the Himalayas.

> **Talk about it**
>
> In your group, consider how a leisure centre might target a family of two adults and two children under 10?

Life cycle categories

Targeting a market segment by age or life cycle classification, as shown in the chart below, can give leisure and tourism organisations an excellent focus. The life cycle puts a person into one of nine categories which are based on where that person is in his or her life cycle.

> **Talk about it**
>
> In your group, can you identify people you know who fall into the life cycle concept? Do you agree with the different categories?

> **Activity**
>
> ▶ Saga Holidays and Club Med cater for specific age groups. Using brochures from travel agents, describe the type of holidays on offer.
>
> Write down how Club Med and 18–30 holidays are promoted in holiday brochures.

Gender

Leisure and tourism organisations have recognised the needs and interests of both genders. For example:

- women tend to prefer to take part in non-contact sports and activities such as yoga and aerobics.
- a number of leisure centres now have a beauty salon offering a range of beauty treatments for women
- women may prefer all-female classes for their workouts.

Name of category	Life cycle
Bachelors/spinsters	Young single people with a reasonable level of personal disposable income. Enjoy nightlife, music and package holidays in Spain/Greece
Newlyweds/parties living together	Higher disposable income. Eat out a lot. Holidays in Florida/India/Far East
Full nest 1	Young couple/married/living together, youngest child less than 6. Family trips to zoo, parks. Self-catering holidays
Full nest 2	Young couples with children, youngest over 6. Falling disposable income. Less money to spend on leisure activities
Full nest 3	Older couple with older children who are still dependent, probably studying. Lower disposable income. Home is base for entertainment, e.g. TV, video, radio, computer
Empty nest 1	Older couples, no children or children left at home and dependent. Disposable income not restricted. Weekend breaks, eating out, theatre, and annual holidays abroad
Empty nest 2	Older couples, chief breadwinner retired. Income once again restricted. Home entertainment: home improvements, gardening, TV
Solitary survivor 1	Single/widowed person. Restricted income. Gardening/home-based leisure
Solitary survivor 2	Single person retired. Little spare cash. Little to spend on leisure

A women-only session. Leisure and tourism organisations recognise the needs of different groups and market them accordingly

> **Talk about it**
> In your group, discuss whether you think that women should be able to play football or rugby with men.

> **Talk about it**
> In your group, discuss what sort of leisure activities could be aimed specifically at each gender, for example a 'knit and natter' club for women over 60 or a parent and toddler swimming group.
> Think of some activities specifically for men and women. Does this encourage sex discrimination? What about boxing for women?

> **Did you know?**
> It's not so long since some pubs had a male only bar – no women allowed. Nowadays, pubs encourage women and families by providing a warm welcome and providing facilities like family rooms.

It's important that organisations recognise the need to cater for each gender as this could improve business and improve the image of the organisation. For example, hotels can make the effort to cater for businesswomen as well as businessmen.

Nowadays, women do things which were previously the domain of men, for example in athletics women now take part in the pole vault and triple jump. Women jockeys race alongside men. However, there are still some sports where women cannot compete against men, for example football and rugby, although women have their own football and rugby leagues.

Social group

This is sometimes referred to as socio-economic grouping. It is a way of categorising people under the headings of marital status, education, jobs and income. In general, people who have similar incomes and similar jobs have similar leisure interests.

The most widely used method of grouping people for marketing purposes based on income and occupation is shown in the chart below.

Grouping	Social status	Occupation	Products and services
A	Upper middle class	Lawyers, chief executives	Expensive holidays, exclusive golf club
B	Middle class	Doctors, teachers	All-inclusive holidays
C1	Lower middle class	Supervisors	Fly/drive holidays
C2	Skilled working class	Plumbers, electricians	Package holidays
D	Working class	Semi-skilled, unskilled labourers, cleaners	Cheaper package holidays
E	Unskilled	Casual workers, pensioners, widows	Coach holidays, day trips

Social status and leisure activities
Registrar-General's Social Classification

It is assumed that people in each category have similar amounts of disposable income and buying habits. It is also assumed that people in social grouping A have the highest level of disposable income.

However, there are a number of problems with this type of classification system. For example:

- It's a big drop from social groupings A to E – and this can happen if the director of a national leisure company is made redundant.
- Some people in C1 and C2 may have a higher disposable income than those in A and B, who might decide to pay for private education for their children or private health care for all the family.
- It is a good way of categorising, however the divisions between each group are unclear.

Talk about it

If a hotel targeted people in the A social category, the price of rooms, decor, style and exclusiveness of the place would reflect this, whereas a seaside hotel might consist of basic, friendly accommodation and service to the C1 and C2 categories.

In your group, discuss whether it is right to categorise people like this.

Whether you agree or disagree with categorising people in this way, it should be remembered that this classification system is used purely for marketing purposes – for selecting market segments to match the products and services available.

Talk about it

In your group, discuss whether you think this method of categorising people is accurate? What newspapers would you expect A and B groupings to read? What newspapers would you expect people in C1 and C2 to read?

What difference in income would there be between A and E groupings?

Lifestyle

Efforts have been made to look at groups of people according to their lifestyles, that is the way they live, their interests and opinions, and their activities.

Advertisers, in particular, look at lifestyles and target their advertisements to hit the right target market. Examples include services such as banking (credit cards) and insurance, both of which have been heavily marketed.

One method of marketing research is ACORN – 'A Classification of Residential Neighbourhoods'. This method classifies people under the following categories:

- **Mainstreamers** – average people doing ordinary things, buying branded products like Heinz beans and Adidas sportswear.
- **Aspirers** – these people tend to go for exclusive and expensive products like fast cars and luxury holidays.
- **Succeeders** – people who have been there and done it, and have achieved by ambition. A powerful group who can afford a lifestyle to which they have become accustomed.
- **Reformers** – people concerned about the quality of life, for example preserving the environment.

Leisure and tourism organisations might target these groups in the following ways:

- An exclusive health club – Aspirers.
- A local leisure centre – Mainstreamers.
- A five-star hotel – Succeeders.
- A natural health food shop – Reformers.

Activity

▶ In your group, design and make a collage for each of the lifestyle categories and include a family that would go with it.

Ethnicity

Different cultures and races have different interests and needs. Leisure and tourism organisations need to take religious customs, food and language into account when promoting products and services for different ethnic groups. Here are some examples:

- A London hotel may have to change its menu to suit overseas visitors. A group of American tourists may want to be served burgers, not cottage pie, chips and gravy.
- Special Saturday morning films at the cinema may be shown to attract the Asian community, as this is part of their culture.
- Sports and leisure centres may provide women-only swimming sessions for strict Muslim women. Female lifeguards only will be on duty, a provision which respects the Islamic religion.
- A Caribbean centre acts as a meeting place for people of West Indian origin, where they can take part in activities such as singing, dancing and organising fund-raising events for local charities.

Case study

Danny, restaurant manager

Danny manages a high-class restaurant in Stratford-upon-Avon. It is a very popular venue with tourists who flock to Stratford for the Shakespeare experience.

Danny's main responsibility is to make sure all his customers, mainly tourists, are well looked after and are served with what they ask for.

Danny says:

> If you want a challenge mixed with variety, then this is certainly the job to be in. Talk about pleasing everyone. Americans love burgers, Germans love sauerkraut, the French love garlic and Australians will eat and drink just about anything! Surprisingly, our Chinese diners absolutely love fish and chips!

How else could Danny cater for the needs of his multi-cultural diners?

Check your knowledge

1. Define target marketing in your own words.
2. What does the term 'potential customers' mean?
3. Who would be the target market for:
   a a nightclub
   b McDonald's
   c a disco on ice?
4. Which market segment is most likely to be targeted by a travel agent offering holidays that include parties, barbecues and fun?
5. A restaurant in York is promoting a range of midweek lunches. What market segments are being targeted?
6. How can a hotel cater for different groups of people?
7. What activities would you market for the group 'Empty Nest 1'?
8. How can hotels cater for businesswomen as well as businessmen?
9. What products and services would appeal to 'aspirers'?
10. What does the term 'ethnicity' mean?

Chapter 3 — Market research

Market research is a tool that helps organisations to find out their customers' needs. This chapter looks at what market research is, how organisations might benefit from its use and the various market research methods including postal surveys, telephone questionnaires, personal surveys, observation and the Internet.

What you will learn

- What is market research?
- How organisations benefit from market research
- Carrying out successful market research
- The market research process
- Market research methods

What is market research?

Market research helps an organisation find out what people think of its products

Talk about it

In your group, discuss why you think organisations need to ask customers about their products?

What do members of the group think about Mars Bars? What conclusions can you draw from this? How could this help the company that manufactures the Mars Bar?

Case study

Tara, market researcher

Every Monday, Wednesday and Friday Tara heads for the town centre ready to start her day and talk to as many people as she can. With her clipboard in hand, she carries out surveys by asking passers-by questions and then writing down their responses. We call this market research.

Tara's main task today is to find out what newspapers people read. She is employed by an agency which carries out market research for large organisations. The questions Tara asks go something like this: Which daily newspaper do you read? What do you like about it? Do you think it gives good value for money? What is your favourite section of the paper? Do you look at the advertisements?

1. Why is Tara asking these questions?
2. How would the organisation who receives the information benefit from this market research?

Fact file

Market research is a tool that helps organisations to find out their customers' needs.

Market research gathers together the likes and dislikes of consumers so that an organisation can act on the information and improve the product.

Anyone involved in making decisions will appreciate the value of accurate and up-to-date information such as that collected by Tara in the case study. The better the information, the more likely organisations are to successfully sell their products and services.

How organisations benefit from market research

Market research enables organisations to answer the following questions:

- Who will be our typical customers?
- What will they want?
- Why will they buy from us and not our competitors?
- How much will we sell as a result of our market research?

There are other questions that can be answered too:

- How can we improve an existing product?
- How much are customers prepared to pay?
- How often will they buy it?
- What sort of image will sell the product?
- What new products should we develop?

Market research involves forecasting. Forecasting is predicting the type of product that people want to buy. Good forecasting can reduce the risk of bad decision-making, so market research helps with product or service development. In other words, marketing research helps take the guesswork out of decision-making.

Activity

▶ Visit a health and fitness centre in your area and pretend you want to join. This will give you information about membership, fees, equipment and training programmes. Ask as much as you like because if they think they have a potential customer, it is guaranteed that they will do 'the big sell'.

Remember that 'mystery shopping' is an accepted practice. It goes on all the time. The aim is to gain information and ideas and then use them.

Think about it

Write down some examples of organisations, not necessarily in leisure and tourism, which you think might employ mystery shoppers.

Carrying out successful market research

There are many sources of information for market research and an organisation has to work out which are the most useful.

Imagine that you run a health and fitness centre. Figure 2.3 shows some of the groups of people who might be of great help to your research.

To find out what your competitors are doing, you will need to find out what facilities they offer and what they charge. Organisations often employ 'mystery shoppers' for this purpose.

The market research process

There are five stages in the market research process:

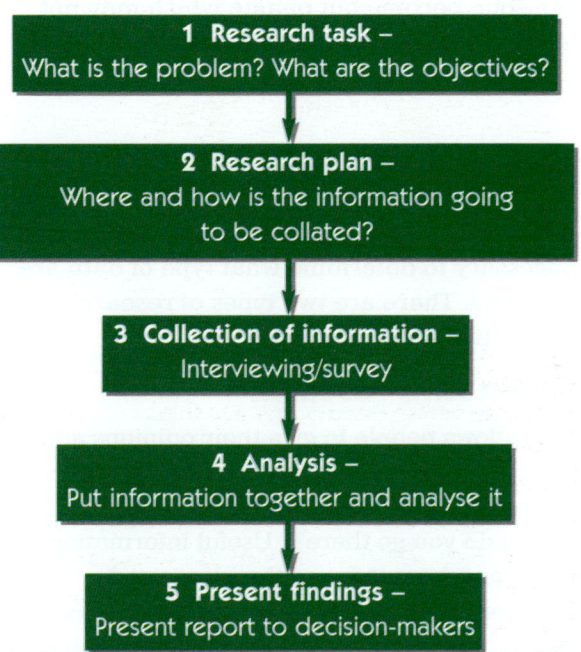

Figure 2.3 Sources of information for your market research

Chapter 3 — Market research

Market research methods

Research involves collecting and analysing information. There are two types of market research: primary and secondary research.

Primary research

Primary research, also known as field research, involves collecting and analysing information at first hand using face-to-face interviews and surveys. The information collected is called primary data.

The advantage of primary research is that the data are original and up to date. However, it can be expensive in terms of paying people to go out and ask questions and it can also take time to collect.

Secondary research

Secondary research, also known as desk research, involves using material that has already been published such as government reports, newspaper articles, published company accounts and financial records. This is secondary data. There is a wide range of data available and it is usually free. However, it can soon become out of date which may not make it relevant to the research.

Types of research

Before carrying out a research project, it is necessary to determine what type of data are required. There are two types of research: qualitative and quantitative.

Qualitative research

This allows people to give their opinions and involves using open questions like 'Why do you go there?', 'How often do you use the gym?', 'When do you go there?'. Useful information can be gained from this and the ideas used. However, there will be a lot of different opinions which makes the analysis more complicated.

For example: The way people regard Alton Towers (perception), what makes them go there (motivation), how they feel about its location, prices and customer service (attitudes).

Quantitative research

This gives factual information by asking closed questions (requiring only a simple yes or no answer) which make analysis relatively easy. This type of research is connected with statistics. It records what people do.

For example: At Alton Towers, the number of rides you went on, the number of times you went on them, the number of people you went with, the number of times you have visited.

Snapshot

The Octagon Theatre

The Octagon Theatre had a problem. Attendances were falling, the owners were concerned about its financial situation and a new theatre was opening less than 20 miles away.

The manager decided to carry out some qualitative research in order to find out who did and who did not use the theatre and why.

A quantitative analysis of ticket sales showed that sales for the twice-weekly showing of films was declining. Qualitative, attitude research revealed that people preferred to see up-to-date films, not ones which had been on the circuit for several weeks.

The results also showed that not everyone was aware of the wide variety of activities that went on at the theatre.

Armed with this information, the manager negotiated a deal with the film distributors to show new releases at the same time as purpose-built cinemas. He then promoted this development and the other activities by advertising in the local newspaper, putting up posters around the town and direct mailing theatre-goers whose addresses he had on a customer database.

Market research is about collecting information. There are five widely used methods for collecting primary marketing research data:

- postal surveys
- telephone questionnaires
- personal surveys
- observation
- the Internet.

Case study

Sveta, health and fitness club manager

Sveta is manager of a health and fitness club. Recently, attendances have been falling, mainly due, it is thought, to the local authority leisure centre opening its new fitness suite. Sveta has been asked by her directors to do something to increase attendances.

She went to the new fitness suite in the leisure centre as a paying customer to find out its attractions and why it was drawing her customers away. During her workout she listened to what other users were saying and watched as they enjoyed their session there.

Sveta knew she was up against stiff opposition. She put together a questionnaire and asked her existing customers what they wanted from a health and fitness suite. She also asked people in town. Her aim was to find out how her club could regain its popularity.

She interviewed more than 250 people. She then collated all the information and found that people wanted a variety of things when they exercised, namely good facilities, friendly staff, and a place to relax.

Sveta presented her report to her directors and made the following recommendations:

- Introduce new state-of-the-art exercise equipment.
- Create packages that would attract customers such as early morning fitness sessions followed by a healthy breakfast.
- Introduce personalised training programmes for individuals.
- Send staff on a Welcome Host/Customer Care course.
- Provide staff with uniforms and name badges.

Can you recognise the five stages in Sveta's market research process?

Adventureland
Customer Questionnaire

We would be extremely grateful if you could spend a few minutes of your time to complete the following questionnaire about your visit to Adventureland. We rely on customer feedback to provide the best quality facilities for an enjoyable family day out.

1. How many times have you visisted the theme park?
   1–2 ☐ 3–4 ☐ 5+ ☐
2. How many people are in your party?
   1–2 ☐ 3–4 ☐ 5+ ☐
3. How many rides did you go on?
   none ☐ 1–3 ☐ 4–6 ☐ 7–9 ☐ 10+ ☐
4. How many times did you go on the 'white knuckle' rides?
   none ☐ 1–3 ☐ 4–6 ☐ 7–9 ☐ 10+ ☐
5. How long did you stay at the park?
   less than 2 hours ☐ 2–4 hours ☐ 4–6 hours ☐ more than 6 hours ☐
6. How many catering outlets did you use?
   none ☐ 1–2 ☐ 2–4 ☐ more than 4 ☐
7. Did you buy any merchandise? If so, what did you buy?
   mug ☐ key ring ☐ t-shirt ☐ toy ☐
   other (please specify) ☐ ……………………………………
8. Which age group do you fall into?
   16–24 ☐ 25–45 ☐ Over 46 ☐

Example of quantitative research

Postal surveys

Postal surveys are a very common method of research used in leisure and tourism. It involves the posting back of a completed questionnaire, so it is important to remember to send a stamped-addressed envelope. It is unlikely that people will reply if they have to pay for the response themselves.

Postal surveys can reach a lot of people in a very short time. There is no interviewer training required and it is usually cheaper than a face-to-face interview in terms of time. Respondents also have time to consider their answers, which can be an advantage or disadvantage, depending on the question.

One way of encouraging people to complete postal surveys is to offer incentives such as: 'Complete and return this very simple questionnaire in the pre-paid envelope and you could win a holiday for two in the Caribbean'. Quite tempting isn't it? You don't even have to buy a stamp!

Some travel agents send out questionnaires to find out if customers were satisfied with their holiday and all the arrangements that go with it including transfers, excursions and the service provided by the holiday representative.

```
Cheap 'n' Cheerful
Travel
1 The High Street
ANYTOWN
Yorkshire
AN1 2CC
```

On a scale of 1–5 where 1 is excellent and 5 is poor, how would you rate the following?

	1	2	3	4	5
1. Service provided by the travel agent	☐	☐	☐	☐	☐
2. In-flight service	☐	☐	☐	☐	☐
3. Hotel facilities	☐	☐	☐	☐	☐
4. Holiday representative	☐	☐	☐	☐	☐
5. Entertainment	☐	☐	☐	☐	☐
6. Accommodation	☐	☐	☐	☐	☐
7. Overall enjoyment	☐	☐	☐	☐	☐

A postal survey

Advantages	Disadvantages
Data can be collected cheaply from a large number of respondents	Not many returns and surveys that are returned don't answer the questions
No problem with the behaviour and appearance of the interviewer influencing results	Responses may be largely from people who have strong opinions on the subject
Respondents have time to consider answers and consult others if necessary	No check on whether respondents have really understood the questions
Postal methods may be the only way to contact some respondents	No control over who actually completes the questionnaire
Easy to set up	No opportunity to observe respondents' reactions to the questions
	Cannot expect to collect respondents' spontaneous answers
	No control over order in which questions answered
	Respondents are limited to the question-and-answer options presented and their real views may not be revealed

Advantages and disadvantages of postal surveys

Talk about it

A travel agent sent out a postal questionnaire to find out the holiday habits of 100 people. The results were as follows:

- 50 per cent of replies were from senior citizens.
- 15 per cent of replies came from 18–25-year-olds.
- 35 per cent came from 35–50 year olds.
- 50 per cent of the senior citizens went abroad for two months to avoid the English winter.
- The 18–25 age group wanted sun, sea and fun.

In your group, decide what sort of holidays the travel agent should promote based on these statistics?

Why might a hotel use a telephone survey?

Talk about it

Have you ever been questioned about a product or service on the telephone? In your group, discuss what you think are the advantages and disadvantages of telephone questionnaires.

Postal questionnaires can be distributed in a number of ways:

- Travel agents may post the questionnaire to clients as soon as they have returned home.
- Some facilities, e.g. hotels, theme parks, may have the questionnaire on 'site' at reception or in the rooms. They can be posted back when they have been completed.
- They can be given out at the end of a coach trip or on the flight home from a holiday and posted back.

Postal questionnaires can be expensive for the organisation in terms of postage costs. One way to avoid these costs is to ask clients to complete questionnaires straight away and place them in a sealed box before they leave.

Telephone questionnaires

Telephone surveys are growing rapidly as a means of obtaining a quick response to an event or activity. For example, organisers at an exhibition centre might phone exhibitors after the event to find out if everything had been satisfactory for them.

You might have thought of the following advantages:

- A larger number of interviews can be carried out covering a wide geographical area.
- There are no transport costs for the interviewers – they do not need to visit respondents (interviewees).
- Costs per interview are low.

Disadvantages may include the following:

- Only a short questionnaire can be used because of the time factor.
- There is a general distrust by customers of speaking to people they cannot see and have never met.
- Telephone surveys can be soul destroying for the interviewer if they receive nothing but negative responses.

It is difficult when conducting telephone surveys to convince people you are not trying to sell them anything. This is because we receive calls from double-glazing companies, motoring organisations and insurance sales reps, all trying to sell us something by phone.

Case study

Nicola

Nicola works for a well-known motoring organisation. Her job is to phone existing customers about the service they receive from her company.

Nicola's background is in telesales, followed by two years as a receptionist in a tourist information office.

Her telephone conversations with customers go something like this:

NICOLA:	Good morning Mr. Ablewhite. My name is Nicola and I work for the XYZ motoring organisation. As one of our members, I wonder if you would mind answering one or two quick questions for a survey we are carrying out.
MR ABLEWHITE:	I hope you are not going to be long because I have to go to a meeting in 10 minutes.
NICOLA:	OK. It will only take a few minutes.
MR ABLEWHITE:	Very well then, but I hope you are not going to try and sell me anything.
NICOLA:	No. It's just a survey. Mr. Ablewhite, do you have any additional services with us such as house insurance, loans, or car insurance?
MR ABLEWHITE:	I've got my car insured with you.
NICOLA:	Would you mind if I gave you some details about our other services?
MR ABLEWHITE:	As long as you can save me some money, but be quick about it please.
NICOLA:	At the moment we are able to match any of our competitors' car insurance quotes and then cut them by 20 per cent.
MR ABLEWHITE:	Yes, I've seen that offer on television.
NICOLA:	Well, as you have been a member for 15 years this offer is extended to house insurance for our members.
MR ABLEWHITE:	How much would that save me?
NICOLA:	On average, £150 per year. How does that sound?
MR ABLEWHITE:	That sounds interesting. Send me the details.
NICOLA:	I will put everything in the post now and will ring next week to confirm your decision to go ahead with this special offer.
MR ABLEWHITE:	Thanks. Now I must dash.
NICOLA:	Goodbye and thank you.

1. What telephone techniques does Nicola use?
2. Why do some customers resent this type of call?
3. What is 'cold calling'?

Activity

In your group, write a script for the first couple of minutes of a telephone survey. After you are all satisfied with the script, see if you can try it out on another group. How successful was it?

A good way to start a telephone survey would be:

'Good morning. I am a student from Anytown College and I'm doing a survey about how much exercise people take each week. I'm not trying to sell you anything. I only want to ask you a few simple questions. It won't take up too much of your time. Would you mind please?'

The request is harmless and it's not going to cost anything, so the chances are that people will take part in the survey. However, you must always remember that the person being interviewed may give you any answer because they are in a rush or they may also give you an incorrect answer e.g. a smoker might respond 'No' to the question 'Do you smoke?'.

Personal surveys

Personal surveys sometimes involve a group of people giving their reactions to a product they have tried to an interviewer. What sorts of product might leisure and tourism organisations wish to find out more about in a personal survey?

> **Talk about it**
>
> In your group, discuss how you might feel if you were stopped in the street and asked to help complete a survey.

Personal surveys involve face-to-face interviews with either an individual or a group of people. The interview may be structured around a questionnaire upon which answers are recorded and analysed. On the other hand, an interview can be in the form of a discussion, with the interviewer having a list of topics of interest to discuss. The interviewer can also create questions and seek responses as the interview progresses.

Questionnaires can:

- tell an organisation about its customers
- give the organisation its customers' opinions
- tell an organisation about its customers' habits
- gives respondents/customers the opportunity to air their views.

Advantages	Disadvantages
Very good response rates are possible	Time-consuming interviews can mean that only a small, unrepresentative sample is chosen
Interviewer is available to clarify questions and prevent misunderstandings	Interaction between respondent and interviewer can lead to distorted answers being given
Pace of questioning can encourage spontaneous responses	Respondents are limited to the question-and-answer options presented, and their real views may not be revealed
No uncertainty over who actually answers the questions	
Interviewers can observe and collect useful background data	
Uniformity of interview technique and content makes quantitative analysis of the data possible	

Advantages and disadvantages of personal surveys

It is important to design the questionnaire in such a way that the required information will be received. Questionnaire design and asking the right questions is a skilled job and can take time. Here are some basic rules:

- Keep questions simple.
- Leave questions about age, occupation and marital status to the end of the questionnaire, after some type of relationship has been built up with the person being interviewed.
- Don't ask questions which have nothing to do with your aim of finding out what customers want.
- Ask no more than eight questions.
- Ask open questions by using the words 'what', 'why', 'how', e.g. 'What do you look for in a holiday?'
- Interview a large enough sample, to give valid results.
- Do not include questions which test the respondent's memory, e.g. 'How much did you spend on food each day during your first week here?'

It is common practice to test or 'pilot' a questionnaire to check if the right questions are being asked and to see if they are easily understood.

Types of questions

There are two types of question – closed and open.

Closed questions usually require an answer to be selected from a range of options, including yes or no. Closed questions are used in quantitative surveys. They can be answered quickly using a tick box, and are often used because of the ease with which they can be analysed later.

Examples of closed questions

Do you come swimming on your own?
Yes ☐   No ☐

Have you stayed in this hotel before?
Yes ☐   No ☐

Do you watch television every evening?
Yes ☐   No ☐

Open questions allow respondents to express an opinion and show their feelings. Although these questions give useful information, the results are more difficult to analyse because people have different opinions.

Examples of open questions

What do you think about this swimming pool?
What do you look for in a holiday?
What improvements would you like to see in the fitness suite?

LEISURE AND TOURISM QUESTIONNAIRE

I'm doing a survey. Can I ask you some questions?

1. How old are you?
2. Where do you live?
3. If you won the Lottery where would you go?
4. How much would you pay to go on holiday?
5. Are you a non-smoker?
6. How many children have you got?
7. How much did you spend on food per day for the first week of your holiday?
8. Don't you agree that rail travel is expensive?
9. How much does the main breadwinner in your home earn?
10. Who decides where you go on holiday?

An ineffective questionnaire

Think about it

Analyse the ineffective questionnaire above, and the effective questionnaire on page 117, then discuss your findings with the rest of your group.

Activity

▶ Your group has come up with the brilliant idea of setting up a health and fitness club in your area. Design a questionnaire which would give you sufficient marketing research evidence to see if your idea would work.

Divide your group into pairs. Each pair should interview ten people, using the questionnaire you designed.

As a group, analyse your results and present your findings to your tutor.

TOURISM QUESTIONNAIRE

Good morning/afternoon. I am carrying out a survey on holidays and tourism for a national travel company. Would you mind if I asked you a few questions? It won't take long.

1. Did you go on holiday last year?
   Yes ☐   No ☐

2. How often do you go on holiday each year?
   Once ☐   Twice ☐   More often ☐

3. Where do you go?
   UK ☐   Europe ☐
   USA ☐   Elsewhere ☐
   Include destination and country
   _____

4. Who goes on holiday with you?
   Family ☐   Friends ☐
   Please give details
   _____

5. When booking your holiday how do you make your arrangements?
   Make your own ☐
   Use a travel agent ☐
   Go direct to a tour operator ☐

6. If a new travel agency was to open in this area, where do you think would be the best location?
   On the high street ☐
   In a shopping centre ☐
   In a side street off the main shopping area ☐
   Elsewhere ☐

7. What opening times would attract you to visit the travel agency?

   Monday – Friday   **Saturday**
   9–12 noon ☐   9–12 noon ☐
   1–5 pm ☐   1–5 pm ☐
   5 pm onwards ☐

   Sunday
   10–1 pm ☐
   1–4 pm ☐

8. What sort of holiday would you like to see on offer?
   _____

9. What type of travel arrangements would you like to see on offer?
   _____

10. Where do you live?
    _____

11. Which age group do you belong to?
    16–24 ☐   25–39 ☐   40–59 ☐   60+ ☐

    Observation
    Male ☐   Female ☐

Thank you very much for taking part in this survey. The answers you have given will be treated in strict confidence.

An effective questionnaire

Personal interviews have their disadvantages. They can be time-consuming and this therefore limits the number that can be carried out in a day.

However, there are also advantages. Interviews can take place in the street, at a tourist attraction, at home or at work. A face-to-face interview gives you the opportunity to find out what customers:

- want
- think of your competitors
- think of you
- think about your product
- think about the name of your organisation – is it easy to remember, can they pronounce it?
- think are the best words to describe what you offer, e.g. 'value for money', 'cheap', 'good quality'
- think of your advertising and promotional material.

Interviewing may be costly in terms of time but it is an investment well worth making. By asking the right questions you will get the answers which will tell you about your product and organisation.

A face-to-face interview can yield excellent qualitative information (feelings) which could lead researchers to identify any problem areas. This, in turn, could enable researchers to focus on the questions to ask in the next interview in a more structured, quantitative way (numbers, statistics).

Discussions

This method of market research is used to generate new ideas when finding answers to questions like 'What new activities would you like to see in the leisure centre?' or 'What type of performances would you go to watch at the theatre?'

Discussions can also be used to find out what consumers think about a new promotion or idea before it is widely available, for example a different colour or type of packaging for a product or even a name change. Sometimes group discussions are recorded or videotaped to assist in preparing a summary of the group's responses.

Observation

Direct observation allows a researcher to see exactly how something is done at first hand. How might direct observation techniques be used in a leisure centre?

> **Fact file**
>
> **Observation** means studying by looking.

Observation is a popular and useful research technique. Well-organised observation has several advantages:

- You can observe what people actually do, not what they tell researchers they do. People are studied in their own environment and should be expected to behave naturally. Observation can detect 'taken for granted' behaviour that subjects are not aware of, and would thus not report if asked in an interview.
- Observation can be done over time, allowing changes in groups or situations to be revealed.

There are two types of observation: direct observation and participant observation.

Direct observation

Subjects are watched as they go about their normal business and observations are recorded by the researcher. Naturally, observations can usually take place only where permission has been granted – otherwise observation could be classed as being unethical.

Examples of direct observation include:

- watching and listening to a hotel receptionist dealing with guests' enquiries
- observing a trampolining instructor coaching a student – the observer could be an examiner watching to see if the coach passes the requirements of the qualification.

Direct observation does not always have to be carried out by a member of staff. For example, it can be done by closed-circuit television (CCTV) which monitors the movements and actions of people, such as in a town centre or at a football match. With this form of direct observation, however, participants do not always give their permission!

Organisations such as libraries use an electronic counter to record the numbers of people using the facility, and turnstiles are used at sports stadia to keep a check on the numbers of spectators coming into the ground.

Participant observation

This means that the researcher becomes part of the group being studied (e.g. a 'mystery shopper'). There is probably no better way of getting to understand the way a group works than to join them.

Examples of participant observation include:

- joining a group of recreation assistants throughout their shifts for a week
- working alongside the kitchen staff in a restaurant.

Think about it

Suppose you were a receptionist in a big hotel. How would you feel if you knew you were being observed by a marketing agency researcher? Would you be able to act naturally?

Cameras capture crime

Street cameras are already beginning to pay dividends in the fight against crime.

Police reports show that the 18 town-centre cameras are pinpointing crime and aiding detection just two weeks after being switched on.

A 24-year-old man has been released on police bail after being filmed allegedly stealing a bag of clothes from outside a charity shop on High Street at 9.30 pm on Monday.

Three juveniles were arrested at 5.00 pm on Sunday on suspicion of taking clothes from outside the same charity shop. An 11-year-old girl and a 10-year-old boy have accepted cautions, and another 11-year-old girl has been released on bail.

Inspector Wood said: 'The camera system has really only just gone online but already it is proving its worth. This system will greatly benefit the town centre, its businesses, its residents and its visitors.'

Think about it

Many town centres now have CCTV. Do you think this takes away a person's liberty and is too intrusive. In other words, is 'Big Brother' watching you?

Would you feel your every move was being watched if there were CCTV cameras in a sports centre?

How can facilities benefit from the use of CCTV observation?

Activity

▶ Bridgetown Leisure Centre is to open in three months' time. The local authority wants to make sure the activities that are put on at the leisure centre are the ones that customers want.

Market research will help find out customer needs. This is what you have to do:

Divide the group into four so that each group is responsible for one method of marketing research: postal surveys, telephone questionnaires, personal surveys and observation.

Helpful hints

Group 1 – design a questionnaire which will give you information about customer needs and wants at the leisure centre. Send out 20 letters and act on their responses.

Group 2 – phone 30 people and find out what they would want to do at the leisure centre. Make sure you have a list of questions to ask them.

Group 3 – design a questionnaire and interview 30 people.

Group 4 – observe the customers at your local leisure centre. What are the most popular activities? On average, how long do people stay there? It is essential that you ask the leisure centre manager for permission to conduct this observation.

When all your information has been gathered, list the activities you would put on at the Bridgetown Leisure Centre and say why.

The Internet

The Internet is regularly used as a market research tool to find out the thoughts and opinions of customers.

Leisure and tourism organisations use the Internet because there is easy access to a wide range of information. It's easy to find out the products and services competitors are offering and it's so quick – log on, access the relevant site, ask questions and analyse the information.

Secondary, or desk research data which we talked about earlier, is usually published on the Internet. Using this facility is less time-consuming than going to the library to look for different publications or phoning government departments for information.

Many organisations publish research and sell products on the Internet. Details of customers who order catalogues or who buy the products are usually put on a customer database. This means there is an opportunity to use these people for market research on existing or new products. Of course, not everyone has access to the Internet so research opportunities may be limited. Despite this, leisure and tourism organisations are able to carry out some worthwhile research by accessing customers one way or the other.

Activity

▶ If you have access to the Internet, try to find some examples of market research by leisure and tourism organisations and others in a non-related industry. Visit www.heinemann.co.uk/hotlinks for a list of suggested websites.

Check your knowledge

1. Why is market research so important?
2. Which groups of people may be of help in the market research for a restaurant opening up in town?
3. What is mystery shopping? Why is it used?
4. What is primary research?
5. Give another term for secondary research.
6. What would an organisation obtain if it did qualitative research?
7. What would an organisation obtain if it did quantitative research?
8. What are the advantages of postal surveys?
9. How can questionnaires help leisure and tourism organisations?
10. Why is it important to pilot questionnaires?
11. What makes a good questionnaire?
12. How can observation help leisure and tourism organisations?
13. What are the advantages and disadvantages of CCTV in town centres?
14. How can the Internet be used as a market research tool?
15. What incentives can be offered to get people to complete questionnaires?

Chapter 4: The marketing mix

The marketing mix is one of the most important concepts in leisure and tourism marketing. This chapter looks at the four factors which together make up the marketing mix – product, price, place and promotion, often called the 4Ps. Organisations need to take these into account when meeting the needs of their customers.

What you will learn
- Product
- Price
- Place
- Promotion

Talk about it

Fantasy Travel has introduced a holiday package with a difference. It's called 'Around the World in 80 Days'. This holiday does exactly what it says, taking in more than 40 countries in an incredible 80 days. It costs a mere £25 000. It will be advertised in a quality Sunday newspaper magazine for just two successive weeks. Tour organiser, Sally Winchester, says, 'It's the trip of a lifetime for anyone with time on their hands and money to spend.'

In your group, discuss what you think about this package. Why is it advertised in a quality Sunday newspaper magazine?

Which of the 4Ps of the marketing mix can you see at work here?

A successful marketing mix of the right product in the right place at the right time, using attractive advertising and promotion, wins customers and makes success more likely.

The marketing mix

Figure 2.4 How a leisure centre uses the marketing mix

Marketing decisions made using the marketing mix can help increase business and boost sales if the organisation gets the right product in the right place at the right price using the right type of promotion.

Some leisure and tourism organisations may adjust the emphasis of the 4Ps, depending on their objectives. Here are some examples:

- A local authority leisure centre has opened a health and fitness centre. As a result, the manager of a nearby fitness centre reduces his prices to compete with his new rival.
- A pub finds that more and more families are coming in for meals so the landlady adjusts her product accordingly, e.g. special children's menus, builds a play area.
- A new restaurant has opened in town. The owner carries out a variety of promotions to raise awareness of the new facility.
- A sports goods shop has decided to expand to a bigger premises so it looks for a place in the centre of town which is easy to locate for a large number of people.

Activity

▶ Draw a diagram similar to Figure 2.4. Instead of using a leisure centre as the example, one group show a hotel, one group illustrate a cinema and another group show a restaurant. Compare your completed work.

▶ Analyse how the marketing mix can help leisure and tourism organisations increase attendances, raise awareness and boost profits.

Product

Fact file

Product describes the goods or services offered for sale by organisations. It is through the product that customers' needs are satisfied.

Product or service features

It is ironic that we should talk about 'products' because leisure and tourism is really a 'service' industry. Although there are products like books, training shoes, squash racquets, and so on, much of leisure and tourism is connected with the customers' experience and how those experiences are delivered to the customer.

Some examples of leisure and tourism products are shown in Figure 2.5.

Figure 2.5 Some leisure and tourism products. Which ones are tangible, which are intangible?

Some products are tangible – you can touch a tennis racquet and can see a theatre and its facilities. Many leisure and tourism products are intangible, for example you can't touch or see a package holiday or a session in the gym, *but* you can experience it.

Activity

▶ List five products and services you would find in a hotel.

▶ Explain how a hotel's products and services can help business people.

Customer satisfaction

Leisure products must satisfy the needs of the customer. There are a number of ways satisfaction is measured for a leisure product:

- Quality of customer service. For example, if a theatre receptionist treated a customer badly, the customer might complain, not return or do both. This emphasises the importance of customer care training for staff.

- Standard of facilities. Nowadays, people expect value for money, not poor quality goods, out-of-date equipment or dirty changing rooms.
- Atmosphere. Facilities should be bright, warm and friendly, creating a welcoming image.

Activity

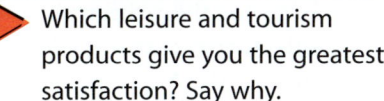

- Which leisure and tourism products give you the greatest satisfaction? Say why.
- How does a theme park attempt to achieve customer satisfaction?

Case study

Felix, customer

Felix loves rock music, so it was no surprise that he bought tickets for the weekend festival of rock near London. He paid a fortune for them but thought that since he worked hard every day on his rounds as a postman, he deserved a treat. He had saved really hard for this once-in-a-lifetime experience.

The music was brilliant. He couldn't have asked for anything more from the bands; they all sounded great. Unfortunately, everything else was not up to the same standard.

There weren't enough toilets and the ones that were available were filthy. There were no litter bins. Hamburgers cost £4.50 and a can of beer was £2.75. Everything was a rip-off.

The music was great. What a pity the rest of Felix's leisure experience didn't match it.

1. Have you had a similar experience to Felix?
2. What elements were missing from your overall experience?

The moral of Felix's story is that leisure and tourism products are made up of different elements, but all these elements should combine to form a satisfying leisure experience. If something goes wrong, it can badly affect the overall experience.

Products have to be continuously improved and developed as customers are always seeking new and improved goods. For example:

- Blackpool Pleasure Beach and Alton Towers open new and exciting rides such as The Playstation and Oblivion each year.
- New adventure sports like paragliding, jet skiing and windsurfing have been developed for those who like adventure and are prepared to take risks.
- Leisure centres provide crèches to allow parents to take part in keep-fit sessions knowing that their children are being well cared for.
- Health and fitness clubs now provide much more than keep-fit classes. The complete package can include personalised fitness programmes, dietary advice, massages and manicures.

This constant development is aimed at satisfying customer needs, maintaining quality and succeeding over the competition.

Talk about it

In pairs, can you think of any other products which have been improved to make them more attractive to customers?

What new products and services could an airline develop?

The brand name

The brand name given by an organisation to one of its products (or services) aims to make recognition of the product easier and to differentiate the products or collection of products from those of their competitors. In other words, it establishes a product in the mind of the customer.

Brand names in leisure and tourism include Reebok, Adidas, McDonald's, Thomson, Holiday Inn and Little Chef. Other well-known household brand names include Heinz,

Kellogg's, Hoover, Nescafé. In the eyes of the customer, these brands tend to suggest quality, trust and reliability so people are prepared to pay a higher price for them because they feel they are superior to other similar products. As a result, organisations encourage brand loyalty to be built up so they can take advantage of this feeling and behaviour by customers.

The brand name gives a product identity and organisations promote it to encourage potential customers to buy. The characteristics of a good brand name are as follows:

- It is easy to remember and pronounce, e.g. Puma, Reebok, KFC.
- The name is short and catchy, e.g. Pepsi, Levis, Donnay.
- The name is adaptable in that it covers a number of different products, e.g. Adidas makes clothes, footwear and aftershave.

Some organisations link a brand name to particular segments of a market, for example an airline may have 'standard' class, 'executive' or 'gold' class seating for specific travellers who fall into those categories.

Activity

1. List some brand names both within the leisure and tourism industries and outside them.
2. Think of a product, for example a chocolate bar. Make up a brand name for it which is easy to remember and catchy.

▶ How do organisations keep brand names firmly in the minds of consumers?

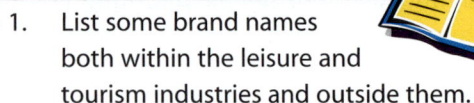
After-sales service

Good after-sales service should provide additional business for organisations. For example, a leisure centre may design a course for people in the fitness suite to help them lose weight. It could be advertised as 'Gym and trim'. The course would be successful if people lost weight, therefore the objective would have been met.

But what about marketing weight loss? Why not put on another course which would help customers maintain their fitness, keep to their reduced weight and keep them motivated? A follow-on course could be: 'Look good, feel good', an aerobics class, or 'Gym, swim and trim', a combination of activities.

Other services should be reviewed to establish a link to increase customer satisfaction and increased income for the organisation. One example could be in a college where students studying for the primary ABTAC – Travel Agent's Certificate – could then progress to the Advanced ABTAC course.

Think about it

Can you think of another service where customers could progress?

Activity

▶ Imagine you are going to carry on studying leisure and tourism after you have achieved your GCSE in Leisure and Tourism. What future qualifications related to this subject are available to you at school or at your local college? You may find the AQA, Edexcel and QCA examination board websites useful. Links to these websites can be found at www.heinemann.co.uk/hotlinks.

The other aspect of after-sales service is ensuring continual customer satisfaction with the product and the service received. For example, selling a holiday and issuing the tickets to the client isn't necessarily the end of the sale for either party. The travel agent could phone the client after the holiday to find out if he or she enjoyed it. This demonstrates three things:

- The travel agent shows genuine concern that the product was right.
- It enables the travel agent to find out if the customer's needs were met.
- It encourages good public relations, that is creating a good image for the organisation.

> **Talk about it**
> In your group, think of some other examples of after-sales service.

After-sales service also includes dealing with complaints. The quicker these are dealt with and sorted out, the more likely it is the customer will return and use the organisation again.

Product life cycle

> **Fact file**
> The **product life cycle** shows the different stages in the life of a product and the sales that can be expected at each stage.

Some products and services may be very popular and sell well for a while. Eventually, however, they lose their popularity and sales start to fall.

> **Talk about it**
> Many pop groups have two hit records and then fade from the scene. In your group, discuss why you think this is.

Figure 2.6 shows the six stages in the life cycle of a product.

Stages in the product life cycle

1 Development
This is when the product is being designed and, as yet, is not on the market, hence no sales are made. At this stage, ideas are tested, suggestions made and a decision to launch the product is taken. Organisations spend a lot of money on research and product development. A large number of new products never progress beyond the development stage if it is felt that they won't sell.

2 Introduction
This is when the product is launched. Costs are still incurred and it is likely that the product will still not be profitable as it takes some time for customers to gain confidence in new products. On the other hand, a product can be an instant hit resulting in rapid sales. Examples of such products include mobile phones, digital cameras and DVD players.

3 Growth
Rapid growth is likely as the product gets established in the market. This leads to profits. At this stage, competitors may launch their own version of the product so there could be a slow-down in sales.

4 Maturity
Sales level off as the product becomes established. Competitors charge a lower price because they haven't had to cover development costs – these were borne by the original manufacturer.

5 Saturation
At this stage, more and more organisations enter the market so there is no longer room for growth.

6 Decline
When new products appear, the original market goes into decline. This is usually due to new technology or a change in customers' tastes.

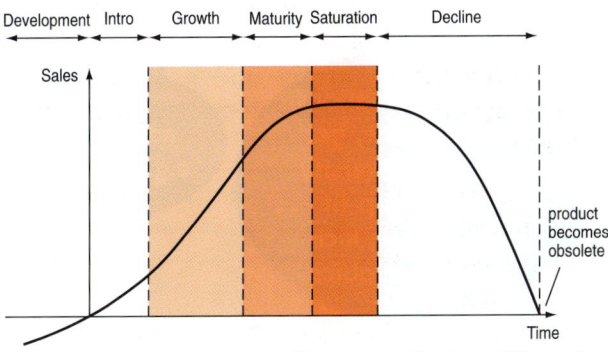

Figure 2.6 Product life cycle

Skateboarding has been through a life cycle

Imagine a gym that provided only circuit training and not much else. It would soon lose its popularity because people today want a whole range of keep-fit sessions such as aerobics, boxercise, kick boxing or even yoga. What's more, they may also require additional advice on diet, lifestyle and exercise, probably leading on to personal fitness programmes.

Managers of leisure and tourism organisations are constantly seeking ways to encourage people to use their facilities. One of the best ways of doing this is to keep up to date with trends and develop new products. It is far better to start a new fashion or trend rather than follow one.

Talk about it

The following 'products' have all been through a life cycle: skateboarding, line dancing, BMX biking, even The Spice Girls. In your group, choose three more examples and show the stages in the life cycle of each one.

Talk about it

In your group, think of some leisure and tourism products like sport, a holiday destination, a pair of training shoes or a hotel. How could you extend their product life cycle? For example, the National Lottery started in 1994 with only the Saturday draw. Since then, the following ideas have been added: Wednesday draw; scratchcards, rollover, Thunderball, Lottery extra, Christmas and New Year jackpots.

Activity

▶ The life cycle of products in the music industry is particularly short. Trace the stages and draw a life cycle of a current single and CD in the music charts.

Extending the life cycle of a product

In order to extend the lifespan of a product, organisations introduce various techniques. These include a change of packaging, special offers on price, extra promotion and adjusting the product so it appeals to even more people.

Ways to extend life cycle of product
- Widen product range, e.g. books into CDs
- Find new markets, e.g. sportswear into leisurewear
- Special promotions, e.g. buy one, get one free, diversify product – keep-fit... aquasplash, kick boxing, aerobics
- Extra advertising, e.g. television

How to extend the life cycle of a product

Price

Fact file
Price describes what a customer will pay for a product or service.

Customers will generally buy products if they feel they are getting value for money. This means the organisation's objectives can be met in that:

- the private sector can make a profit
- the public sector can provide a service at break-even point (that is, the product or service does not make a loss).

The actual selling price

Organisations can stay in business only if customers are prepared to pay the price of their products. This is known as the selling price.

Price → Income (which covers costs) → Profits → Staying in business → Expansion

Many leisure and tourism organisations hope to make a profit. They have to try to set a price for the product or service that the customer will pay and which allows the organisation to make a profit.

Price is the only part of the marketing mix that generates income. Place, promotion and product all create costs. These costs are covered if the right price is charged.

Arriving at a price

When pricing products the following factors must be taken into account:
- the cost of producing the product
- the price customers are prepared to pay
- the price competitors charge
- the profit margin.

Credit terms

Credit terms are arranged when goods and services are supplied yet the customer does not have to pay at the time of purchase. For example, 'Buy now, pay later' is a promotional technique used to encourage customers to make a commitment for the product. In addition, there may be no interest charged. This is an even bigger attraction.

Credit cards entitle the holder to a free period of credit. They can be used for making payments for things like accommodation, meals and holiday bookings. Theatre and concert tickets can also be booked by credit card, usually over the phone.

Profitability

Fact file
Profit is the difference between sales and costs:

Sales – Costs = Profit.

Think about it
What importance do you place on price when buying clothes?

Figure 2.7 below looks at some of the factors which influence pricing.

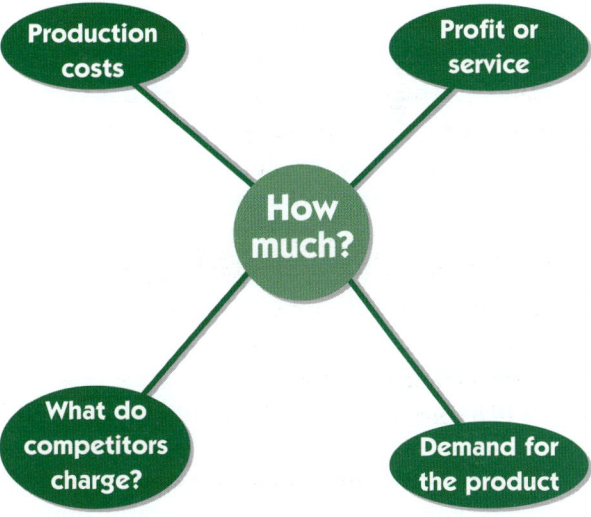

Figure 2.7 Factors which influence pricing

Methods of pricing

Arriving at the right price is not easy. Organisations have to be aware of the value customers put on a product or service. They have to find out what the customer is willing to pay. One way is to use market research. If the organisation has asked potential customers what they are willing to pay, it will have a good idea of what price to charge.

Market-led pricing

Another way of setting a price is to find out what competitors charge. If people shopped around for a similar product, for example a two-week holiday in Crete, and found the same holiday was £200 more expensive at one travel agent than the other, it is likely they would choose the lower priced one. This is known as market-led pricing, when organisations offer similar products and services at a similar price.

One-off pricing

Sometimes an organisation has to work out a special price for a customer because there is no standard price for the product. For example, a businesswoman might want to fly to Thailand for a week, move on to Singapore for three days and finally spend two days in Bombay completing her business before flying back to the UK. This is quite a trip and it certainly cannot be worked out like a package holiday. This is called one-off pricing, as the product is very different from normal travel requests.

Cost-plus pricing

Another method of arriving at a price is **cost-plus pricing**. For example, the owner of a fitness centre works out the costs of operating the business. He then adds on a flat rate or percentage to his products or services in order to arrive at a selling price which covers his cost and creates a profit.

Peak and off-peak pricing

Many organisations in the leisure and tourism industries adjust their prices for the same product at different times of the year, week or even day. For example, a ferry operator might halve the price for its trips between January and March compared to its summer prices. Rail fares can vary for travelling the same distance. For example, a single ticket to London from Newark is £35 before 9.00 am compared to £24 after 9.00 am and at weekends.

Leisure centres often reduce the price of activities during off-peak or less busy times.

These are from 9.00 am to 5.00 pm when most people are at work. The idea behind off-peak pricing is to encourage people to use the centre at quiet times.

Peak times	**Off-peak times**
5–10 pm weekdays	9 am–5 pm weekdays
9 am–6 pm weekends	6–10 pm weekends

Charges Activity	**Peak**	**Off-peak**
Badminton	£1.65 per person	£1.30 per person
Squash	£3.00 per court	£2.00 per court
Swimming	£1.75 per person	£1.25 per person
Hire of hall	£20 per hour	£15 per hour

Holidays in the UK

Low season (cheaper rates) January, February, March	High season (higher rates) June, July, August

Holidays abroad

High season Prices rise during the school holidays, – especially summer and Christmas	Low season Winter (except for skiing) reduced prices

Activity

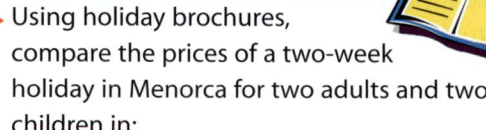

> Using holiday brochures, compare the prices of a two-week holiday in Menorca for two adults and two children in:
>
> a March
> b August.

Group and special discounts

The idea of offering discounts is:

- to offer as many people as possible the opportunity to take part in leisure activities
- to increase usage of facilities
- to increase income.

Discounts are offered to:

- school parties
- senior citizens
- the unemployed
- students
- the disabled.

For example, a leisure centre might offer discounts for the unemployed such as:

- low-cost or free activities
- free equipment hire.

A pub might offer discounts on meals to senior citizens at certain times, such as 'Silver' three-course meals for the over-60s £3.50 every Tuesday, 12 noon–2.00 pm.

Talk about it

In your group, give some examples of discounts offered by leisure and tourism organisations.

Special offers

Below are some examples of special offers:

- A new pub has just opened in town and has a special offer of beer at just 99p per pint for the first six weeks of opening. This is likely to attract customers in the hope that they become 'regulars'.
- Every Thursday evening is 80s night at the local club. Special offers include 80p admission, 80p for drinks for the first 80 minutes. Quite a novel idea. The club is full every Thursday.
- Special discounts on late bookings such as flight only £99 to Ibiza departing this Saturday (three days to book!) or two weeks in Gran Canaria, self-catering, £199 per person, departing next Thursday. Such discounts are aimed at filling the plane ('bums on seats'). You may find someone sitting next to you on the plane who has paid twice as much as they were unable to take full advantage of the special offers.

An advert for a special offer

Place

Fact file

Place refers to the actual location of the facility *and* how the product is distributed to the customer.

Place is concerned with getting the right product to the right people at the right time.

Activity

- Find out where restaurants, cinemas, sports centres and schools are located in your area.
- Write down why you think location is so important.

Types of outlets and facilities used and their location

Facilities in leisure and tourism need to be located near to a well-populated area where customers and potential customers live. Restaurants, theatres, cinemas and concert halls usually have a town or city centre location.

In addition, there should be good signposting and sufficient car parking spaces. Accessibility to the facility is equally important. Are there transport links to the facility? Are disabled people easily able to access the facility, for example wide car parking spaces available, ramp into the main entrance?

Talk about it

In your group, discuss the ideal location for a community centre, a leisure centre and a youth club.

Hotels

Should hotels be located in city centres, on the outskirts of towns, at the seaside or near a motorway?

Since hotels serve the needs of many different customers, they can be found in all these locations because:

Chapter 4   The marketing mix   129

- business people use city centre hotels
- holidaymakers stay at seaside hotels
- travelling sales representatives use hotels near good motorway links.

An example of an ideal location is Blackpool Pleasure Beach. This is located in a town which has other attractions such as:

- Blackpool Tower
- The Illuminations
- Seven miles of golden sand
- The Promenade.

Blackpool is well served by the motorway system and has lots of accommodation. You could even use it as a stopping off place before moving on to the Lake District.

Identification of distribution channels – how the product reaches the customer

Leisure and tourism products and services should be made available to customers when they want them. Some of these products and services can be 'delivered' and paid for at the point of production, for example a game of badminton in a leisure centre, a round of golf at the golf club and a concert at the theatre.

Some products and services are made away from the place where the customers want them so channels of distribution are created as follows:

- Communication – giving advice on ticket availability, information on flight times, directions to destinations. For example, it is easy to book a holiday in Bournemouth as most travel agents could do this and most tourist information centres could supply information about accommodation. This distribution of information allows people to book holidays with the minimum of fuss in the knowledge that the destination is easy to reach. Examples of communication channels for a hotel include:
    - ringing up and making a reservation
    - using the same hotel chain and asking the receptionist to book a room for the customer through a tourist information centre
    - via the Internet.
- Stockholding – making sure there are enough products in stock available for the customer to buy, for example a sufficient number of hotel rooms, training shoes, airline seats or squash racquets.
- Transportation – making sure the product is delivered to the right place at the right time.
- Packaging and display – the product should be displayed in such a way that it looks attractive to customers and at the same time is practical for the shop itself, that is making sure the display does not take up too much space.

Many products are sold through third parties because it is not always possible to sell direct. These intermediaries are usually retailers and wholesalers who deliver the product to the customer.

For example, Figure 2.8 shows the distribution channel for a holiday.

Figure 2.8 The distribution channel for a holiday

It has both advantages and disadvantages as shown in the table below.

Method	Advantages	Disadvantages
Travel agent	Good location, loyal customers. Good image could be presented within premises	High overheads for renting high street location
Tour operator	Reputable and well-known organisation	No face-to-face contact with customers

Advantages and disadvantages of the distribution channel for a holiday

Promotion

> **Fact file**
>
> **Promotion** describes all the methods a leisure and tourism organisation uses to tell customers about its products and services and, hopefully, to persuade them to buy them.

The promotional activities of a hotel, for example, will be geared towards filling its rooms. Similarly, an airline will focus on selling all its seats.

Promotion is the most recognised aspect of marketing. It is all about communication with existing and potential customers so that they react by buying the product. It is highly unlikely anyone will buy a product if they have never heard of it. Promotional activities can be put into action once the product, place and price of the product have been determined.

Promotion aims to:

- make customers aware of the product
- promote understanding of the product
- persuade customers to buy the product (which increases sales)
- encourages customers to return – repeat business.

The main promotional techniques

Advertising

The aim of advertising is to communicate with potential customers so that they will buy the product, thus increasing sales. As many customers as possible within the target market should be reached.

The main methods of advertising include:

- television
- radio
- newspapers and magazines
- billboards
- public transport.

Advertising can be expensive and costs vary according to space, frequency and how long the advertisements run.

One method is to use the 'shotgun approach' – 'spraying' as many potential customers as possible in the hope that some of them will be persuaded to buy the product. For example, local advertising attracts local people, and local radio is one example of shotgun advertising. This type of advertising could be used by a leisure centre wanting to promote its new swimming courses. It would be within the centre's budget, far more so than advertising on television, and it would be targeted at the people who would be most likely to use local facilities.

Money will be wasted if an advertisement does not reach its target audience. But reaching the target audience is not enough – the message must also be put across effectively.

Probably the most expensive form of advertising is on television. A 30-second commercial during the break in *Coronation Street* costs thousands of pounds. This timeslot is classed as peak-viewing time when there is an audience of around 15 million people. The advertising costs would reflect this. Production costs in making a television advertisement should also be taken into account.

Advertising on television is usually restricted to large commercial organisations that are able to afford it. Examples include Adidas, Lunn Poly, Thomas Cook, Coca Cola and Nike.

Newspaper advertising can also be expensive. A full-page advertisement in a national newspaper would cost thousands of pounds whereas one in a local paper may cost only £100.

> **Activity**
>
> ▶ Contact your local newspaper and find out the costs of a half-page and a full-page advertisement.
> Does the cost vary according to its position in the newspaper? Are there any discounts offered if the advertisement is placed over a period of time every week?

Direct marketing

This is sometimes known as direct mail advertising where leaflets are posted through doors to try to get a response from potential customers. These leaflets may be delivered with magazines and newspapers.

Most of us regularly receive direct mail (sometimes known as 'junk mail'). Personalised letters are sent directly to individuals by post from organisations with which they may have had no contact. Examples include finance companies such as American Express, *The Reader's Digest* and double-glazing companies.

These organisations obtain individuals' names and addresses from a database and then write to them to explain the benefits of their special offers and products. The organisations are able to target their market segment accurately and directly by ensuring that they obtain the names and addresses of people in certain age groups on certain incomes.

The most common direct marketing techniques used in the leisure and tourism industries are:

- direct mail
- telemarketing – by phone
- door-to-door distribution – by post
- direct response advertising – where the customer responds either by phoning (to collect a gift) or completing a coupon which will be entered in a prize draw.

Talk about it

In your group, discuss what sort of direct mail you receive. Did you receive incentives like a free gift? Have you ever responded to direct mail?

Public relations

The main aim of public relations (PR) is to boost the image of an organisation. It also aims to:

- show the organisation in a good light – promote a good image of the organisation's products and services
- publicise what the organisation offers.

PR involves organisations contacting the media to inform them of forthcoming events and interesting stories.

Snapshot

Making PR work

Back in 1982, when I was manager of a leisure centre I contacted the local press to say I had an exclusive story which would benefit the local community.

Ours was the first centre to provide a mother and baby changing and feeding room. This allowed complete privacy for mothers to feed and change their babies in a purpose-built room. We even managed to get Boots to provide the nappies free of charge.

This story showed the community that:

- we were a 'caring' centre
- we provided facilities for all ages, even babies.

I saved the newspaper time by writing the story for it. This meant all the information was detailed and accurate.

This story gave us a lot of publicity and what's more, it was free!

Holiday programmes on television are good PR for the destinations featured. They create a favourable image of the places visited which encourages people to go to them.

Travel journalists are often given free holidays by travel companies and overseas tourist boards in the hope that their published articles will give a favourable impression of the area.

Public relations officers help create a good image for their organisation. If, however, an unfortunate incident happens, for example a chemical leakage at a swimming pool, or food poisoning at a hotel, it would be up to the PR officer to limit any bad publicity and give accurate information rather than let journalists speculate.

Activity

▶ Find a story in your local newspaper which creates a good image for an organisation.

Personal selling

This involves face-to-face communication with the seller trying to persuade the customer to buy the product.

Selling also includes giving information about facilities or places. This is the job of receptionists in leisure centres and tourist information offices. The most important thing about selling is *making a sale* – whether it is a holiday, health club membership or sports equipment.

Selling products keeps organisations in business as income is generated, costs are covered and profits are made.

There is every possibility that your first job in either the leisure or tourism industries will include selling. How you inform customers about your products and services and how they match your customers' needs will determine your success as a salesperson.

Tasks of the salesperson

The salesperson's main aim is to sell the product, whether it be a holiday or a pair of training shoes. He or she also has to search for new clients and offer after-sales back-up.

The advantage of personal selling to the organisation is that the salesperson can gear his or her sales presentation to suit the individual. The salesperson can show his or her in-depth knowledge of the product and can therefore answer any queries immediately.

The one disadvantage of personal selling is the high cost attached to selecting, training and operating a sales force.

Displays

A display stand at an exhibition

If you go to a trade fair or exhibition, you will see displays set up by organisations aimed at promoting their products and services. A member of staff will be on hand at the display to answer any queries that potential customers may have.

Displays which attract most interest from passing customers are the ones which have incentives to make people stop and look. Free food and drink may be on offer or even the chance to win a fabulous prize in a competition.

'Hands-on' displays which entice people to 'have a go', for example test a computer or ride an exercise bike, are the most successful.

If you ever have to run a display at an exhibition you will find that there are three types of visitor: customers, potential customers and time wasters. The crucial issue is to identify prospective customers and lead them towards a sale.

Customers mainly come for something new – new ideas, new products, new services. They like to collect information. They walk past a display in about three to six seconds and stay at a major exhibition on average for four hours.

Customers are attracted by noise, music, crowds and demonstrations.

Role of staff on a display stand

- Be open, warm and welcoming.
- Don't cluster in a group talking to each other.
- Don't pounce on customers, but don't ignore them.
- Show a product working, or have a moving object to attract passers-by.

The conversation

- Smile. Approach customers and open the conversation. Ask open questions.
- Show interest and listen. Make customers feel important.
- Find out what they want and provide it if possible.
- Record details so you can follow up later.
- Follow up fast.

The display stand

A display needs to be colourful, attractive and different from all the hundreds of other displays. Staff need to be friendly, knowledgeable and informative. A recent travel trade exhibition in Manchester had over 500 displays with lots of incentives. Here are some examples:

- the Scottish Highlands – a free glass of whisky
- Melton Mowbray – a free pork pie
- the Bahamas – a chance to win a two-week holiday
- Blackpool Pleasure Beach – free tickets to ride on 'The Big One'
- Scarborough – a free stick of rock.

Activity

▶ In your group, think of a holiday destination and design an eye-catching display.

Sponsorship

This has the advantage of getting the organisation's name known to the public.

Organisations sponsor teams or events by providing them with financial assistance. In return, sponsors expect to receive lots of good publicity and increased sales. For example, in 2002:

- Vodafone sponsored Manchester United.
- Going Places sponsored the television programme *Blind Date*.
- Barclays Bank sponsored the Premiership.

Vodafone sponsored Manchester United

Most football teams, both local and national, have sponsors. A walk to the local park on a Sunday morning will reveal teams with sponsors' names on their shirts. Many are even sponsored by the local pub, which makes a lot of sense to the landlord who will reap the benefit of his or her team either drowning their sorrows or toasting their victory in the pub!

Probably the best known sponsor on television is the confectionery manufacturer Cadbury's which sponsors *Coronation Street*.

Sponsorship leads to:

- increased recognition of the sponsor through advertising, for example on football shirts
- the promotion of a favourable image, especially if an organisation is sponsoring a good cause, for example raising funds for the local hospital
- prestige for sponsoring a well-known event, for example The Embassy World Snooker Championship or the AXA FA Cup.

Some sports have found it difficult to gain sponsorship if they are not popular enough, especially for television, for example canoeing, or if they have a poor image, such as boxing.

Think about it

Think of two examples of local and national sponsorship.

Demonstrations

Product demonstrations enable you to see:

- what a product can do
- how it can benefit you.

Watching a demonstration can also tempt you to buy the product.

Imagine you are the manager of a leisure centre and you have decided to buy a state-of-the-art computerised till for your centre. A demonstration would show you the following:

- All receipts issued should reconcile with takings.
- Bookings for each activity on a daily, weekly and monthly basis.
- Trends in usage.

Staff who use the till could also be involved in watching a demonstration as their questions could be answered and they would feel part of the decision-making process. This is good for employee relations.

Imagine you are the manager of the local theatre and you have £10 000 to spend on an up-to-date lighting system. A demonstration of the new system by the salesperson would show its effectiveness and a greater variety of lighting effects. The results could be seen instantly.

Every demonstration should be clear, simple and informative. The benefits of the product to the customer should be stressed throughout the demonstration.

Activity
> Imagine you are a salesperson and you have to demonstrate a product to a group of customers. In pairs, decide what product you could demonstrate and be prepared to give your demonstration to the rest of the group.

Sales promotions

The leisure and tourism industries are extremely competitive. Every organisation does its best to win business. Sales promotions offer customers something extra within a specific time limit. Below are some examples:

> One child goes free if you book your holiday before the end of September

> Buy one meal, get one free until 21 April

> Stay three nights for the price of two this weekend only

> No charge for cars with four paying passengers on all ferry crossings this month

Here are some more examples of sales promotions or incentives which can be offered to customers:

- Taster sessions – try out our health suite for free.
- Coupons – money-off vouchers in newspapers for entry to theme parks, or coupons for discounted meals.
- Competitions – enter our prize draw and win a holiday.
- Special offers – beer 99p a pint this week.
- Free gifts – free T-shirt when you spend over £30.
- Loyalty incentive – Airmiles when buying a product, loyalty points when shopping at the supermarket.

Advantages and uses of sales promotions
- To exploit special opportunities, for example supporting an advertising campaign.
- To motivate staff. This has to be short term or it loses its effectiveness.
- To improve brand loyalty.
- Organisations obtain a direct response which can be evaluated.

Activity
> In pairs, find some examples of sales promotions, not necessarily connected with leisure and tourism.

Promotional techniques and target markets

Promotional techniques such as advertising and direct mail have to be targeted at specific market segments if they are to be successful and therefore effective. For example, the following factors need to be taken into account when promoting holidays:

- Who is the target market?
- What appeals to them?
- What do they read?
- What do they think about price?
- Where do they go?

An 18–30 holiday could be advertised in magazines such as *Hello!* or *OK!* which this age group read. Posters could be located in travel agents and the London Underground. The aim is to reach the target audience with a message which it likes and a product it cannot resist.

A local leisure centre might advertise in local newspapers and place posters in the centre to promote a keep-fit campaign as financial resources wouldn't stretch to television or radio advertising.

Talk about it

In your group, discuss how a local football club could promote a summer soccer tournament.

How could a travel agent promote a four-week Caribbean cruise?

The effectiveness of promotional materials

Advertisements

Effective advertising arouses the interest of customers and can reach a large number of people. It is vital therefore that advertisements motivate customers to buy the product.

Advertisements attempt to persuade potential customers that there is something special about the products being advertised. They claim that the products cannot be matched by any other organisation's.

An advertisement cannot stimulate sales unless it is read. It cannot be read unless it is seen and it cannot be seen unless it gets your attention.

It is, of course the attention and interest of the target market and not the world in general that the advertisement seeks to attract.

Advertising agencies usually prepare advertisements for larger organisations. A team of creative writers put the advertisement together, which the organisation then approves.

Local organisations may prepare their own advertisements to save costs. They are more likely to advertise in local newspapers whereas larger organisations would advertise on television and radio.

Case study

Cindy, shopping complex manager

Cindy is manager of an out-of-town shopping complex. Her main responsibility is to advertise and promote the facility. She always follows a set pattern when creating advertisements which goes like this:

- Who am I aiming this advert at?
- What message do I want to get across about the shopping complex?
- Where is the best place to put the advert?
- What costs are involved?
- What about design?
- Every picture tells a story, so what pictures should I use?

Based on Cindy's format, design an advertisement for Cindy's shopping complex?

Any good advertisement should use the AIDA formula:

Create **Attention**.
Promote an **Interest**.
Motivate the customer to **Desire** the product.
Enable the customer to take **Action.**

A good advertisement will attract attention, arouse interest, create desire and make it easy to take any necessary action to buy the product.

Activity

 Find two advertisements in your local newspaper and show how they use the AIDA formula.

Creating your own publicity

1 White space. Look at a page of advertisements in a newspaper. Notice how a large advertisement with a lot of white space stands out from the rest. It's a brave decision to produce advertisements with a lot of white space because you are paying for the space and not giving in to the temptation to fill it with information. Used properly, this type of advertisement stands out from the rest.

2 **Border.** This can make an advertisement stand out and seem important. Like a frame round a picture, it can make what is inside look really good.

3 **Colour.** Spot-colour in a newspaper draws attention to an advertisement, especially if it is the only one with spot-colour on that page. Evidence suggests that full-colour advertisements in magazines attract twice the readership of black and white adverts.

4 **Illustration.** This is an effective way of getting the reader's attention and interest. Illustrations say things more quickly than words, more vividly too. Don't forget, seeing leads to believing. The best illustration of all is the one which shows that the product or service is being happily used. Happy customers and smiling faces are a powerful way to get across the message. This is especially true if you can use before and after illustrations demonstrating the benefits of the product.

5 **Headline.** You must try to grab the readers' attention and arouse interest. The most important headline words are YOU, FREE and NEW. For example:

- 'Instant hot drinks from 'Supervend' will save you time and money'
- 'A quiet word to the hard of hearing'
- 'How little need you pay for a restful night?'

These headlines:

- mention the target customer
- promise benefits
- arouse curiosity.

Activity

> In pairs, design an advertisement for a leisure product which will grab the readers' attention and act as an incentive for them to buy it.

Newspapers contain two types of advertisements:

- Display ads – these are usually placed among news stories so they stand out and get noticed. They are generally bigger and more expensive than classified advertisements. They use headlines and logos to catch the readers' attention.

- Classified ads – these consist of a few lines of text listed under category headings. They are an essential form of advertising for newspapers as they generate a lot of income. Publications like *Exchange and Mart* and *Loot* are full of classified ads. They don't carry news stories.

Activity

 Find an example of each of the above types of advertisement.

 List the advantages and disadvantages of each.

Brochures and leaflets

A good brochure should turn an enquiry into a sale. Brochures must therefore be informative, interesting and persuasive.

Brochures come in different sizes although most are in colour. A tour operator's summer brochure shows the product (the holiday destination) in a tangible form in that it shows golden sands, deep blue sea, magnificent scenery and happy holidaymakers.

Brochures are displayed on the shelves at travel agents and tourist information offices and because there are so many, it is only the most eye-catching that will stand out from the rest of the crowd.

Using direct mail, brochures can be sent to customers, making it easier for them to take their time and choose what they want.

A tour operator's travel brochure must entice people to pick them up and look inside ... with the aim of making a sale

> **Activity**
> - Go into a travel agent for a holiday brochure. Write down what you think of the brochure as a piece of promotional material.
> - What techniques have been used in the advertisements for different places?

Leaflets are not as expensive as brochures to produce. They are less bulky and are usually in single A4 or A5 format. They advertise things like keep-fit sessions at the local fitness centre or give details of forthcoming events, for example a riverside water festival.

Large organisations tend to produce leaflets which have been designed by a graphic designer. They are usually printed in colour on good quality paper with illustrations to make them stand out.

Smaller organisations do not have large advertising budgets. Their leaflets are usually word-processed and printed in one or two colours at the local printers.

Posters

Posters are seen on billboards, at stadia, on buses and at bus stops. If they catch your attention and if you have time to read them, they can carry a very effective message which can stay in your mind. This is especially true if there is an image or photograph on the poster.

A shop window is an ideal location for posters and you have only to look at a travel agent's window to see some examples.

Black lettering on a yellow background is an effective format for a poster. Have a look at a travel agent's window next time you are in the high street and see the type of posters on display.

One poster campaign which proved to be a great success was the English Riviera posters of the 1986 and 1987 seasons which relied on artistic quality and were widely displayed in London Underground stations.

Posters are used as point-of-sale-advertising within travel agents. However, good quality, full-colour printing on large sheets can be expensive. It is also difficult to evaluate their effectiveness.

A successful poster
English Riviera Tourist Board

Point-of-sale material (POS)

This is an eye-catching display of the product, or information about the service, and is displayed at the point at which it is sold to customers.

The point of sale is the actual place where products are sold, for example the counter in a shop or the reception in a leisure centre.

When customers arrive at the point of sale they are usually in a position to buy. If they do have doubts about products, then there are special offers, promotions and discounts to encourage them to spend their money.

Point-of-sale materials on display in shop windows entice the customer inside.

Examples of point-of-sale materials include pens, key rings, flags, banners and stickers. This is when the assistant should take over and convert the interest into a sale.

Merchandising materials

Included in this group are T-shirts, mugs, calendars, bracelets, books and photographs.

Many tourist destinations and theme parks merchandise their material

A Disney shop is a classic example where merchandising material is on full display. In this case, it would be connected to the Disney theme.

Football clubs sell merchandising materials which include diaries, photographs, shirts, pens, books and scarves. Manchester United Football Club generates more money on merchandising material than it does from its gate receipts.

Many tourist destinations and theme parks merchandise their own materials because they know people want something to remember their visit by.

Talk about it
In your group, say what you think about the price of some merchandising materials. Give your reasons.

Videos
This type of promotional technique is relatively new and highly effective.

Travel agents can sometimes give clients a video about a destination they are interested in. This is an excellent selling tool as a video can give a powerful and lasting impression of a place.

Disney uses videos to promote its facilities and holidays. Potential customers simply call a freephone number to get their free copy.

It is worth remembering that videos portray only favourable images; they never show the bad side of things.

Press releases
Press releases include details of events or activities which can be forwarded to the media in advance of them happening. The main advantage of a press release is that, if published, it creates free publicity.

A good press release will provide sufficient detail to a journalist so he or she can write an article without actually having to attend the event.

If organisations can build up a good relationship with the media they may find that they are able to have their press releases published regularly.

The other big advantage of a press release, apart from the fact it is free, is that people are more likely to read it than an advertisement which may have the same content but is written in a different format.

How to write a press release
Answer questions like who?, what?, where?, when? and why? in the opening paragraph.
Keep the press release as short as possible.
Submit it well before deadline dates.
Put in a quotation from the contact person.
Give details of the contact person.
Use double spacing – this allows for editing.
Include a picture if it will help tell the story.

Activity

Using the guidelines given above and the example, write a press release about a forthcoming event at your school/college.

Internet sites
As most leisure and tourism organisations now have access to the Internet, they have created their own websites to promote their products and services. This is particularly true for theme parks, local authority leisure and recreation departments, airlines, health clubs and even schools.

Chapter 4   The marketing mix

As one in seven people now have access to the Internet, it makes sense for organisations to use it to promote themselves.

Websites should be easily accessible, colourful and interesting. This helps organisations to be seen in the best possible light. Nowadays, buying over the Internet is commonplace, which is advantageous to both buyer and seller as it is quick and convenient.

Activity

 Find two major leisure and tourism websites and compare and contrast them.

 List the disadvantages of buying and selling over the Internet.

Check your knowledge

1. The use of television advertising is an example of what part of the marketing mix?
2. A restaurant is offering 'two meals for the price of one', 5.00–7.00 pm, Monday to Friday. What type of marketing activity is this?
3. A city hotel uses its customer database to send out a mailshot giving information about weekend breaks. What type of promotional activity is this?
4. A sports centre offers reduced prices for daytime use of its facilities. Which group is most likely to benefit from this scheme?
5. What is the term commonly used for direct mail?
6. List five products and services you would find in a cinema?
7. What is off-peak pricing? Give an example.
8. What is the importance of after-sales service?
9. What is meant by the life cycle of a product? Give one example showing the full span of the product life cycle.
10. How does the Internet promote products and services? Give two examples.

Chapter 5: SWOT analysis

All leisure and tourism organisations need to know how they are performing. This chapter looks at how SWOT analysis enables them to do this.

What you will learn

What is SWOT analysis?
Using SWOT analysis

What is SWOT analysis?

SWOT analysis is used by organisations to help them find out how they are performing. A SWOT analysis involves looking at an organisation's:

- **strengths** – its strong points, e.g. experienced and qualified staff
- **weaknesses** – the problems it has which will affect its performance, e.g. poor facilities, out-of-date equipment
- **opportunities** – things that may benefit the organisation in the future, e.g. new markets
- **threats** – negative things that may damage the organisation, e.g. lack of finance, too much competition.

Strengths and weaknesses are internal factors that the organisation should be able to control. Opportunities and threats are external factors outside its control.

Using SWOT analysis

When an organisation has undergone SWOT analysis the results should show:

- the strengths that can be built on
- the weaknesses that can be overcome
- the opportunities that can be taken advantage of
- the threats to be aware of and eliminated.

The action taken after a SWOT analysis has been completed is very important. It could mean more advertising is required, staff training should improve or plans for expansion should be put into action. The main aim of SWOT analysis is to ensure that the organisation benefits from it and that necessary action is taken.

Case study

The Pitstop Café

Joe Delaney bought the Pitstop Café two years ago. It is located in the middle of town and is open from 9.00 am to 5.00 pm, Monday to Saturday. Joe's customers range from those who just pop in for a cup of tea and a sandwich to regulars who enjoy Joe's full English breakfast.

Trade has declined recently so Joe decided to carry out his own SWOT analysis to find out how things could improve.

Strengths
Excellent, friendly service
Good location in town
Good reputation for value-for-money meals

Weaknesses
Some people prefer restaurants to cafés
Limited variety of meals
Old fashioned furniture and decor

Opportunities
Untapped markets, e.g. business people, senior citizens
Space to expand – Joe owns an adjoining empty property
Adjust opening times

Threats
Competition from mobile caterers on market days
Out-of-town shopping complex

Case study continued

On the basis of his SWOT analysis, Joe decided to take the following action:

- Issue staff with attractive uniforms and name badges to strengthen the image of excellent, friendly service.
- Change the name from the Pitstop Café to the Market Square Restaurant to make it sound more attractive.
- Introduce vegetarian meals and trial foreign cuisine such as curry and lasagne.
- Refurbish the restaurant with modern furniture and bright welcoming decor.
- Change the opening hours to 7.30 am–4.30 pm so that early morning breakfast specials can be served.
- Introduce special offer two-course lunchtime meals for £3.99 to attract office workers and business people.
- Introduce 'silver savers' every Thursday lunchtime for senior citizens when they could have a three-course meal for £3.75.
- Liaise with town centre shops and offer 10 per cent discount voucher schemes.
- Increase promotional activities, e.g. sandwich board outside showing menus of the day, mailshots to local town businesses, grand opening day for the launch of the Market Square Restaurant.
- Long term – possibly expand using adjoining property.

The main aims of Joe's new marketing objectives are:

- to survive as a business
- to increase profits
- to establish the restaurant as the place to be.

Suggest other ideas Joe could put into practice as a result of his SWOT analysis?

Activity

▶ Carry out a SWOT analysis on Stella's Gym using the following information:

Stella Stevens opened her gym last year. Her main users are people aged 18–35 who want to exercise on a regular weekly basis.

A new local authority leisure centre is due to open nearby next week and Stella thinks attendances at her gym will suffer.

▶ On the basis of your SWOT analysis, what action should Stella take? Give your reasons.

Check your knowledge

1. How can a SWOT analysis help a leisure and tourism organisation?
2. Write a brief SWOT analysis of your nearest leisure facility.
3. What threats would a small independent travel agency have?

Chapter 6: Promotional campaigns

Leisure and tourism organisations need to plan their promotional campaigns carefully in order to achieve maximum impact and to make the best use of resources such as staff and finance. This chapter looks at the objectives of promotional campaigns, their target markets, promotional techniques and materials, how campaigns are monitored and their success evaluated.

What you will learn

- Objectives of a promotional campaign
- Identifying target markets
- Techniques used in promotional campaigns
- Promotional materials used in marketing campaigns
- Monitoring and evaluating the success of a promotional campaign

The many products and services in the leisure and tourism industries need to be promoted in such a way that customers will be encouraged to buy them. Promotion is done by means of a promotional campaign:

- The local leisure centre wants to encourage more people to join a 'healthy lifestyle campaign' so it uses the local media to advertise it with a series of features on leisure facilities in the local community.
- A national sportswear company decides to promote a new range in sweatshirts and so, as part of a wider campaign, places advertisements on television and in national newspapers.

Objectives of a promotional campaign

All promotional campaigns, no matter how big or small, should have objectives.

Objectives enable organisations to focus on what they want to achieve with a particular campaign. The success of the campaign can be judged on whether the objectives have been met.

Promotional campaign techniques

Objectives should be SMART:

Specific – aimed at one area of operation
Measurable – the effectiveness of the campaign can be assessed
Achievable – realistic enough to ensure objectives can be met
Realistic – fit in with the aims of the organisation and what it stands for
Timed – deadlines can be met.

Examples of promotional campaign objectives

- Visitor attraction – to attract 15 000 visitors per month over the next six months.
- Travel agent – to sell ten summer holidays by the end of next week.
- Leisure centre – to double the number of senior citizens using the indoor bowls centre next season.
- Theatre – to reduce overtime by 10 per cent during July and August.
- Health and fitness centre – to increase club membership by one-third between now and the end of the year.

Snapshot

The Palace Theatre: a promotional campaign

This 99-year-old variety theatre is owned by the local authority and sponsored by a building society and a local newspaper.

> In 1984, the theatre was refitted, refurbished and re-opened after having fallen into a state of disrepair. Since then, it has flourished, offering a variety of entertainments to a wide audience.
>
> June 2002 marked the 100th anniversary of the theatre opening and the manager has planned a week-long celebration to mark the event.

The product

The week-long celebration will include a play by local school children, guided tours, a theatre workshop, a pantomime, a concert by the local brass band, a special showing of The Full Monty, Voulez-Vous, a tribute to Abba, and on the last night a music hall variety concert, with a well-known personality as compère. This would be a grand finale as the very first performance in 1902 was a music hall variety show.

Planning for this campaign started a year before the anniversary.

Objectives

- To celebrate 100 years of the Palace Theatre
- To raise awareness of the theatre both in the town and the surrounding area
- To get as much media coverage as possible and therefore create a high profile
- To get the community involved in the campaign

Market research

The manager went out into the community to ask for ideas about the centenary celebration. She did this by face-to-face interviews.

She also rang up an old friend who managed a theatre 200 miles away, who had just put on a similar campaign. In a way, this was secondary market research.

Target markets

- Senior citizens who would enjoy a good night out
- School children who would watch a pantomime
- Regular theatre-goers who would enjoy a backstage tour
- Cinema-goers who would like to see The Full Monty

Promotional methods

- Advertising – paid advertising placed in the local newspapers
- Publicity – a press release written by the manager and interviews on local radio
- Sponsorship – local companies invited to sponsor individual performances
- Direct mail – to existing customers, names and addresses obtained from customer database
- Posters and leaflets around the town

Type of media

- Local radio and television
- Point of sale in the theatre foyer
- Direct mail – of leaflets
- Local newspapers – advertising publicity

Now, let's look at the objectives of a promotional campaign in more detail.

Raising awareness

Customers cannot buy an organisation's products or services if they are not aware of them. Attracting the attention of customers is an essential first step in communicating with them.

Informing customers

Promotional campaigns are all about sending messages to potential customers about the product or service the organisation provides.

Holiday destinations, accommodation, new facilities, discount prices and new facilities like a restaurant can all be promoted.

Leaflets and brochures could be used for this type of promotion where a lot of information is being given out.

The type of media used to inform customers will depend upon the size of the market and the target market the organisation is informing.

Motivating people to buy the product and improving sales

Promotional campaigns are aimed at motivating customers to take action and buy the product, which will lead to increased sales and greater use of the facility.

Selling, sales promotions and displays are aimed at getting customers to take some form of action, for example visiting a theme park or buying a holiday.

Promotional campaigns use advertising to increase sales. Good advertisements, as we have already seen, should grab the reader's attention (AIDA) and motivate people to buy the product.

Sales can be increased through the use of promotions like 'Buy two, get one free', offering free gifts and reduced prices. Direct mail and personal selling do the same job.

Improving the image

Leisure and tourism organisations try to promote a good image to look good in the eyes of their users and the public in general in the hope that people will continue to buy their products and use their facilities. This can be achieved by:

- improving products and services
- creating an up-to-date impression
- reaching out to a new target market.

Facilities sometimes receive bad publicity. A promotional campaign could attempt to put that right.

Snapshot

Chemical leakage at local authority swimming pool

A swimming pool had a chemical leakage and had to be evacuated. Fortunately, no one was injured and the accident was not caused by negligence. However, in the eyes of the public, the pool was considered to be unsafe so the damage had been done.

The manager invited the press to watch him and his two young daughters be the first people to take the plunge in the pool once the leak had been repaired. This was done in the hope that it would show the public that the pool was perfectly safe. He also organised a public meeting where people could voice their concerns over the incident. At the meeting the manager gave a full explanation of what had happened. He slowly regained the confidence and trust of his customers. Rebuilding the image of the pool was a long and difficult task.

Case Study

The European Blue Flag Campaign

The European Blue Flag campaign is an annual award given to beaches and marinas across Europe. The award is given to places that have met very strict criteria for water quality and environmental management. Beaches and marinas have to display notices that tell the public all about their facilities, including parking, first aid, lifesaving and toilet facilities. They also have to display information about water cleanliness for bathers. The information must be correct and officials are employed to check that the attraction meets the highest standards.

At the moment there are 535 beaches that are monitored as part of this campaign. In 2001, only 270 achieved the necessary water-quality standards and only 51 achieved the Blue Flag. As you can see, the standards are very high and this is an extremely valuable achievement.

Tidy Britain Group

Activity

 Imagine you are the marketing assistant at a seaside resort that has just been awarded the Blue Flag for its beaches, how would you use this to promote your resort?

1. Carry out research into the Blue Flag awards in the UK and find out which beaches received awards in 2001.
2. At the same time, can you also find out which were the dirtiest beaches? You might like to discuss whether you have been to any of these and if the findings were what you expected!
3. What can individual visitors do to make sure that beaches and marinas are kept clean?

Attracting new customers

Below are some examples for attracting new customers:

- A new leisure centre is to open next week. New customers will be attracted to the facility by advertising in newspapers, direct mailing of leaflets and writing press releases.
- Imagine a pub has just opened a bistro. Why not offer two meals for the price of one between 12 noon and 2.00 pm for the first month. Better still, invite the press for a free meal which they can then write about in the local paper. That would be an offer they couldn't refuse!
- A theatre has recently undergone a major refurbishment programme which has brought it into the twenty-first century. New plays, new concerts and up-to-date films will create a new image to attract new customers.

Maintaining existing customers

Customers who enjoy using a facility will more than likely return regularly and stay loyal to it. They also usually tell their friends about how good it is. Customer loyalty should be rewarded. Why not introduce a system whereby regular customers receive discounts?

A loyal customer base is essential. Don't let them go to your competitors.

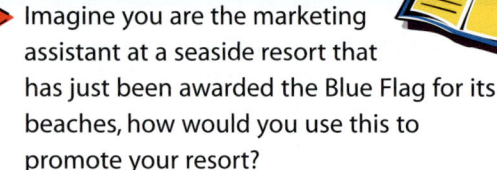

Completely refurbished

Enzo's Pizzeria

under new management

- Authentic Italian atmosphere
- Come and enjoy family friendly dining in comfort
- Children's portions
- Live music – Fridays and Saturdays

For month of February only: Children eat free!

Identifying target markets

Market research helps define what group of people – the target market – the promotional campaign should be aimed at. It will also help organisations decide what type of promotion is best for a product or service by using research techniques such as:

- observation – who is using the facility?
- questioning – why do you use this facility?

Market research also enables organisations to choose the right mix of promotional techniques. As we found out earlier, this is known as primary or field research. Secondary or desk research, for example in libraries, can tell us how people spend their leisure time, and how much disposable income different groups have to spend on their leisure activities.

The objectives of a marketing campaign should therefore state what market the organisation wants to target. By doing this, precise targeting of what it wants to put across can save money and ensure an effective response and a successful outcome.

Techniques used in promotional campaigns

The big question organisations have to ask themselves when they are about to embark on a promotional campaign is, 'How do we get the message across to our target market?'

Techniques	Advantages	Disadvantages
Advertising	Reaches a large audience	Can be expensive
	Stimulates interest	May not be seen/heard
	Targets the market	Hits people not interested in the message
Publicity, e.g. press release	Increases awareness	May not hit target audience
	Presents good image	May not be read/heard
Sales promotion	Rapid increase in sales	
	Moves slow items or times (e.g. off-peak usage)	Short term
		Provides little information
Selling	Increases sales	Expensive
	Good for targeting customers	Limited target audience
	Interactive and responsive	Takes a long time to cover a large audience

Advantages and disadvantages of promotional techniques

The choice includes advertising, publicity, sales promotion and selling.

Advertising is an excellent way to create awareness and interest in a product. However, it doesn't always get people to act or buy the product, so it is advisable that promotional campaigns use two or more techniques to get the message across.

The chart above shows some of the advantages and disadvantages of promotional techniques.

Promotional materials used in marketing campaigns

No matter how much money is invested in promotional materials, it will be wasted if they are not used effectively. Selecting the right media to provide the campaign is essential for success.

The choice of media is wide, ranging from television and radio advertising to magazines, posters and point-of-sale material.

The type of media used depends on the objectives of the campaign, the target market the organisation is trying to reach and what it can afford. For example:

- A tour operator may decide to promote a new holiday destination, so one objective of its promotional campaign would be to attract as many people as possible across the country. The most suitable media for such a campaign would be television and national newspapers and magazines.

- A local theatre may want to increase attendances for its Tuesday and Wednesday film evenings as its main objective. In this case, advertisements in the local press and the use of direct mail of leaflets would be suitable.

There are certain ways a message can be put across because promotion, after all, is about sending messages to customers.

Where movement and sound are considered to be necessary in adding impact to the message, television, radio and video (for example Disneyland) would be the most appropriate media.

Messages delivered by using printed materials such as leaflets, brochures, advertisements in newspapers, can also be very effective. If these messages are sent via direct mail they can provide a lot of information over longer periods of time.

Monitoring and evaluating the success of a promotional campaign

Two of the most common reasons for monitoring and evaluating promotional campaigns are:

- to show that money has been well spent
- to show that the promotional campaign has contributed to sales.

Monitoring

Many promotional campaigns aim to increase sales. This is done by motivating people to buy products or services, attracting new customers and retaining existing customers.

Monitoring can take place by checking the till rolls to see how much income has been generated, counting visitors on an electronic counter or seeing how many rooms have been booked in a hotel.

Evaluation

This is the final stage of a promotional campaign. Evaluation enables you to assess the success, or otherwise, of the marketing campaign. Questions to ask as part of an evaluation programme are:

- Did we meet our objectives?
- Did the campaign increase business?
- Was it all worth it? Did we make a profit?
- Did we improve our image?
- Did we achieve what we set out to do?

Evaluation should not be gut feeling and guesswork. There are a number of methods which can be used for evaluating a campaign:

- Face-to-face interviews by market researchers could ask for people's views on the products recently advertised.
- Existing customers could also be asked face to face or they could be sent questionnaires (their names and addresses would be on a customer database).
- Sales of the products or services could be analysed before and after the campaign. This could be done by checking the till roll and comparing the income before and after.
- A sports centre would be able to count the new members joining up after the campaign.
- Staff could ask people in a friendly and informal way how they thought the campaign had gone. Comments and suggestions could be invited.

Evaluating the performance of the promotional campaign team

A promotional campaign is usually a team effort because of the very nature of the task involved. Individuals within the team could evaluate their own performance and the overall team performance could then be evaluated.

The team could evaluate the effectiveness of a promotional campaign

Self-evaluation

- Did I do what I was supposed to do?
- Could I have improved my performance?
- How might I do it differently next time?

Team evaluation

Hold a team meeting based on the principle that all comments will be constructive, no one will be criticised or blamed for anything and everyone will come out of the meeting having learned from the experience and be ready to improve and contribute fully to any future promotional campaign.

Marketing – a summary

- Marketing is finding out what people want and then providing it for them.
- Market research helps find out what the customer wants and answers the question, 'Who will be the typical customer for this product?'
- Target marketing matches the right product to the right customer.
- A market segment consists of people with similar characteristics and likes.
- The marketing mix, or the four Ps, enables the right product to reach the right customer at the right price.
- There are many ways of advertising and promoting products and services. The skill is to choose the one which is the most cost effective.
- A good promotional campaign should raise interest in a product and increase sales.

Check your knowledge

1. What could be the objectives of a library's promotional campaign?
2. Following the staging of a riverside festival, the organising committee meets to discuss how successful the event has been. What part of the promotional campaign is this?
3. A leisure centre runs an open day which includes free entry to the swimming pool for children. How will the centre benefit from this promotion?
4. A theatre has run a promotional campaign in the local newspaper with discount vouchers. How could this promotion be evaluated?
5. What part of a promotional campaign involves a group of people meeting to discuss ideas?
6. A theatre produces a brochure showing forthcoming events. What is the main marketing reason for doing this?

Assessment

This unit is assessed through your portfolio work. The work for this assessment will be your mark for this unit.

Scenario: Your school has been approached by a leisure and tourism organisation. It wants you to carry out an investigation into its marketing activities. It wants to put your research to good use by putting your findings into practice. It has offered a substantial prize for all entries that show evidence of research and effort.

This is what you have to do: You need to produce an investigation into the marketing activities of a chosen organisation from the leisure industry. You will also need to find out about a promotional campaign for a different leisure and tourism organisation to compare it with your chosen organisation.

To achieve grades GG, FF, EE you will have to:

1. Identify the products and/or services, with pricing structures, for the chosen organisation.
2. Identify at a basic level how the products and/or services are made available.
3. Identify at a basic level the market research activities undertaken by the organisation to meet the needs of different customers.
4. Comment briefly on the promotional materials/marketing mix of both organisations.
5. Produce a SWOT analysis for your chosen organisation.
6. Produce a piece of promotional material that includes the basic information for an identified target audience.

To achieve grades at DD, CC, BB you will also have to do the following tasks:

1. Provide a detailed description of the products and/or services and pricing structures for the chosen organisation.
2. Describe fully how the organisation makes its products and/or services available.
3. Provide a detailed description of the market research activities undertaken by the organisation to identify market segments.
4. Suggest other relevant promotional techniques and materials both organisations could use to promote themselves and their products/services.
5. Produce a SWOT analysis for the chosen organisation.
6. Produce an item of promotional material that shows imagination and is appropriate for a stated target audience.

To achieve grades BB, AA, AA* you will have to complete these tasks in addition to the previous tasks:

1. Analyse the products and/or services provided by the organisation in relation to the pricing structures.
2. In addition to a full description, recommend **one** alternative approach which the organisation could take to improve the availability of its products/services.
3. Evaluate the market research activities undertaken by the organisation in terms of cost effectiveness.
4. Compare the promotional techniques and materials used by your chosen organisation with those used by another leisure and tourism organisation.
5. Analyse the SWOT technique for your chosen organisation, identifying areas which the organisation needs to consider for future development.
6. Demonstrate an ability to plan and produce your promotional materials, stating aims, objectives, target audience and evaluate the finished product.

Unit 3: Customer service in leisure and tourism

Leisure and tourism organisations cannot survive without customers. Customers buy and use the products and services provided by facilities like cinemas, sports centres and travel agents.

It is important therefore to treat customers with the best service possible so that they will keep coming back and new customers will be attracted.

This unit shows why customer service is so important to leisure and tourism organisations or indeed for any other organisation. It covers the following topics which you will need to put into practice when dealing with customers:

- the different needs of customers and how they are met
- communicating with customers
- the importance of personal presentation when dealing with customers
- why it is important to keep customer records.

Many people think that providing good customer service is simple and straightforward. Well, it isn't! There are certain skills and techniques required to handle complaints, create a good first impression and to keep and maintain customer records accurately.

This unit links in with the first two units you have studied. It can also play a part in gaining an additional, nationally recognised qualification called 'Welcome Host/Customer Care' run by the English Tourism Council. The course may also contribute to work-based qualifications in Travel Services and Sport and Recreation.

Fact file

Welcome Host/Customer Care is a training programme and qualification administered by the English Tourism Council. The training is geared towards dealing with customers.

Assessment

Unit 3 is assessed through portfolio work. You will find more details about this at the end of the unit.

What you will learn

Chapter 1 What is customer service?
Chapter 2 Different types of customer
Chapter 3 External and internal customers
Chapter 4 Benefits of customer service
Chapter 5 Communicating with customers
Chapter 6 Personal presentation
Chapter 7 Handling complaints
Chapter 8 Keeping customer records

Chapter 1: What is customer service?

Customers are the most important part of any successful organisation, so all leisure and tourism facilities must aim to make sure their customers are happy with the products and service they receive.

Customer service includes all contact with the customer, both face to face, for example when selling the organisation's products and services, or indirect contact, for example when dealing with a letter of complaint.

Good customer service means putting the needs of the customer first and this should be the main aim of everyone working in the leisure and tourism industries. Good customer service means putting yourself in the position of your customer. You need to think how you would like to be treated if you were the customer and act accordingly.

This chapter looks at what customer service and customer care mean, how staff should be trained in the skills of customer service and what customer service involves.

What you will learn

Customers and customer service
Caring for customers
Training for customer service
Situations in which customer service is provided

Talk about it

What annoys you most when you go into a shop or supermarket? How could the way you are treated or the way you feel be improved? In your group, discuss your feelings.

Customers and customer service

First, we need to look at the overall idea of customers and customer service.

Customer service is all about looking after customers so well that they want to return. Customers come first.

Leisure and tourism organisations cannot survive without customers. Giving excellent customer service plays an important part in helping organisations to keep their customers and attract new ones.

Once you have customers, you have got to look after them. Why? *Because unhappy customers don't come back*. If customers are upset by poor service like a grumpy receptionist, or poor facilities, like dirty toilets, they will take their custom elsewhere. And where will they go? *To your nearest competitor*.

Activity

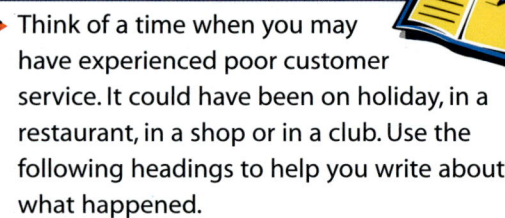

▶ Think of a time when you may have experienced poor customer service. It could have been on holiday, in a restaurant, in a shop or in a club. Use the following headings to help you write about what happened.

- Which organisation?
- How were you greeted?
- How do you think you were regarded by the person dealing with you?
- How do you feel you were treated?
- What do you think of the organisation?

▶ Write down why customers expect to be treated properly and outline the consequences when they are not.

Talk about it

In your group, discuss what you think gives an organisation a bad name.

Leisure and tourism are service industries. Whether you become a flight attendant or a sports centre supervisor, a waitress or a holiday rep, you will have to deal with customers.

Some customers may ask you questions, such as 'How far is it to the beach?'

Some may not feel well – 'I think I've had too much to drink'.

Some may not be very pleasant – 'I'm sick and tired of this hotel, I want my money back'.

Some may even say, 'Thanks very much, you've been very helpful'.

In other words, dealing with customers can be very hard work. So when you've been on your feet all day, you are hungry and you want to go home, you must still treat every customer as if they were your first. Whatever happens, don't use the following phrases:

- 'Oh yes, everybody complains about that.'
- 'Ah well, you can't believe everything the sales department tells you.'
- 'It's nothing to do with me.'
- 'I can't help you with that. Besides, I'm on my coffee break.'

Instead use these phrases:

- 'I'll take care of that for you right away.'
- 'Is there anything else I can help you with?'

Your customer care skills will keep your customers happy. Happy customers not only bring their custom back, they also bring their friends and relatives.

How to care for your customers

customers face to face. The cleaner in a travel agency never meets the clients as he/she may start and finish work before the shop opens. The housekeeper does not always see the hotel guests. But all these staff play a vital role in making sure the customer is satisfied with both the product and the service. In all these cases, the customers would not be happy if the dishes weren't sparkling clean, if the toilets were dirty and if the beds weren't made properly. When staff don't meet customers, it is called indirect contact.

Activity
 Write down some other words and phrases to use which show good customer service.

Fact file
Customer service is looking after customers so well that they want to return. Customers come first.

Caring for customers

Is it caring *for* customers or caring *about* them? It is both, and all staff play an important part in providing good customer service, even if they do not all come into contact with customers. For example, the person washing the dishes in a restaurant may never meet

Talk about it
Can you think of other examples of indirect contact? Can you give examples where staff come into direct contact with customers, for example a hotel receptionist greeting guests. List your examples and, in your group, discuss them.

When you work in leisure and tourism, always put yourself in your customers' shoes. Think about how you like to be treated, how annoying it is to be ignored, how good it feels to be made to feel important. Whatever you do, don't treat your customers like this travel agent did:

CUSTOMERS: Good morning, we'd like to go to Goa.
TRAVEL AGENT: Hang on a minute, I'm not ready yet.

CUSTOMERS: Have you got any information about Goa?
TRAVEL AGENT: Goa. Where's that, then? Eve, Jude, these two punters want to go to Goa. Any ideas?
CUSTOMERS: Actually we've changed our minds. Bye.
TRAVEL AGENT: Grief, there's no pleasing some people!

Case study

Our day out

This is a true story. The plan was to hire a mini-bus and take ten Leisure and Tourism students to Skegness for a day out as an end-of-year treat. I went to collect the mini-bus and found it wasn't ready. They were still cleaning it up from the previous day's booking. I had to wait 25 minutes which obviously meant we were late setting off.

Oh no! There was no radio or cassette player. I had asked for one. How can students survive a 120-mile round trip without music? Being late is bad enough, having no music is a disaster!

Unfortunately, once one thing goes wrong, or in this case two things, then there's more to follow.

I always thought that when you went to the seaside for a day out you were meant to have a good time and enjoy yourself. I also thought that whenever you went you would be made to feel welcome. Not so. There we were, having a game of bingo and having a brilliant time, laughing and joking when, all of a sudden, the attendant came up to us and shouted, 'Keep the noise down you lot'.

Charming! Anyway, excitement grew as one of my students got 'all four corners' and shouted out at the top of her voice, 'BINGO, Housey Housey, I've won!' To our amazement, we were told to leave for making too much noise. She didn't even get her prize!

Fortunately, the fish and chips were good and we made the best of a bad day. It was all a bit of a let-down as a result of some very poor customer service.

How could I prevent the same disasters from happening on future trips?

Ten rules of customer service

1. Never underestimate the importance of good customer service.
2. The customer is always right.
3. Always be positive and enthusiastic.
4. Communication must be open and honest.
5. A customer is satisfied when his or her needs have been met in a friendly and professional manner.
6. A customer is loyal when he or she has received consistently good and friendly service.
7. Treat each customer as an individual.
8. Every member of staff is responsible for effective customer service.
9. As a customer, expect and demand good service.
10. All customers are different and all customers are special.

Good customer service

Examples of good customer service might include:

- a recreation assistant showing you how to use the new locker system
- in a fish and chip shop, not only do they provide a plastic bag, but they also put the fish and chips into it for all the customers.

Snapshot

Zoe

Zoe went into town with a friend and her friend's mum, Linda, to have her belly button pierced. She had the money, she had plucked up the courage and she had even chosen the shop.

Before the girl doing the piercing got started, she asked if anyone had any last questions. Linda asked: 'Zoe is going to Majorca in two weeks' time. Does that matter?'

The assistant then advised Zoe not to have it done until she returned from holiday, as there was a risk of infection either from swimming pool water or sand.

This was sound, honest advice and an example of good customer service. It would have been easy for the assistant just to do the piercing and collect the fee. Instead, she put the customer first and showed she was caring for the customer.

Training for customer service

Customers who are treated properly by staff usually return. Staff are trained to ensure that this happens since repeat business is the lifeblood of any leisure and tourism organisation.

Customer service includes all contact with the customer, whether it be face to face or dealing with letters of complaint. These two elements of customer service play a big part in any organisation's training programme.

Imagine a situation on your first day at work in a travel agency or a leisure centre. Your first customer is becoming quite rude and aggressive towards you, through no fault of your own. How would you deal with a situation like that without proper training? The answer is, you couldn't. In fact, you might even make things worse. That's why leisure and tourism organisations should provide quality training before allowing staff to deal with the public.

It should be emphasised to staff during training that good customer service is one of the main aims of the organisation. That is why role-play situations are introduced so that new staff are either put in the customers' shoes or they play the part of sales staff. This gives them a good idea of what it is like, in real life, to be a customer on the receiving end of service by staff, both good and bad.

Private sector leisure and tourism organisations have two main aims: to make a profit and provide excellent customer service. In order to make a profit, they need to sell their products and services to customers. It is with these aims in mind that leisure and tourism organisations train their staff to sell as many products as possible.

Selling products is a very specific technique and well-trained staff can turn a potential sale into a real one. If customers are pleased with what they have bought, are happy with the way they have been treated and satisfied that they have got good value for money, they will usually return. As mentioned above, this is repeat business.

It is important to see the link between good training in customer service and customer satisfaction. Successful organisations provide staff with the necessary customer care skills in the hope that staff have the skills to serve customers confidently and effectively.

Situations in which customer service is provided

Talk about it

In your group, imagine you work in a theme park. What sort of information would you expect to give to customers?

Providing information

The more you know about your organisation, the area in which you work and the leisure and tourism industries in general, the more you will be able to help your customers.

For example, imagine you are working in a big hotel during your college holidays and a guest asks to see the manager to make a complaint. Do you know the manager's name? Do you know when she is on duty? Do you know the procedure for handling complaints? Do you know where the deputy manager is? Well, you should. The customer would certainly expect you to know. The customer will not care if you have only worked there for two days. He has paid his money and expects answers. It is a

Staff should receive training in customer service

good idea to find out straight away as much as possible about your organisation so that you can provide information confidently and accurately rather than say, 'Sorry, I don't know'.

> ### Think about it
> 1. Think of some questions customers might ask the following people:
>   a a hotel receptionist
>   b a sports centre supervisor
>   c a flight attendant.
> 2. What are the best ways of finding out how your organisation operates?

Customers expect you to know most things about your organisation and the particular facility you work in. A thorough knowledge of your workplace will create a good image of both yourself and your organisation.

Giving advice

Some customers need advice: which wine to drink with their meal, which is the fastest train to catch to London, which is the best club in town? Holidaymakers especially often seek reassurance because they are on 'unfamiliar territory' and they constantly want to know if they are going to the right places or doing the right things. As a result, they need to ask lots of questions. You may have even asked similar questions yourself such as:

- Which club plays the best music?
- Is it safe to drink the water?
- Is it best by taxi or bus?

Leisure and tourism staff are often bombarded with questions so they should:

- be trained in when and how to give advice
- know about the area they work in
- ask someone in authority if they don't know what advice to give.

Receiving and passing on messages

There is a big difference between hearing and listening. You may hear something but not necessarily take in the message. For example,

> ### Case study
> **Sophie, potential customer**
>
> Sophie loves ten-pin bowling so she called in at the newly opened Megabowl to get some details.
>
> Sophie: Can you give me some information about the competitions and leagues you hope to run?
> Receptionist: Haven't a clue. I haven't been told anything about that. Anyway, I don't think the boss wants that sort of thing.
> Sophie: OK. What about membership? How much is that? Can I join and then play at any time?
> Receptionist: We have got membership schemes but to be perfectly honest, they're a bit complicated and I don't really understand them. You see we've got student and family discount rates but I'm not sure what we've got for individuals. The boss will probably let me know when he's ready.
> Sophie: How much is a game for an adult?
> Receptionist: Sundays is double – they call it peak price – Saturdays is half price and weekdays is somewhere in between. I can never remember the exact price.
> Sophie: Thanks a lot. I must say you have made everything as clear as mud. Do you know of any other bowling alleys around here?
>
> 1. Why is it important for staff to have a thorough knowledge of their organisation's products and services?
> 2. How would you deal with a situation where staff don't know enough about the organisation they work for?

you may hear your tutor at the front of the class but are you taking in what is being said? If you listen, and listen carefully, you should be able to absorb what is being said.

When receiving information

- Make eye contact with the person who is speaking to you. This shows that you are interested in what the person is saying.
- Give your full attention by facing the person, nodding and commenting to show you are listening. This also encourages people to continue talking.
- Check every now and again that you have heard correctly by giving a quick summary.
- Make a note of the main points if there are quite a few.

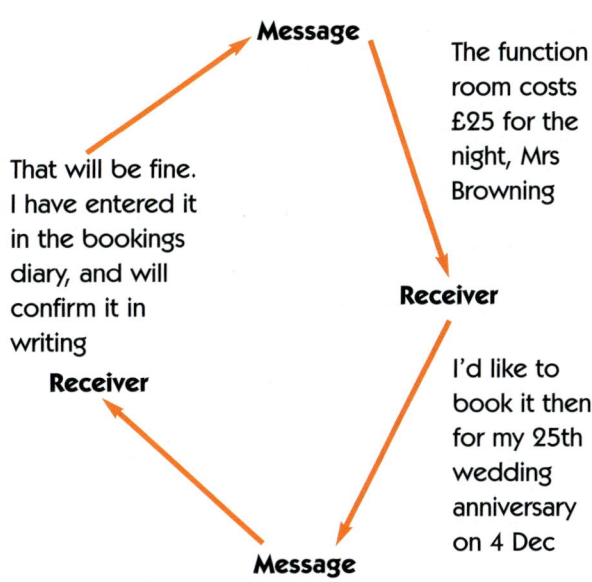

Figure 3.1 A simple feedback loop – how messages are sent, received and understood

Talk about it

In pairs, tell each other about your family, your home, the area where you live and your interests. This is a listening exercise. When each person has finished talking, make a note of everything you've heard and then tell the rest of the group what you have discovered about your colleague.

Activity

▶ Chinese Whispers is a simple party game which shows what can go wrong when messages aren't passed on accurately.

In groups of ten (or if that is not possible, the nearest to that number) stand in one long line. The person at one end of the line has to pass the following message to the next person, who passes it on to the next person and so on:

'The 8.45 train leaving London's King's Cross will arrive in York at 12.30 pm, stopping at Stevenage, Peterborough and Newark. All passengers for Lincoln change at Grantham. There is a buffet car available.'

The message must be whispered so that only the sender and receiver can hear it. In theory the last person to receive the message should be able to repeat exactly what the first person said. Your tutor will help organise this exercise.

Was your team successful? Did you communicate effectively? If not, why not?

When passing on a message

- Speak clearly. This may seem obvious but it is not easy to do when you are concentrating only on what you are saying, not how you are saying it.
- Check that the other person has understood what you have said by asking him or her.
- Vary the tone and pace in which you speak so that your voice is interesting to listen to. In other words, don't send the other person to sleep!

A simple **feedback loop** (Figure 3.1) shows how messages are sent, received and understood. It is always a good idea to check that the customer has understood the information you have provided. This ensures that:

- you have recognised their needs
- you are providing the right product
- the customer knows what is being provided.

Keeping records

This plays an important part in customer service and is dealt with fully in Chapter 8.

Providing assistance

As you know, when working in the leisure and tourism industries it is your job to help customers as much as possible by providing them with all the assistance they need. This may include helping to carry their luggage or directing them to the beach.

Sometimes it may seem that customers do not want your assistance, especially if you ask a closed question like, 'Can I help you?' to which the automatic natural reply could be, 'No, I can manage'. It would be better to ask, 'How may I help you?' It is very difficult to say 'No' to this open question.

The following phrases show how you can offer assistance:

- 'I'd be glad to help.'
- 'I'll go and get it for you myself.'
- 'I don't know but I'll ask someone.'
- 'I'll get him to ring you as soon as he gets back.'
- 'We'll do all we can to help.'

No matter how you are feeling, you must always provide the very best assistance to your customers. This may include:

- using a master key to open a customer's locker because he has lost his key
- helping a tourist fill in an insurance form after having her handbag stolen
- helping to carry someone's luggage into the hotel foyer.

Dealing with problems

When working in leisure and tourism, you may be asked to deal with a wide variety of problems. For example:

- Table 4 has been double booked at 8 pm by two parties of six.
- The showers in the changing rooms are freezing.
- The till has 'crashed' and the assistant can't take money or issue tickets.
- The safe keys are lost and the centre is due to open in ten minutes.
- The roof is leaking and the main hall floor is under two inches of water.
- There is a chemical spillage in the boiler room which is spreading outside.

Before trying to solve any problem, think about the process involved:

- Keep calm, don't panic and think clearly – go and see the problem for yourself.
- If the problem is life threatening, act straight away and call the emergency services.
- If you can solve it safely, do so.
- If you need assistance, send for it.
- If the problem has occurred previously, think about what action was taken before.
- Think of the consequences of your decisions – 'If I do this, what will happen?'
- Make a note of the incident and the action you took.
- If the problem cannot be solved immediately, make alternative arrangements.
- If the problem is going to affect staff and customers, erect hazard signs.
- Alert customers due to arrive if the problem is going to affect their use of the facilities.

Talk about it

In groups of three, choose one of the problems shown previously and using the guidelines given, say how you would solve it. Report your solutions to the rest of the group.

Dealing with dissatisfied customers

All the customers quoted below were dissatisfied with the service they received (or didn't receive) or the state of the facilities:

- 'My chips are cold. What are you going to do about it?'
- 'The toilets are filthy. When was the last time they were cleaned?'
- 'I've paid good money to watch this show and it's a load of rubbish.'
- 'This is the second time my squash court has been double booked. I want to see the manager.'
- 'The hotel was a mile from the beach, the entertainment was non-existent and the pool wasn't supervised. I want my money back.'

Remember the golden rules:

1. The customer is always right.
2. If the customer is ever wrong, re-read rule 1.

The first thing to do is to *listen* to the reason for the complaint. The customer can then say what he or she wants. This also gives you time to think of a suitable response.

Secondly, apologise and be sincere about it – really show your concern but don't admit liability.

Thirdly, take whatever action is necessary to try to diffuse the situation. Say you will do something about the complaint as soon as you have carried out the necessary investigation into the problem.

You may have to offer a full or part refund or another booking in the future depending on the problem. A written apology may be needed, probably from your manager or the head of the organisation.

Talk about it

Have you ever had cause for complaint with a product or service? In your group, describe the situation. What was done about it?

Offering extra services

We know about the products and services which leisure and tourism organisations provide – cinemas show films, travel agents sell holidays, and so on. These are standard services. But what about the extra services that leisure and tourism organisations offer?

- Cinemas provide booking by phone using your credit card so you can collect your ticket from a machine in a wall – no queuing necessary.
- Theatres allow you to order interval drinks from the bar.
- Travel agents sell insurance, exchange currency and book theatre tickets.

Talk about it

In your group, can you think of extra services provided by:

- shopping centres
- leisure centres
- hotels?

What extra services does an airport offer passengers waiting for flights?

Providing something extra can encourage customer loyalty and gives an organisation a good image, showing that it cares for its customers.

Check your knowledge

1. Why does a hotel provide information about evacuation of the premises on the back of the door in every room?
2. What is the importance of providing excellent customer service?
3. Leisure and tourism are 'service' industries. What does this mean?
4. Give one example of direct contact and one example of indirect contact with customers.
5. Why is it important that we should be positive and enthusiastic when dealing with customers?
6. Give an example of good customer service in a hotel.
7. Why is it important that staff receive training in customer service?
8. What information can a leisure centre receptionist give customers?
9. Give one example of a member of staff giving advice to a customer.
10. What is the difference between hearing and listening?
11. Give two examples of the type of service that makes customers unhappy.
12. What does going the 'extra mile' for customers mean?
13. Why should staff in leisure and tourism facilities be familiar with the products and services they offer?
14. Who would give information to holidaymakers on an all-inclusive package holiday?
15. What are the two most likely outcomes for a restaurant if its customers leave feeling they have received good value for money?

Chapter 2: Different types of customer

Leisure and tourism facilities are used by people of all ages, types and nationalities, including those with specific needs, such as disabled visitors and people with young children. This chapter looks at the many different types of customer that you will be expected to deal with and considers the basic needs of all customers.

Did you know?
Customers have four basic needs:
- to be understood
- to feel comfortable
- to feel welcome
- to feel important.

Establishing the different needs of different customers can be quite a complex task as it is not possible to ask each and every customer what his or her needs are. So organisations often use some of the following methods to try to establish customer needs:

- direct discussion with customers
- feedback from staff
- analysis of customer complaints and comments
- market research (see Unit 2)
- questionnaires – written, phoned or personal interviews
- user group discussions.

Below we look at some of these different types of customer.

What you will learn
- Individuals
- Groups
- People of different ages
- People from different cultures
- Non-English speaking customers
- People with specific needs
- Business men and women
- The basic needs of all customers

Think about it
Customers come in all shapes and sizes and all age groups. Imagine you work in a travel agents. How would you deal with a couple over 60, a family group, four 18-year-old 'lads'?

To provide excellent customer service, you will need to identify and meet the needs of a variety of customers, for example:

- individuals
- groups
- people of different ages
- people from different cultures
- non-English speakers
- people with specific needs, for example, sight and hearing impaired, wheelchair access, facilities for young children
- business people.

Individuals

An individual is a person who comes into a facility on his/her own and is dealt with on a one-to-one basis. Dealing with people on a one-to-one basis means you can give them your full attention, thus enabling you to find out their needs. For example:

- In a hotel, you may find out that a business person wants *The Financial Times* newspaper left outside the bedroom door every morning.
- Working as a flight attendant, you may find out that one of the passengers is a vegetarian.
- A first-time user of the gym may need advice about how to use the equipment and what training programme to follow.

It is quite easy to find out an individual's needs. You just need to ask, but make sure you use open questions. Instead of 'Can I help you?', say 'How may I help you?'

You ask the questions, let the customer do the talking.

> **Talk about it**
>
> In pairs, think of other examples of individuals using leisure and tourism facilities and identify their needs. Discuss your answers with the rest of the group.

Customer service in practice

This is what some people working in the leisure and tourism industries have to say about customer service:

'Making it our responsibility to give individual paying customers a quality leisure service – it's not just a top management job, we all need to do it' – theme park supervisor.

'Providing customers with customer satisfaction – giving them a level of service that satisfies their leisure needs in every way' – sports centre manager.

'Making customer satisfaction our most important sale. Yes, we are actually selling enjoyment not just holidays' – travel consultant.

'Creating a positive image of our organisation by the way we speak, listen and behave' – flight attendant.

'Viewing every guest as a valued customer and treating them all in a very special way' – hotel manager.

Case study

Heather, tourist information centre employee

Heather works in the local tourist information centre. She gets a great deal of job satisfaction by helping people new to the town. Obviously, these people need directing to the local facilities and it is Heather's job to give out accurate information in a friendly and professional way. Her conversations with customers go like this:

Heather: Good morning. Welcome to Retford. What can I do for you?

Tourist: Morning. It's our first visit to Retford. We are hoping to stay for three days so we need some accommodation.

Heather: Well, we have a range of accommodation, including hotels, guesthouses and bed and breakfasts. Which do you prefer?

Tourist: A nice little guesthouse would do. We also want to get an idea of what we can do during our stay.

Heather: There's a nice little guesthouse called The Mowbray half a mile from here. I can phone them to see if they have any vacancies. I will also give you a brochure about the town and show you where all the facilities are.

Tourist: Thanks. Anywhere we can grab a bite to eat?

Heather: There's a café round the corner that does a great steak pie and chips special. Brilliant value for money. Why don't you pop in there and I will bring you all the information you asked for.

Tourist: That's great. Thank you. See you later.

What customer service qualities has Heather shown that have met the needs of her customer?

Chapter 2 Different types of customer

How might a holiday rep 'go the extra mile' for his or her customers?

Groups

A group is considered to be a number of people who want to take part in the same activity. For example holidaymakers gathered together to listen to a rep's talk would be classed as a group. The group might be made up of families, young couples, senior citizens and people holidaying alone. Although the holiday rep may look on these guests as a group, he or she must also remember that the group is made up of people who should be treated as individuals.

Different groups have different needs, as shown in the chart.

Group	Needs
Holidaymakers	Information about attractions, entertainment, restaurants, shops, foreign exchange, excursions
Families on holiday	Activities for children, baby-sitting service, crèche, pubs which will accept families
Conference delegates	Four-star hotel, access to fax machines

Needs of different groups

Activity

Match the group with the needs.

Group	Needs
Senior citizens' day trip to Blackpool	Stopping-off points for refreshments, early arrival at ground, location of pubs, safe journey back
Club 18–30 holidaymakers	A tour guide who can speak their language, lots of tourist attractions, opportunities to take photos and buy souvenirs
Foreign visitors on a tour of London	Lots of fun and parties, great nightlife, sun, sea and sand
Children's birthday parties	Interesting lessons, day trips, guest speakers, great tutors, relevant assignments, new friends
A coach of football supporters	An entertainer (magician), bouncy castle, sandwiches, crisps, balloons, games, prizes, fun
Leisure and tourism students	Lots of toilet stops, friendly driver who tells jokes, Jim Reeves on tape, fish and chips, and a good old sing-song.

It can be daunting to stand up and talk to a group, although some people make it look easy such as:

- a tour guide speaking to visitors from overseas
- a sports coach talking to a class of children
- a business person talking to conference delegates.

You need to prepare your talk well beforehand, make your voice sound interesting and look around the group to make sure they are all listening. It takes practice, and then more practice. But once you have acquired the skill, you never lose it.

Activity

▶ Imagine you are a holiday representative. Your task is to give a first-day welcome to 20 holidaymakers who have just arrived in Majorca. Take 5 minutes to prepare your talk and then go for it!

▶ Write down the type of planning you would do when preparing to give a talk to a group on 'How the foot-and-mouth epidemic affected tourism in the UK'.

Case study

Innocent, a children's holiday rep

Innocent is a children's holiday rep for Longcroft Tours, a company specialising in family holidays in Tenerife. Innocent says:

> My job is to look after the 6–10-year-olds and provide fun activities for them. This means that parents can have a break from their children in the knowledge that they are being well looked after. The activities we organise include sport, fun swimming, painting, nature trails and, of course, there's the bouncy castle which keeps them occupied for ages.
> We create a fun atmosphere as the emphasis is placed on enjoyment and having a good time. Obviously, we have to take into account all the safety regulations because I am responsible for the children and if anything happened to them their parents wouldn't be too happy with me.
> We keep an eye on the possibility of sunburn, we check all the equipment before we use it and, most importantly, we make sure the children don't wander off. We have to be strict on this point.
> The children's activity session lasts from 9.00 am to 12 noon and restarts at 2.00 pm till 4.00 pm. It's a tiring and busy day, especially in the heat. I finish my day with a nice relaxing swim in the sea—not a bad way to round off the day.

1. Produce a day's programme of activities for ten 7-year-olds on holiday in Tenerife.
2. What qualifications would you need to become a children's holiday rep?

Case study

Wayne, an adventure holidays courier

Wayne is a courier with Trekstar Holidays, a tour operator which specialises in adventure holidays abroad.

These trips don't come cheap. A two-week adventure holiday in Colorado, USA, costs £5000. Activities like rock climbing and white-water rafting offer great fun, risks and adventure in some of the wildest and remotest areas of the state. That's why at the end of the day the accommodation the adventurers stay in is luxurious. No expense is spared. There is a jacuzzi in each room, the food is à la carte and saunas and massages are given at the end of the day.

Wayne says: 'It's a mixture of roughing it in the wilds and recovering in luxury. We seem to have hit on a winning formula. Our guests are used to the good life, staying in five-star hotels yet as they have become older and more adventurous they are prepared to take the rough with the very smooth.'

1. What type of jobs do you think Wayne's customers have?
2. How do you think Wayne should treat his customers?

People of different ages

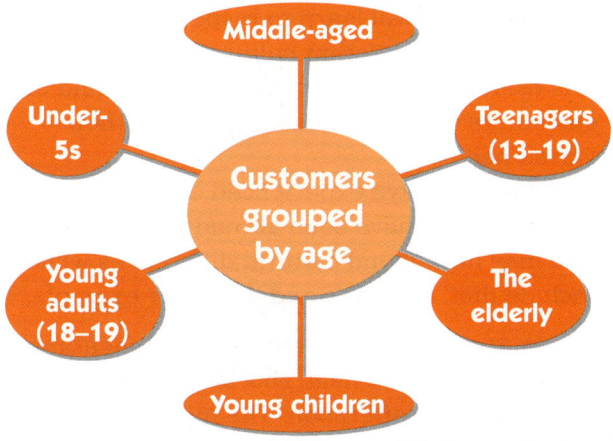

Note: there may be some overlap between age categories

Customers can be grouped together by age

Customers have different needs and groups of customers are often made up of different age groups, for example grandparents, mum and dad and three children. This complicates matters slightly as they all have different needs – gran and grandad want to relax by the pool, mum and dad want to go down to the beach, Ravi, Sanjit and Hira want to join the other children in the organised games.

Activity

> Imagine you are the assistant manager of a leisure centre and are responsible for programming activities. What would you put on for:
>
> a   senior citizens
> b   under-5s with their parents
> c   teenagers aged 17–19 years?
>
> Find out how tour operators cater for different age groups.

People from different cultures

Culture can be a difficult word to define. It relates to the character, history and traditions of people.

People from different cultural backgrounds have different needs. When you start your career in the leisure and tourism industries you will learn to respect the beliefs of people from different cultural backgrounds. It is useful to know the cultural background of customers so that you can provide for their varied needs.

You may have experienced different cultures if you have been abroad on holiday. You may have found cultural differences which include diet, language and dress, for example:

- In Spain, shops usually close at lunchtime because of the heat, so a siesta is taken during the afternoon. The nightlife may start at 11.00 pm and finish at 6.00 am.
- In Scandinavia, breakfast might be pickled herring and dark rye bread.
- In France, breakfast often consists of a bowl of coffee and a croissant.
- In Australia, Christmas dinner could be a barbecue on the beach.

Talk about it

In your group, discuss some other examples which show cultural differences.

Non-English speaking customers

You may become involved in helping the many foreign visitors who come to the UK who cannot speak English.

This barrier can be overcome in a number of ways by providing:

- leaflets in different languages
- headphones and tapes in different languages, e.g. on a guided tour
- guides and translators who can speak the language of overseas visitors.

In order to communicate with non-English speaking customers, remember:

- Smile.
- Do not shout – they can hear you.
- Speak slowly and clearly.
- Use maps to help with directions.
- Use gestures.
- Be patient.
- Keep checking to see if they have understood by asking, 'Do you understand, yes?'
- If there is a real problem, see if you can find a translator.

Patience is the key word. Remember, you are providing a very valuable service to these customers. It is reassuring to them that they are dealing with someone who can help them.

Symbols in signs assist non-English speaking customers

Activity

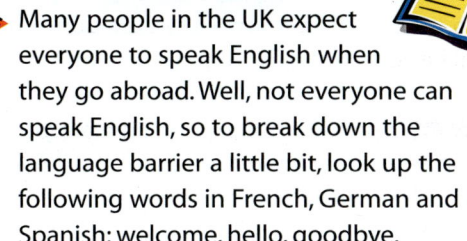

▶ Many people in the UK expect everyone to speak English when they go abroad. Well, not everyone can speak English, so to break down the language barrier a little bit, look up the following words in French, German and Spanish: welcome, hello, goodbye.

▶ Have a go at translating these phrases:

a Where is the railway station? (German)
b How much is this? (Italian)
c Can you direct me to the Post Office? (Spanish)

- wider car parking spaces
- car parking spaces near the entrance to the building.

Visually impaired customers

When helping people who are visually impaired, consider the following tips:

- When guiding a blind person, ask how he or she would like you to guide him or her. Most prefer you to walk slightly ahead while they take your arm.
- Explain exactly what obstacles are ahead, e.g. a set of stairs going up.
- Try to avoid intrusive background noise, such as loud piped music – blind people rely far more on their hearing than sighted people.

Customers with specific needs

All customers have their own special needs and wants. Some customers have more specific needs and require extra understanding and sensitive treatment. These customers include people with disabilities who usually like to be as independent as possible and to be treated in the same way as other people. Remember that if customers with disabilities are accompanied by someone, you should not ignore the disabled person by directing all your attention to the helper. An understanding of customers with disabilities is essential for all employees who come into direct contact with customers.

Knowledge of the facilities which are available for people with disabilities would also be very useful. It is worth remembering that we should see customers as people with particular needs not difficult people.

Snapshot

Describing the view

I once took a blind student up the Eiffel Tower. He asked me to describe the view overlooking Paris. This was quite a challenge since the student had been blind from birth. I found myself trying to describe colours, shapes and sizes. It was amazing – putting myself in his position. We had a great time. He said he felt like he was on top of the world.

Hearing impaired customers

Consider these points when dealing with customers who have hearing difficulties:

- Face the customer on the same level, with your face to the light.
- Speak the words clearly.
- Do not shout as it distorts the visual effect of words.
- Allow more time for customers to work out what you are saying.

Customers with restricted mobility

These range from people in wheelchairs to those suffering with stiff joints. Many buildings are equipped to deal with this by providing:

- lifts
- ramps

Think about it

What sort of special facilities are provided in places like leisure centres and cinemas for people with disabilities?

Chapter 2 — Different types of customer

Activity

▶ Try this exercise which your tutor will organise. One person will be blindfolded and the other has to lead that person and give all the necessary warnings of obstacles and explanations. This will give you a good idea of what it is like being visually impaired and is good practice for when you have to deal with this situation.

Other special needs

There are other customers, as well as people with disabilities, who have special needs. These can include parents with young children who may be restricted by the needs of the children.

In the example of a leisure centre, these needs can be met by providing breastfeeding and crèche facilities, baby changing rooms, and programming sports activities for families.

Another group with special needs is people who are unemployed. They may not be able to take part in sports activities due to lack of money, lack of adequate sports equipment and lack of confidence. The ways these customers may be encouraged to take part in sport and recreation activities include off-peak pricing, free use of equipment and the provision of special sports sessions.

Business people

People on business, especially if they are staying away from home, use many of the facilities which we normally associate with holidaymakers. They eat at restaurants, travel by taxi from the airport and stay in hotels. In addition they will use fax machines, Internet facilities and may need a meeting room.

Snapshot

Mark, businessman

Mark is the chief executive of an engineering firm. His business frequently takes him all over the UK and sometimes abroad.

Mark says:

> A typical business trip would mean flying down to London, staying overnight and meeting clients. I usually stay in a hotel which has facilities to allow me to work, such as email, fax and a photocopier. I make sure there's a desk and chair in my room along with the other usual facilities. One thing I do need is a trouser press because looking smart plays a big part when meeting clients.
> After I've completed my work in my room, I enjoy a nice meal in the hotel restaurant and a quiet drink in the bar. This sets me up for another busy day tomorrow.

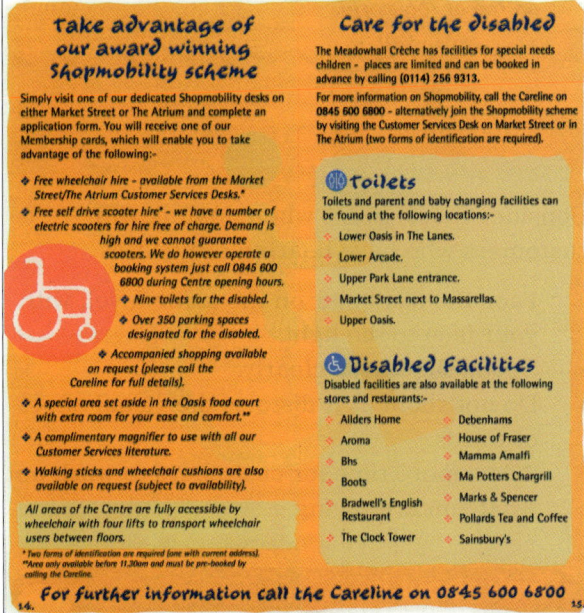

© Meadowhall Centre Limited – correct at time of print, July 2002

Meadowhall customer-needs brochure

Excellent customer service comes as a surprise. If you receive the type of service you expect, there will be no surprise. However, if you really want to impress your customers, you have to give them more than they expect.

Good customer service is about detail. It's about getting lots of little things right. In other words:

Detail makes the difference.

Activity

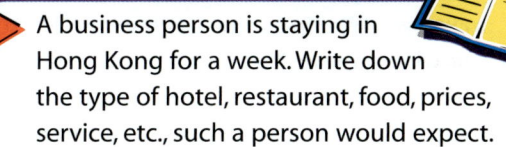

- A business person is staying in Hong Kong for a week. Write down the type of hotel, restaurant, food, prices, service, etc., such a person would expect.
- 1. Why do people go overseas to find business?
- 2. What is the role of the business travel agent?

The basic needs of all customers

Remember, the four basic needs of customers are: to be understood, to feel welcome, to feel important and to feel comfortable.

More specifically, customers need:

- help
- advice
- information
- the right product – at the right time in the right place
- security
- safety.

Below are examples of these.

Help

- Directing a family to the nearest McDonald's.
- Carrying a guest's luggage from the car to the hotel.
- Showing a wheelchair user to the lift.

Advice

- 'Which is the best wine to accompany my meal?'
- 'Which hotel is suitable for families?'
- 'Which show do you think I should see first?'

Information

- 'What are the opening hours of the leisure club?'
- 'What type of visa will I need for visiting South Africa?'
- 'How often do the trams run to the Pleasure Beach?'

The right product – matching the product to the customer

- Honeymooners wanting a trip to 'Paradise'.
- Families wanting value-for-money accommodation.
- Young people wanting designer clothes.

Security

- Personal belongings will be safe.
- Night-clubs do not tolerate violent behaviour.
- Airports check all luggage.

Safety

- Sports equipment, e.g. trampolines, checked regularly.
- Fairground rides well maintained.
- Fire exits kept clear.

Case study

Carmen

Carmen works as a secretary in a school office. She is in charge of a team of four – the examinations assistant, the clerical assistant, the finance clerk and the receptionist.

Things have become a little tense recently in the office and tempers have begun to fray. Carmen called a meeting to get to the bottom of the problem. She knew that it wasn't as a result of personality clashes because her team worked really well together and always supported each other. The real problems came out at the meeting.

- There was open access to the office for teachers, students, caretakers, cleaners and deliveries, meaning there were too many interruptions.
- There was no space to move. Desks were shared, there was little storage space and there was a danger of tripping over computer wires.
- It was very stuffy. There was only one shared fan which added to the feeling of being cramped.
- Furniture and chairs were out of date and uncomfortable.
- The whole environment was dull and dreary.
- The school safe was located in the office which presented security problems.

1. How would you go about making Carmen's office a better place to work in?
2. How important do you think it is to have a comfortable and safe working environment?

Check your knowledge

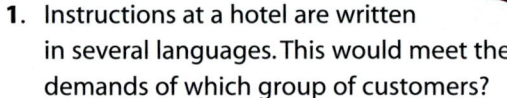

1. Instructions at a hotel are written in several languages. This would meet the demands of which group of customers?
2. In customer service we use open questions to find out what customers want. Give two examples of open questions.
3. What needs would a group of football supporters travelling to an away game have?
4. How would you prepare a speech to be made to a group of holidaymakers?
5. On holiday, how do the needs of senior citizens differ from the needs of the 18–30 years age group?
6. How would you direct a non-English speaking customer to a local restaurant?
7. How could a cinema cater for the needs of disabled people?
8. How would you communicate with a hearing impaired customer?
9. How could a hotel help a business person make the most of his or her business trip?
10. How can a leisure centre provide for the needs of families?

Chapter 3: External and internal customers

Customer service includes providing service to both external customers and internal customers. This chapter explains who external and internal customers are and why it is so important to treat them well.

What you will learn
Who are external customers?
Who are internal customers?

Think about it
Imagine you weren't feeling well. In fact, you probably shouldn't be at work but there's no one else available. How would you treat your customers?

Who are external customers?

External customers are the visitors or consumers who use the facilities of an organisation and pay for its products and services.

They play a vital role in the leisure and tourism industries because without them, there would be no business! They must be given the very best customer service so that they return and use the facilities again. External customers will also recommend an organisation to their friends if they feel they have been treated well.

Fact file
External customers are people from outside the organisation who use facilities or buy the products and services on offer.

Snapshot
Good news ... bad news

> *I always like going to our local sports centre because the staff are so helpful and friendly. Nothing seems to be too much trouble for them. We play badminton there every Sunday morning. It's now become a social event as we meet our friends there and have a drink and a meal in the bar after our game.*

> *I just knew I wasn't going to enjoy my meal as soon as I walked in. The tables were full of empty plates and the ashtrays were full to overflowing. We had to wait 20 minutes before someone took our order. When the food eventually arrived, it was cold and I'm sure I didn't ask for a child's portion. Sorry, but we won't be going back there again.*

Who are internal customers?

Internal customers are the people you work with, that is other employees of your organisation working in another department. It might seem strange at first to think of your colleagues as customers, but you have the same responsibility to each other as you do to your external customers. We shall look at internal customers in more detail at the end of Chapter 4.

Fact file

Internal customers are people who work within the same organisation and support each other. An internal customer should be treated as well as an external customer.

The European Working Time Directive

The conditions for working (number of hours a day, minimum time for breaks, etc.) are usually laid down by law. A European Union Directive is a law or regulation that all the member states of the European Union have to abide by.

These particular conditions were set out in 1998 and state that:

- people are limited to working 48 hours a week (although some people can discuss working longer hours with their employers)
- there should be minimum daily and weekly rest periods
- people should work an average of only 8 hours a day
- there must be rest breaks at work.

You can see that there could be problems with this for people working in the leisure and tourism industries. Long and sometimes unsociable hours are part of the job for many employees. For example, holiday representatives may work 12-hour shifts.

Talk about it

In groups, discuss the following:

a   Do you think the European Working Time Directive is generally a good idea?
b   What might be the advantages and disadvantages for the leisure and tourism industries?
c   What are the advantages and disadvantages of working shifts both for the employee and the organisation?

Check your knowledge

1. What is an internal customer? Give one example of an internal customer in a theme park.
2. Who are the external customers at Alton Towers?
3. Why is it important to treat internal customers properly?
4. How can an organisation benefit from the good customer service it gives its external customers?
5. List four methods of customer service that staff can give to external customers.

Chapter 4 — Benefits of customer service

Excellent customer service brings a number of benefits for leisure and tourism organisations such as increased sales, satisfied customers, repeat business, a better public image and an edge over the competition. It is also very important that all members of staff give a high level of service to each other.

This chapter looks at how good customer service benefits the organisation and its staff. It also considers the importance of the internal customer chain.

What you will learn

Benefits for the organisation
The internal customer chain
Benefits of providing excellent customer service to internal customers

Talk about it

Retail organisations like Marks & Spencer spend a lot of money training their staff so that they treat their customers properly. In your group, discuss what you think Marks & Spencer gets out of this?

Benefits for the organisation

Excellent customer service brings a number of benefits for leisure and tourism organisations as can be seen in Figure 3.2.

Figure 3.2 *How good customer service benefits the organisation*

Increased sales

Good news travels fast. An organisation that has a good reputation and is recommended by existing customers to other people will find the number of its customers increasing. This means more people will spend their money on the products and services of the organisation as Figure 3.3 shows.

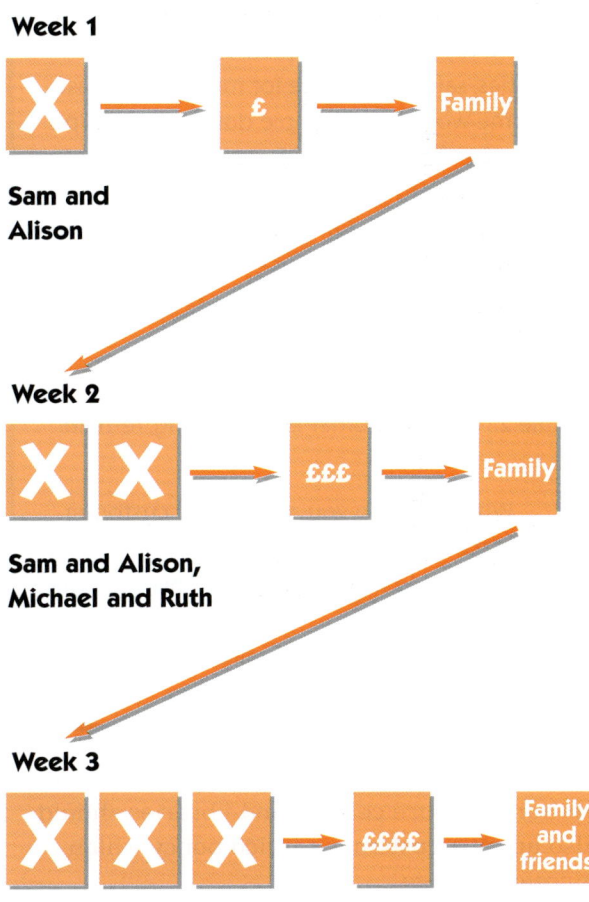

Figure 3.3 *A good reputation leads to recommendation and to increased sales*

Private sector organisations like restaurants and travel agents aim to make a profit. Increased numbers of customers brought in by excellent customer service leads to higher sales and increased profit.

> ### Case study
>
> **Richard, theme park manager**
>
> Richard manages one of the biggest indoor water parks in the country. It has slides, flumes, fountains, rapids, waves and a beach area. He calls it an indoor paradise, plum in the middle of Birmingham, miles away from the nearest coastline.
>
> Richard's staff are trained in lifesaving and first aid and they have additional qualifications in customer care, something he puts at the top of his priority list alongside health and safety.
>
> He knows people want to enjoy themselves in their leisure time and a big part of that enjoyment depends on how they are treated. Richard says: 'I know people want top-class facilities, safety and value for money but these become worthless if people don't get the type of service they deserve. After all, they are paying good money to come here.'
>
> Everyday Richard meets his team and reminds them of the importance of excellent customer service. In fact, Richard has put a large notice in the staff room which reads:
>
> 'Rule 1: The customer is always right
> Rule 2: If the customer is ever wrong, re-read rule 1!'
>
> 1. What value do you as a paying customer place on customer service?
> 2. How could Richard find out if his customers were happy?
> 3. Have you ever been 'spoiled' at a place like Richard's?

- Getting the details right first time and every time.

Good customer service encourages customer loyalty and spreads the word to potential customers. So why do organisations lose customers? The Welsh Tourist Board gives a number of reasons as follows:

1 per cent of customers die.
3 per cent of customers move away.
4 per cent of customers float from one organisation to another.
7 per cent of customers change organisations on recommendation of their friends.
8 per cent of customers are chronic complainers and buy according to their needs.
9 per cent of customers change because they can buy more cheaply elsewhere.
68 per cent of customers stop dealing with organisations because the staff giving the service are not bothered and show little interest in them or their problems.

Satisfied customers

> **Satisfied customers** are customers who are happy with the products and services they have paid for and the way they have been treated.

> ### Think about it
> What do you think makes a satisfied customer? Think about a time when you bought a product or service and were happy with it. Compare your notes with those below.

Satisfied customers are happy because they have:

- had value for money
- been very well looked after
- been given accurate information about the product or service
- had their wishes fulfilled.

Satisfied customers can also motivate staff. Customers who have been treated well will sometimes show their appreciation to staff by thanking them and smiling. This means that staff are then motivated to deliver the same type of service to the next customer.

Public sector organisations such as local authority leisure centres and libraries should also adopt a customer service policy which increases usage.

The English Tourism Council has the following customer service policy:

- Exceeding customers' expectations.
- Putting the customer first and at the centre of things.
- Finding out what the customer wants and making sure that it is delivered.
- Making sure that every customer recommends us.

Satisfaction spreads

- If customers thank you for a job well done, it makes you feel good.
- If you feel good about your work, you tend to be enthusiastic and motivated – you want to work!
- Recognition by customers will put a smile on your face and your work will be so much more enjoyable.
- Everyone will feel good about working in an atmosphere of teamwork and enthusiasm.

The postcards below show one satisfied customer and one not-so-happy one.

Wish you were here?

Dear Mum

Hotel lousy – still building it. Staff ignore us. Food dreadful. Pool has no water. Air conditioning broken. Cockroaches love it here.

See you soon.

Love Peter

PS How's Sheila?

Mrs J Gill
16 First Avenue
Blackpool
Lancashire B1 2XX
ENGLAND

… or here?

Dear Mum

Hotel superb. Staff treat us like royalty. Food magnificent, pool perfect. Everyone happy. Must dash, staff have organised karaoke party.

Love Sheila

PS How's Peter?

Mrs J Gill
16 First Avenue
Blackpool
Lancashire B1 2XX
ENGLAND

> **Activity**
>
> ▶ Look at the Ten Commandments of Customer Care and the Ten Magical Rules of Customer Service of Alton Towers below. In pairs, make up your own Customer Care Charter for a leisure and tourism organisation of your choice.

Statistics show that it is five times cheaper to retain a customer than it is to obtain a new one, and that if you upset a customer, they tell at least 12 other people about it. That's why in today's fiercely competitive environment, customer service will be the key to survival in the twenty-first century.

'dissatisfied customers tell an average of 12 other people about it'

TEN COMMANDMENTS OF CUSTOMER CARE

1. **Our customers** are the most important people in our business
2. **Our customers** are not dependent on us – we depend on them
3. **Our customers** like to be welcomed and recognised, listened to, smiled at, cared for, thanked and invited back
4. **Our customers** are not an interruption to our work but the reason for it
5. **Our customers** are not people to argue with or match wits with
6. **Our customers** are not cold statistics but human beings with feelings and emotions just like our own
7. **Our customers** want value for money and enjoyment, quality products served correctly and promptly in relaxed and welcoming surroundings
8. **Our customers** give us an opportunity to serve them
9. **Our customers** are deserving of our most courteous and attentive treatment
10. **Our customers** are the lifeblood of our business and have paid for our service

'Ten Commandments of Customer Care' (Alton Towers)

TEN MAGICAL RULES OF CUSTOMER SATISFACTION

1. **Warm welcome** – the key to a successful attraction
2. **First impressions** – are lasting and our visitors will remember the impression you give
3. **Stars of the show** – you are part of the show, your presence can bring the attractions 'alive'
4. **Appearances count** – you are on show, look the part to meet our visitors
5. **Excuse me** – know the park/hotel and be ready to answer questions
6. **Fun, fun, fun** – you are in the entertainment business, show you enjoy your work
7. **Be prepared** – for unexpected emergencies and know how to handle any situation
8. **Positive thinking** – take the initiative, make suggestions to make your attraction even better
9. **Litter** – is everyone's problem, so take pride in your site
10. **Winning team** – work together and use your talents to the best

'Ten Magical Rules of Customer Satisfaction' (Alton Towers)

More customers through repeat business and recommendations

Did you know?
An unhappy customer will tell between 10 and 15 other people of their unhappy experience.

Good customer service can lead to repeat business, that is existing customers coming back for more. In fact, if they continue to return, they will tend to build up loyalty to an organisation. This is also the best and most cost-effective way of advertising – recommendations by word of mouth. There is no better phrase than 'I recommend'. For example:

- 'I recommend you go for a meal there' will lead you to that restaurant
- 'I recommend these boots to anyone' means you may well buy some
- 'I recommend Ritzy's Nightclub' means you will go there rather than anywhere else.

Fact file
Repeat business is when customers who are happy with the products and services of an organisation return for more.

Customers usually trust organisations where they have received good service and build up loyalty towards them.

Talk about it
In your group, discuss if there is a leisure facility or shop which you keep going back to? Why would you recommend it?

A better public image

All leisure and tourism organisations like to promote a good public image. This is a way of showing customers that the product they are buying is good value and that the service they receive is second to none. The good image will not exist without the excellent customer service.

Leisure and tourism organisations promote a better public image by using endorsements from satisfied customers to promote their products. They also use pictures of people having the time of their lives as a result of using the organisations' products and services. The aim of this is to encourage new custom and to build up loyalty.

Luigi's Restaurant

'The food was superb, the service was excellent.'

'The staff are so helpful, they couldn't do enough for us.'

'The setting is perfect. The staff knew just what we wanted.'

Talk about it

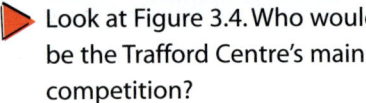

In your group, list the things which give organisations good and bad reputations. How can a restaurant overcome a bad reputation?

Activity

- Look at Figure 3.4. Who would be the Trafford Centre's main competition?
- List the type of customers who benefit from the centre's customer care policy.

An edge over the competition

By providing excellent customer service – better than that of your competitors – you will give your organisation more chance of maintaining existing customers and also attracting new ones. A travel agent may, for example, sell the same package

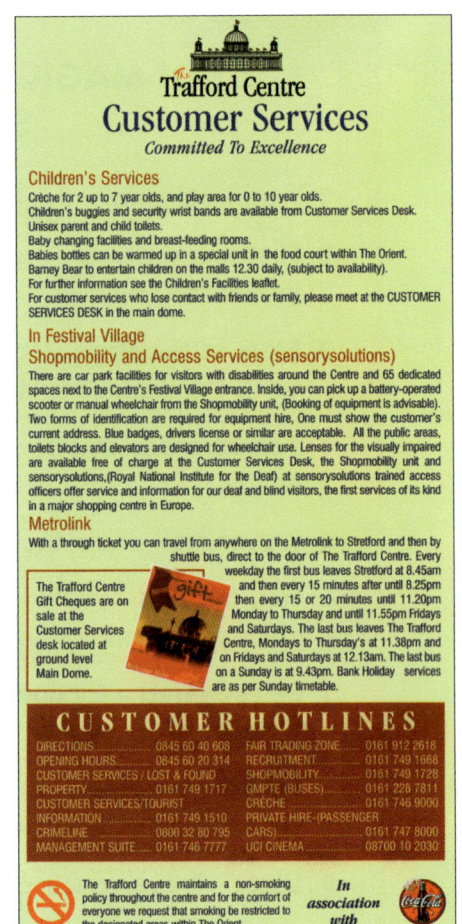

Figure 3.4 Trafford Centre customer services leaflet

holiday at the same price as a competitor, but it is the one which gives the very best in customer service that will attract the business.

Benefits to staff and the organisation

In Chapter 3 we learned that internal customers are the people you work with – your colleagues. You must try to treat your internal customers the same way that you treat your external customers.

It is important to remember that all members of staff should give a high level of service to each other as this leads to benefits for staff and the organisation.

Imagine you work in a travel agency. You know that your external customers are the people who want to book a holiday or arrange travel insurance, etc. To reach that stage in the transaction head office would have provided you with the posters to advertise the holidays,

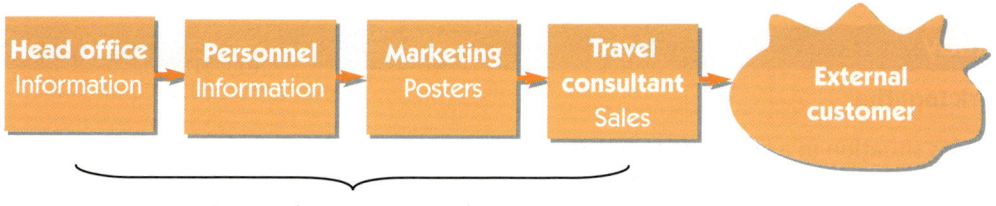

Figure 3.5 The internal customer chain

the computer systems to enable you to make the reservation and the skills you need to operate the computers.

In this case, **you** are the internal customer because you need the product, that is the advertising material, the equipment and the necessary skills to do the job properly. All these things are provided by your organisation (Figure 3.5).

The internal customer chain enables holidays to be sold to the external customer.

Imagine you work as a waiter or waitress in a restaurant. It's very busy and customers just keep piling in as your restaurant is renowned for its value-for-money meals and excellent customer service. Your job is to take the food and drinks to the tables. The following people enable you to carry out your work:

- The table cleaners make sure the tables are clear and clean.
- The dishwashers make sure the crockery and cutlery are clean.
- The kitchen staff make sure the meals are prepared.
- The cashier makes sure the customers pay.
- The manager makes sure everything runs smoothly.

In other words, there is a great deal of teamwork, where everyone relies on each other. Imagine if one link in the chain was weak, the whole operation would suffer.

Talk about it

In pairs, make a list of all the internal customers you can think of and show how they all have to help each other in the following organisations:

a cinema
b sports centre.

How could you promote a spirit of teamwork?

It takes a bit of getting used to thinking of your colleagues as internal customers. However, it must be remembered that staff who come into direct contact with customers cannot provide them with good customer service unless they receive the same type of service and support from their colleagues.

> We believe in teamwork. Every member of staff is important and we all treat each other with importance. Our external customer service is reflected in our internal customer service – Hotel manager.

Benefits of providing excellent customer service to internal customers

A more pleasant place to work

Imagine what it would be like if you had a job and, for some reason, you didn't enjoy it – perhaps it was boring; perhaps the pay wasn't that good. Now imagine if you were working with people who didn't help you, talk to you or listen to you. That would be even worse, and what is more, it is likely that your feelings would be apparent to your external customers, which would be really bad for the organisation.

On the other hand, if colleagues were friendly, polite, supportive and helpful, the result would be a happier you and a happier workforce, providing better service for external customers.

So, remember, it is important to:

- cooperate with colleagues at all times
- work well together
- be friendly and polite
- help and support each other.

Case study

Let's work together

Consider this situation in a leisure centre when one employee asks a colleague to do a task.

Request 1: 'Dave, could you set up the main hall for badminton please and then go and check the squash bookings?'

Answer A: 'Grief. Who do you think I am, Superman or something? Look I've got one pair of hands and I can't work miracles!'

Request 2: 'Andrea, could you check the first aid box and then put out the lane ropes for the swimming club when you have finished on the poolside?'

Answer B: 'No problem. In fact, I know we need some plasters and scissors so I'll pop up to reception and get some. Also last week the swimming club asked for floats and armbands so I'll organise that as well.'

Answer A is obviously unhelpful and downright rude. There's no doubt about it, Dave has a severe attitude problem towards his colleague.

Answer B is helpful, friendly and professional. This type of response ensures both internal and external customers will benefit.

1. What makes a good working atmosphere?
2. How would you deal with an employee like Dave?

A happier and more efficient workforce

People who work well together usually enjoy their work more. A happy workforce leads to teamwork and greater efficiency. This is good news for the external customer who, as a result, should receive some truly excellent customer service.

Snapshot

All right on the night

I once had to organise a New Year's Eve dinner dance for 300 people as part of my job as entertainments officer with a Borough Council. This task meant working with colleagues to make sure everything was all right on the night. This is how our internal customer chain looked:

We all had to work together and treat each other with the same respect as we would treat external customers. All this led to:

- teamwork
- high staff morale
- a sense of achievement.

At 3.30 am we finished, exhausted but happy, knowing we had done a good job.

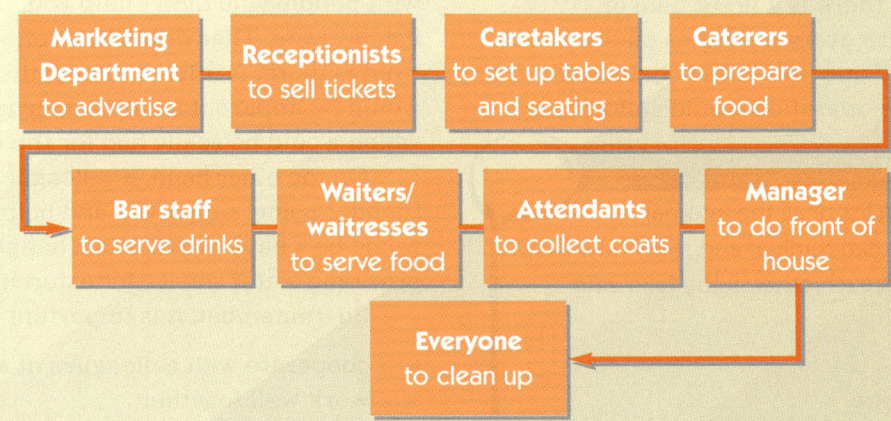

Marketing Department to advertise → Receptionists to sell tickets → Caretakers to set up tables and seating → Caterers to prepare food → Bar staff to serve drinks → Waiters/waitresses to serve food → Attendants to collect coats → Manager to do front of house → Everyone to clean up

Improved job satisfaction

If employees are treated in the same way as external customers, there will be improved job satisfaction – employees will enjoy their work and take pride in it. An organisation should give a level of service to internal customers which should include:

- being valued
- keeping them informed of how the organisation is performing
- being treated with respect
- receiving appropriate training.

Fact file
Job satisfaction is the degree to which employees enjoy their work and feel motivated to do so.

Job satisfaction leads to a sense of pride in the organisation, an increase in self-confidence and competence, and the motivation to continue to do well.

Improved chances of promotion

If you take an interest in your job, attend training courses and work well with others in your organisation, the chances are that your enthusiasm and positive attitude will be noticed by the management. People who can work well with others have a habit of motivating them. This is especially useful in supervisory and management positions. Providing excellent internal customer service can result in cooperation from colleagues, recognition from management and the chance of promotion.

Customer service – a quick reminder
- Treat your customers, whether external or internal, as you would want to be treated yourself.
- You are more likely to be promoted if you provide excellent customer service to both external and internal customers.

Check your knowledge
1. What does the term 'value for money' mean?
2. What motivates employees to work better?
3. Why are recommendations about a facility important for an organisation?
4. What is meant by having a good public image?
5. What can give a restaurant a bad reputation?

Chapter 5: Communicating with customers

Most people working in the leisure and tourism industries will at some time come into contact with customers. Receptionists, waitresses and sports centre assistants deal with external and internal customers every day, while cleaners or lighting technicians in a theatre may be expected to come into contact only with internal customers.

However, all leisure and tourism staff need to know how to communicate with customers and use different skills in different situations. Whatever job you do, you will be expected to communicate with customers. You will become more confident in communicating as you get to know more about the job and the organisation you work for.

This chapter looks at the types of communication and gives guidance on their use.

What you will learn
Types of communication
Communication working methods

Think about it
Imagine you are a receptionist. A customer is about to come in. What are the best ways of communicating with that customer?

Types of communication

When communicating with customers, you will need to use appropriate:

- language
- pitch and tone of voice
- pauses and silences
- body language.

Language

The way in which we say things is just as important as what we say. Our verbal communication, either face to face or on the phone will affect what our customers think of us.

Imagine you are a receptionist who wants to tell a guest the opening times of the hotel restaurant. In simple terms, it looks like this:

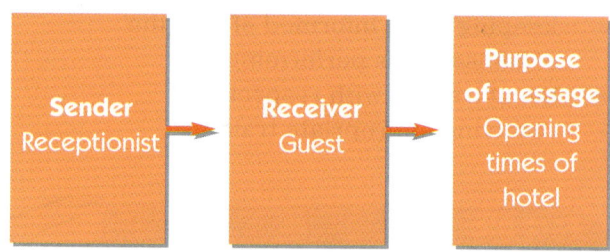

Examples of face-to-face communication include:

- sharing ideas and opinions – group discussion
- working with other people – teamwork
- giving instructions and awaiting feedback – supervisory roles
- offering information and advice, e.g. giving the opening times of a restaurant or suggesting a certain wine with the meal.

In a customer service situation the language you use with your customer should be simple and therefore easy to understand. After all, communication is not only about sending a message, it is about receiving it and understanding it.

Activity

▶ We have seen that there are many different types of customer, so our communication and therefore our language must be geared towards the individual customer. In pairs, write down what sort of language you would use and how you would speak to the following customers:

a   a young child
b   a foreign tourist.

▶ Select a newspaper article and analyse the type of language used in it.

When speaking to customers, try to avoid using the following:

- Jargon – language specific to your industry, e.g. 'Your ETA is 20:00 hours'. Customers might not understand that ETA means 'estimated time of arrival' or even that 20:00 hours is 8.00 pm.
- Slang – words and phrases that are not standard English, e.g. 'innit' (isn't it), quid (£), wanna ('want to'), ain't that right ('isn't that right').
- Colloquialism – words or phrases used in a specific locality, e.g. 'mardy' (bad tempered), 'moidered' (worry about), 'appen so' (that may be the case).

Activity

▶ Imagine you are the holiday rep described previously. Prepare a welcoming speech to your guests – use your imagination as to the location and type of accommodation. Prepare to give your 'welcome' to the rest of the group.

▶ Imagine you have to explain directions to a foreign tourist who can speak little English. She wants to find a hotel which is half a mile away. Try to give her the right directions.

Helpful tips
- Don't complicate what you say with difficult language.
- Speak clearly and concentrate on what you are saying.
- Ask the other person questions to check what you have said.
- On the phone, try to vary your voice so you don't send the caller to sleep.

Pitch and tone of voice

What happens if someone speaks to you in a dull, monotonous tone? The chances are that you would stop listening. Think about this sentence:

'Put some life into your voice.'

Customers will not want to listen to someone whose voice is boring and monotonous.

Talking to groups

Imagine you are a holiday rep and one of your first tasks is to introduce yourself to the group and tell them all about the hotel, the nightlife and the do's and don'ts. Here are some points to remember if you are ever in that situation:

- Face all the guests – don't turn your back on any of them.
- Plan what you are going to say and say it with confidence.
- Be prepared to answer the questions that members of the group may fire at you.
- Don't just look at one person in the group, speak to them all.

Think about it

Read out the following news story, adjusting the pitch and tone of your voice:

'Last night England won the World Cup by defeating Germany 3–0 at Wembley. Street parties broke out throughout the country and the Prime Minister declared that everyone could have the day off work.

Fans filled the streets in a mood of great joy and happiness never seen in the country. Flags flew, glasses chinked, car horns blasted out and the national anthem rang out in every village, town and city.

No one, but no one could ever remember such scenes of joy and happiness. Every football fan in the land cried tears of joy.'

Did your voice go up and down? Did it range from loud to soft? If it did, you were altering the pitch and tone of your voice which would have made it easy listening.

Making your voice sound interesting takes practice.

The pitch and tone of your voice – whether it is high or deep – is often affected by fear and nervousness. The muscles in your throat and your vocal chords tighten so the sound becomes a squeak or high pitched.

> **Think about it**
>
> Take a deep breath and, as you breathe out slowly, say a few short words like 'I love to talk'. You should find your voice sounds better since it is physically impossible to breathe out and keep your muscles tight at the same time.

It's not what you say, it's the way that you say it. You can, if you want, sound angry, full of life, enthusiastic, bored or downright miserable. Customers can tell by your voice what mood you are in and how you feel. The way you talk about something will affect their judgement of it.

For example, if you talk enthusiastically and positively about a local hotel, the customer will feel it would be worth staying there. At the same time, if you talk in a boring and unenthusiastic manner about a show at the local theatre, you would hardly be encouraging people to go and see it!

> **Activity**
>
>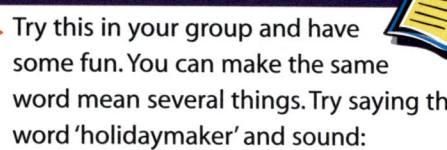
> Try this in your group and have some fun. You can make the same word mean several things. Try saying the word 'holidaymaker' and sound:
> - bored
> - surprised
> - pleased
> - overjoyed
> - angry
> - tired.

Adjusting the pitch and tone of your voice to situations takes practice and time. It is worth it because people will listen to you and your message will be received and understood.

Pauses and silences

People can absorb only so much information in one go and they tend to switch off when they cannot take in any more. This is worth remembering when dealing with customers because you want to keep their attention and interest when you are talking to them. That is why it is important to pause now and again and also to maintain silence at the appropriate time. Using these techniques will give:

- the customer time to absorb the information you have given them
- the customer the opportunity to comment or ask questions
- you the opportunity to think what you are going to say next.

> **Case study**
>
> **Selling and silence**
>
> In a selling situation the 'sound of silence' can win or lose a sale. The following example illustrates this:
>
> Assistant: How can I help you?
> Customer: I'd like to look at some training shoes.
> Assistant: What size do you take?
> Customer: Size 10.
> Assistant: What colour would you like?
> Customer: Blue with white stripes.
> Assistant: These are the latest design in your size. Sit down and try them on. They look great. How do they feel?
> Customer: Very comfortable.
> Assistant: OK. There's 10 per cent discount on those at the moment. Would you like me to take them over to the counter and I can put them in a box whilst you pay for them?
>
> 1. At which crucial moment must the assistant pause and keep quiet while the customer is making up his mind?
> 2. When should the assistant let the power of silence take over?
> 3. What might the consequences be if the assistant rushed the customer?

Activity

- Using pauses and silences is a skill that takes practice. Try this exercise. Work in pairs. One of you be the customer, the other be the sales assistant. Sell the following items using the 'pause and silence technique':
  - a holiday
  - a mobile phone.

Body language

Fact file

Not all face-to-face communication involves using words. We can also convey our feelings, thoughts and attitude without speaking by using gestures or facial expressions. This is known as non-verbal communication or **body language**.

In fact, 80 per cent of all communication is non-verbal. Being able to read someone's body language will be a big help when you are dealing with customers as you will be able to work out how they are feeling. It will also be useful for you to monitor your own body language so that you know you are sending out the right signals.

You can usually tell by looking at people's faces if they are feeling happy or angry – a smile will show happiness, a scowl will show anger. In fact, the face is probably the most expressive area of our body as it can show many emotions, including:

- fear
- anger
- surprise
- disgust
- interest
- sadness
- terror.

Talk about it

In groups of four, take it in turns to try to depict the above words by facial expressions. Remember not to use any words!
Discuss how a hotel receptionist might use body language when dealing with guests.

You will be able to tell if a customer is angry merely by looking at him or her. This will give you time to plan your reaction. Likewise, if you see someone is distressed you can be ready to be understanding and sympathetic.

Some body language gestures are open and positive, for example leaning forward with open palms facing upwards shows acceptance and a welcoming attitude.

Some others are closed and defensive such as leaning backwards, head down and arms folded. This may show someone is not interested or can express rejection.

If you use plenty of gestures other people interpret you as being warm, enthusiastic and emotional. This would be appropriate if you want to generate enthusiasm for a new idea. Using gestures only now and again would make you seem cold, reserved and logical. This might be useful if you had to convey cold facts or bad news.

Using eye contact is a way of acknowledging customers, making them feel welcome and showing that you are really listening.

Talk about it

In your group, discuss how you would describe the following examples of body language.

Activity

- One 'volunteer' stands in front of your group and performs an example of body language which the rest of the group has got to guess within 20 seconds. Did you find this easy or difficult?

You can gain a general impression of customers by a combination of their facial expressions, head movements and gestures. Being able to judge what the other person is thinking through his or her body language is a very powerful tool which you can use when dealing with customers.

Communication working methods

Dealing with customers can be hard work. Your job is to try to handle confidently every situation which may occur, such as giving someone directions, sorting out a complaint, finding accommodation for tourists or selling souvenirs.

Work accurately

In order to provide good customer service you will need to be able to work accurately. For example, if you are making a reservation for someone wanting to stay at the hotel where you work, it is important that you give them accurate information about:

- room charges
- meal times
- methods of payment
- room service
- types of accommodation
- local entertainment.

Customers expect you to be accurate because they are paying for the service and they are relying on you to help them.

If you know you are giving customers the right information, this will increase your confidence and make you feel good about doing a job well. At the same time, if you do not know the answer to a question asked by a customer, you should say 'Sorry, I don't know, but I will find out straight away'.

Listen and respond to customers

One of the most important yet under-used skills in customer service is that of listening. You have to really concentrate when someone is speaking to you. You must also resist the temptation to interrupt – this puts people off what they were going to say.

Most people love to talk about their favourite subject – themselves! Many of your customers will tell you their life story, given half the chance. This example sums up the point: 'He was one of the most brilliant conversationalists I've ever met. He stood and listened to everything I said the whole night'.

The important point to remember is that by listening to customers carefully, you will find out what they want.

Ask appropriate questions (using open and closed questions)

Open questions

These allow customers to give an answer other than 'no'. For example:

- Where would you like to go?
- How long would you like to go for?
- What type of accommodation would you like?
- How many people are going?
- When would you like to go?

Open questions are particularly useful in selling. An expression used by salespeople is 'Selling isn't telling, it's asking'. So a sales assistant will ask, 'How can I help you?', to which the customer may reply, 'I'd like to look at some training shoes, please'.

Talk about it

In pairs, think about the reasons why open questions are used. Make notes of your answers and then compare them with the list that follows (don't cheat by looking at the list first!).

Open questions begin with the words 'Who', 'What', 'Where', 'When', 'Why'.

Why do we ask open questions? Some of the reasons are:

- to give customers the opportunity to talk
- to show interest
- to find out how customers feel

- to keep control of the conversation
- to make customers feel important
- to understand any complaints
- to understand exactly what the customer wants.

Use open questions to gain as much information as possible. If you feel a customer is ready to buy a holiday and you have asked plenty of open questions, you can close the sale by using a final open question, 'How would you like to pay?'

You may feel that this is a bit pushy and you may not have the nerve to do it. Try to remember that people expect to be sold things, so don't be embarrassed.

Obviously, you won't be selling things all the time. The point to remember is that open questions give you information and make customers feel that someone is interested in what they want.

Closed questions

These begin with 'Is', 'Can', 'Does', 'Have', 'Are'.

A closed question would be 'Can I help you?', to which the answer could be simply 'yes' or 'no'. A reply of 'no' is a real conversation killer especially when you are trying to sell something, that's why we always try to use 'open' questions when selling something.

Another example of a 'closed' question is 'Have you seen anything you like?' The answer could yet again be 'no' or, if you are lucky, 'Yes, I like that dress in the window'.

Check your knowledge

1. Which type of communication skill is most important for an instructor in an outdoor pursuits centre?
2. What is body language?
3. How can body language help when communicating with customers?
4. Why is it important to listen closely to what customers say?
5. How can 'putting life into your voice' help when dealing with customers?
6. Why do we use pauses and silences when communicating with customers?
7. How can the 'power of silence' help in a sales situation?
8. How can you tell if a customer is angry?
9. Why should you make eye contact when dealing with customers?
10. Why do we use open questions in a sales situation?

Chapter 6: Personal presentation

First impressions count, particularly in the leisure and tourism industries where dealing with people is an important part of the work. The way you and the organisation you work for present themselves to customers has a direct impact on customer enjoyment, your job satisfaction and the success of your organisation.

This chapter looks at why first impressions are so important and what you can do to create a good impression. It also looks at telephone techniques, and how to make a good impression in writing.

Talk about it
In pairs, think of an example of a good and bad first impression you have experienced as a customer. It may have been a greeting from a sales assistant in a shop, a receptionist in a doctor's surgery or an attendant in a leisure centre.

What you will learn
- First impressions
- Telephone techniques to make a good impression
- Good impressions in writing

Think about it
What do you think is meant by creating a good first impression?
What would *not* impress customers?

Snapshot

The receptionist – first to make an impression

When it comes to making a good first impression, there's no one more important than the receptionist. That crucial first impression makes all the difference as to how customers see your organisation.

A receptionist should be:
- *able to put customers at ease*
- *able to listen and understand the needs of customers*
- *tactful, reliable and self-motivated.*

Dealing with customers – a receptionist's duties
- *Customers come first – whatever other tasks you may have, your first duty is to look after your customers.*
- *Personality – aim to be friendly, polite, calm, friendly and approachable at all times.*
- *Be organised – keep your work area as clean as possible. Make sure you are familiar with the layout of the building and where other members of staff work.*
- *Accuracy – take messages accurately, remembering to record the date and time the message was taken.*

First impressions

Whether you like the idea or not, customers will judge you and your organisation by the way you look – your appearance – and the way you treat people – your attitude.

You may think that how you look and how you behave is your own business, and so it is away from work, but at work you represent your organisation, and this is important. If you present a 'good' image, then customers will be impressed with both you and the organisation you represent. You never get a second chance to make a good first impression!

Smartly dressed, smiling receptionists

Appearance is important, but what is acceptable in one situation may not be in another. For example, if you work in a nightclub, then a stud in your tongue and gothic make-up may be acceptable. However, if you work in an upmarket health and fitness club, where the annual membership is around £2000, and the clientele drive BMWs and Mercedes, then this is very unlikely to be acceptable.

Be on the safe side! See what your boss wears and gauge your appearance on him or her.

> *We encourage our staff to create a really positive impression. Their uniforms are extremely smart and everyone wears a polished name badge – along with a big smile!*
> *Regional manager, a national travel agency.*

The way you present yourself to customers has a direct influence on their enjoyment, your job satisfaction and the success of the organisation that employs you.

How to make a good first impression
- Make a habit of greeting customers as soon as they enter the facility.
- Greet all customers courteously.
- Where appropriate, using a customer's name creates a favourable impression and provides a personal touch.
- Treat your colleagues courteously (internal customers) – you may be overheard. Always be supportive of colleagues in customer service situations.

In particular, you should understand the importance of:
- dress
- personal hygiene
- personality
- attitude
- behaviour.

Depending on whether you deal with customers face to face, over the telephone or in writing, some or all of the above may be important.

Dress

Many organisations provide staff with uniforms. There are many advantages in this because:
- they are functional
- a professional image is presented
- staff can be easily recognised as being part of the organisation
- staff can be easily found by customers
- staff feel a sense of belonging to a team.

If you are not provided with a uniform, make sure your clothes are clean and ironed. Polish your shoes and get them re-heeled when they need it – this means they will last much longer, as well as looking smarter, so it does make sense!

Fact file
Customers judge staff, and therefore the organisation for which they work, by the way they look and act, i.e. appearance and attitude. It is vital that staff create a good **first impression** because first impressions are lasting impressions.

> **Activity**
>
> ▶ Make a list of all the staff you can think of in the leisure and tourism industries who wear uniforms. What impression does this give?

As we have said, what you wear is part of how customers judge the organisation; it is part of the image.

> **Case study**
>
> **The Rutland Hotel**
>
> **Standards for staff**
>
> *Uniform*
> To be worn at all times when on duty. To be cleaned and well maintained.
> Shoes – black, well polished
> Jewellery – men: no earrings
> Hair – tidy and smart; men: no pony tails
> Personal hygiene – clean, fresh, no body odour; no excessive perfume/aftershave
> Nails – clean and tidy
> Tattoos – none to be visible
> Shaving – clean shaven (no moustaches or beards)
> Make-up – conventional and not excessive
>
> 1. What do you think about these standards?
> 2. Would you be able to work in this hotel? Discuss this in your group.

A good way of remembering the importance of first impressions is to think about when you go for a job interview. At an interview you need to impress the interviewer, who is going to be looking for someone who will please the customers, both internal and external, and conform to the standards of the organisation. In other words, someone who will make a good first impression. You might think that the way you dress is a statement about yourself. It is. But you want to impress your potential employer and think about putting the customer first. You may not do so if you wear jeans, a casual top, training shoes, a ring through your nose and a stud in your tongue.

Some leisure and tourism organisations have coined slogans to emphasise to their staff the importance of creating a good first impression:

- 'First impressions are lasting impressions.'
- 'Customers can always see your attitude.'
- 'Take pride in yourself and your appearance.'
- 'You are always on show – play the part.'

> **Activity**
>
> ▶ Write down two or three expressions of your own which show the importance of customer service.

Personal hygiene

Customers notice details – they notice dirty nails, untidy hair and unwashed, dishevelled clothes. So make sure you attend to your personal hygiene.

> **Talk about it**
>
> Imagine you work in a travel agency as a consultant. Recently, one of your colleagues has started to come in looking scruffy and unwashed. In your group, discuss why this matters. What would you do?

> **Activity**
>
> ▶ Staff who work in catering have to ensure that personal hygiene is a top priority, especially if they are handling food. Find out what additional hygiene precautions they have to take.

Personality, attitude and behaviour

There is more to making a first impression than simply being polite and friendly. It also means doing something extra – 'going the extra mile'.

The following list outlines the type of attitude, behaviour and personality that customers look for in staff:

- A friendly smile goes a long way – customers like staff who are friendly and welcoming.
- Customers don't want to hear your problems. Your facial expression will reveal your problems.
- Act positive, think positive; act enthusiastic, be enthusiastic – these attributes tend to spread.
- Having a bad day? The customer doesn't care if the world is against you.
- A good positive attitude will enable you to build up a speedy relationship with the customer.
- The way you look and behave will affect the way the customer regards you and your organisation.
- Customers want to enjoy themselves in leisure and tourism organisations; they don't want misery, they want enjoyment and your attitude should promote that feeling.
- You need patience – lots of it! You may have been asked the same question a dozen times already today. You may even have answered it all week, but this is the first time that this customer has asked it. Be patient, smile and act as if it is the first time you have been asked.

Remember, your behaviour will influence the customer.

No one can see your thoughts or feelings. People can see only the resulting behaviour. It follows then that the impression people have of you is based on the behaviour they see as well as the words they hear.

Your behaviour is like a beacon, sending out signals to all the people with whom you have dealings. The signals you send are vital because they are a major influence on the reactions of the other person. They can help or hinder every transaction you make with people.

Case study

Jacinta, travel consultant

Jacinta works as a travel consultant in a high street travel agency. She knows that first impressions are formed in the first three seconds of meeting someone. That's why she likes to look very smart for her customers. In fact, a smart uniform, pleasant surroundings and a friendly smile create the right atmosphere for Jacinta to deal with her customers and provide them with what they want.

Jacinta says:

> I treat every customer as if they were my first. I let them do the talking. That way I can find out what they want. I show a keen interest and give them all of my attention. It is hard work. I start at 8.30 am and finish at 6.00 pm. To be honest, some customers go on and on. Still, I keep smiling, listening and selling our products.
> I have a very positive attitude and believe all problems can be solved. In fact, we don't have problems in our office, we have opportunities to put things right.
> If I ever feel tired I just think about my discounted holiday in the sunshine of Mexico next month. It is only going to cost me £90 all in for two weeks. Not a bad perk is it?

What sort of personality would you need to be a:
a   flight attendant
b   sports centre supervisor
c   hotel receptionist?

First impressions of the reception area

Of course, it isn't just a member of staff who gives a good first impression, it is also the place itself. For example, imagine walking into a cinema foyer where the carpets are dirty and the

First impressions are important

litterbins are overflowing with empty cans and popcorn cartons. If this isn't enough, the toilets are smelly and there is no toilet paper or soap. What sort of impression does this give you?

You gain your first impression as soon as you walk through the door. In fact, even before that; the outside of the building gives you a good idea of what to expect inside.

Activity

▶ Think of a place where you go regularly, for example a fast-food restaurant. Picture the place itself and write down your impression of the building, the decor, how clean it is, how welcoming it feels.

▶ What are your first impressions of McDonald's? What sort of standards does the fast-food chain set? Write down your thoughts.

The reception area says as much about an organisation as its staff

How to make the reception area welcoming
- Clean and tidy entrance.
- Doors clearly marked 'Reception' and 'Welcome'.
- Reception area tidy, with fresh flowers.
- Brochures and leaflets neatly on display.
- Receptionist smartly dressed in uniform.
- Receptionist deals with customer's enquiries.

Telephone techniques to make a good impression

The telephone can play an important part in any good customer service strategy, providing it is used properly.

Talk about it
In your group, look at these two slogans and say what you think they mean.
'Smile as you dial and dial a smile'
'Don't phone a groan'

Checklist for dealing with customers by phone
- Give all your attention to the customer.
- Ask for the customer's name, write it down, and use it.
- Ask for other details e.g. address, telephone number, and write them down. Use a specially prepared form.
- Ask plenty of questions.
- Listen hard and show the customer you are listening.
- Keep your voice interesting by varying the speed and emphasis.
- Pause, to show you are thinking about what the customer has said.
- Keep it fresh – remember, the customer is an individual not part of a crowd.
- At the end of the conversation, summarise what you have agreed.

The first slogan says that if you actually smile when you are making or receiving a call your voice will automatically reflect that smile – it will make your voice sound more assertive and friendly. Try it some time and then keep practising it. You will find it works and is far more welcoming than a voice full of misery, which sums up the second slogan.

The receptionist and the telephone

A receptionist should:

- always answer incoming calls in a friendly and professional manner
- take messages quickly and accurately
- be able to answer questions about the organisation's products and services.

Telephone frustrations

- Not getting an answer quickly enough when you know someone must be there.
- Coming across an incompetent telephonist who puts you through to the wrong extension and/or cuts you off and/or isn't sufficiently clued up as to who's who and where to find the individual.
- Being left hanging on without an explanation of what is happening and/or being left on hold listening to piped music.
- Being greeted by an answering machine during the working day.
- Being put through before you've finished what you are saying.

Communicating with answering machines

Telephone answering machines have a tendency to strike some callers dumb. They just can't bring themselves to talk to a machine. Perhaps that's how you feel. But why waste your time by not leaving a message? Here are six tips for making the most from a recorded message:

- Ignore the fact that you are talking to a tape. Imagine a human being at the other end. Say hello and don't apologise for calling. The person you're calling obviously wants to hear from you, otherwise the machine wouldn't be on!
- Say the date and time of your call. That way it won't get overlooked.
- Speak more slowly and more clearly than usual.
- Repeat names, addresses and phone numbers. They may be hard to catch first time round.
- Keep your message brief.
- Be sure to wait for the beep before starting to talk. Otherwise part of your message might be lost.

Good impressions in writing

The way you present a piece of information in writing can affect the customer's impression of the overall service given by your organisation. In other words, poor grammar, spelling mistakes and a badly set out format gives a bad impression.

Activity

> 3 Main Street
> High Wycombe
> Bucks
>
> 29/4/2002
>
> Dear Mr Johnson
>
> I am writing to confirm your booking for a two week holiday in Gran Canaria between June 29thX 30th June and July, 13th, 20002.
>
> Your tickets will be sent when I have received the full payment of the accommodation which you have requested and I hope you have a good time.
>
> Yours faithfully
>
> J Painstakinly
>
> Mannager
>
> Twilight Travel Services

What would Mr Johnston's impression of Twilight Travel be? Find the 8 errors in the letter.

Written communication should:

- be easy to understand
- be properly set out
- use language and grammar correctly
- be spelt correctly.

First impressions – a summary

- Be enthusiastic – enthusiasm spreads.
- Be confident – customers will put their trust in you.
- Be welcoming – everyone likes to be liked and approved of.
- Be polite.
- Show you care – treat customers as individuals and make them feel important.

Check your knowledge

1. Why is it important to make a good first impression?
2. How can a travel consultant create a good first impression?
3. What type of personality do you think people working in leisure and tourism need?
4. How can reception areas help create a good first impression?
5. Why do organisations provide staff with uniforms?
6. Why should you show an interest in your customers?
7. How can you show a professional image on the phone?
8. A guest at a hotel reception is asking for details of prices but reception is very busy. What is the best way to help?
9. What gives a poor impression in written communication?
10. How do you overcome the fear of dealing with telephone answering machines?

Answers to Activity on page 193

a Address should be top right-hand side.
b No postcode.
c Date should also be on the right-hand side.
d 29thX should be 29th.
e 20002 should be 2002.
f Second paragraph should read: Your tickets will be sent when I have received the full payment **for** the accommodation which you have requested and I hope you have a good time.
g The letter should be signed off with Yours sincerely not faithfully.
h Manager has been misspelled.

Chapter 7 Handling complaints

Everyone in the leisure and tourism industries has to deal with complaints at one time or another. A customer who complains is giving you the chance to put things right. It is the unhappy customer who does not complain that is bad for your organisation, for he or she just says nothing but goes elsewhere in the future.

This chapter looks at what makes people complain and how to handle a complaint correctly.

What you will learn
What makes us complain?
How to handle a complaint

Think about it
What makes people complain? How would you deal with complaints?

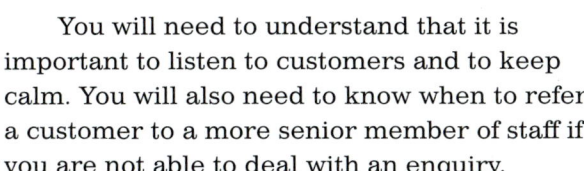

You will need to understand that it is important to listen to customers and to keep calm. You will also need to know when to refer a customer to a more senior member of staff if you are not able to deal with an enquiry.

A complaint which is handled properly tends to bring the two complaining parties closer together.

What makes us complain?

- Products and services that do not live up to what manufacturers claim they will do, e.g. 'You said these trainers would last for a year – they've fallen apart after two months'.
- Queuing up and waiting – there's nothing more frustrating, e.g. 'I've been in this restaurant for 25 minutes and still no one has taken my order'.

Snapshot

Suffering in silence

As a nation, the British tend not to complain, possibly because we are too reserved and probably because it is not in our nature.

I remember when I was 10 years old my parents took my sisters and me to a fish and chip restaurant for a treat.

We had to wait 15 minutes before our order was taken, even though it wasn't too busy. When our meals did arrive, they weren't what we ordered. My dad was unluckiest because he ordered haddock, chips and peas but instead got faggots in gravy.

He mumbled his dissatisfaction to all of us and also claimed his food was cold. When the waitress came up to our table, she asked, 'Is everything OK?', to which my dad replied, much to my mother's astonishment, 'Oh yes, everything's fine'.

We 'complained' by not going back there and obviously telling all our friends and relatives about our bad experience.

- Poor customer service, e.g. staff not listening to the customer.
- Mistakes, e.g. being given the wrong meal.

Case study

Sunil's complaint

Sunil and his mates loved going to watch their favourite Premiership team every Saturday. It was a tradition that at half time they would buy a hot pie and a cup of coffee.

This Saturday was no exception. The first half was exciting and the score was 2–2 when the half-time whistle went. Sunil treated his mates to hot pies and he had a Cornish pastie.

Twenty minutes into the second half, Sunil collapsed. The ambulance took him to hospital where he was diagnosed as suffering from food poisoning. He was admitted for two nights.

Two weeks later he went back to the snack bar where he had bought the pastie and told them about his illness. They took no notice and denied everything.

Sunil complained to the local authority who sent its environmental health team to investigate Sunil's complaint. It found that the snack bar was selling food which was past its sell-by date. It turned out that they were reheating pies and pasties several times over and therefore caused a real health hazard.

The snack bar was closed down and Sunil received compensation.

1. Was Sunil right to complain?
2. Who deals with complaints of this nature at your local authority?

How to handle a complaint

When people complain, they tend to show a range of human emotions, including anger and frustration which can lead to aggressiveness. Handling complaints properly means:

- staff don't suffer verbal abuse
- the customer doesn't blow a fuse
- the image of the organisation isn't tarnished.

Here is some guidance on how to handle a complaint:

- If you can't handle the complaint, refer it to your supervisor or manager.
- Don't admit liability.
- Keep calm – this way you won't get involved in a shouting match with the customer.
- Listen and don't argue – this will help you to get the full story and give yourself time to decide on a suitable reply.
- Don't take complaints personally. This will avoid you over-reacting and becoming defensive. Try to think of a complaint as a cry for help.
- Be sympathetic – the customer has a complaint, but don't necessarily accept the blame.
- Don't blame others, e.g. 'It's the advertising department again. They got the dates wrong'. This is no consolation and it gives a bad impression of the company.
- Use open questions to find out as much as you can about the complaint.
- Try to come to an agreement which will satisfy the customer. Make sure whatever has been agreed is carried out as soon as possible.

Case study

Greengrass Holidays complaints hotline

Greengrass Holidays is a tour operator with a hotline specifically set up to deal with complaints.

Greengrass: Morning, Greengrass Holidays. What do you want?

Client: Our tickets haven't arrived yet and we fly to Greece tonight.

Greengrass: Why didn't you tell us earlier? There's not much we can do about it now.

Client: You said our tickets would be sent to us in plenty of time and we have kept reminding you over the past week.

Greengrass: No. What we said, madam, was that your tickets would be sent to us and you would have to collect them.

Client: Then why didn't you let us know when they had arrived?

Greengrass: Look madam. They are your tickets. It's up to you to organise your holiday.

Client: Then what are you getting paid for?

Greengrass: I'm only following the rules, madam. You've got about half an hour to collect them because it's half-day closing on Wednesdays.

1. What was wrong with Greengrass Holidays' handling of this complaint?
2. How should it have been handled?

Case study

Gareth's CD Centre

Gareth: How can I help you, sir?

Customer: Last week I bought a CD personal stereo from your shop and it seems to have packed up.

Gareth: I'm very sorry about that, sir. Can I take a look at it please? How often have you used it?

Customer: Every night when I take the dog out for a walk.

Gareth: Is there a chance it got wet when you were out walking?

Customer: Well, it did rain a bit the other night but I always attach it to my belt and it's covered by my jacket.

Gareth: I think I know what's happened. These personal stereos are particularly sensitive to damp and if they come into contact with even a small amount of water, then the interior resistor lead is damaged. In other words, you won't be able to turn it on.

Customer: I must admit, I didn't read the instructions.

Gareth: Don't worry, sir. Very few people do. What I can do is replace this with a new model and give you a protective case which will prevent the same problem happening again. Let me know how it goes.

Customer: Thanks. I will be back next week to buy some CDs for my son's birthday. See you then.

How do you think this complaint was handled? Analyse each step.

Talk about it

In your group, share experiences of making a complaint. How was your complaint handled? How did you feel when you were making your complaint?

Handling complaints well gives a good impression of your organisation. It also shows that you care for your customers.

Check your knowledge

1. How would you deal with a customer who complains that she didn't get value for money from her two-week holiday in Majorca?
2. How do you think customers feel about organisations which deal with complaints in a positive and constructive way?
3. What's the best way of dealing with complaints?
4. Give three examples of what makes people complain.
5. Why should you not blame colleagues when dealing with complaints?

Chapter 8: Keeping customer records

Many leisure and tourism organisations keep records of their customers. They record relevant information about customers that may be used for future membership and marketing purposes. Creating and using up-to-date records gives an organisation a clear picture of its business and helps it to plan for the future. For example, a health club might have records of its members' names, addresses, telephone numbers and personal fitness plans.

This chapter looks at why organisations keep customer records, creating them and keeping them up to date, and the importance of accuracy and confidentiality.

What you will learn

Why keep records?
Internal customer records
Creating customer records
Finding and changing existing records
Accuracy and confidentiality

Why keep records?

Talk about it

In your group, discuss why hotels keep records of their guests.

Let's look at some examples of keeping customer records:

- A hotel keeps guests' names and addresses.
- A leisure centre has an activity booking sheet to show who is playing a particular sport.
- A fitness centre shows the progress of members in their fitness programmes.

On some occasions, it is actually a legal requirement to keep records, for example for VAT purposes and the Inland Revenue.

Health and safety records

Another example of record-keeping is the accident report book which gives details of accidents that happen in the leisure and tourism facility, including:

- details of the casualty – name, address, telephone number, age and gender
- details of the accident – date, time, place, what happened, nature of injuries
- names and addresses of witnesses
- action taken – first aid given, casualty taken to hospital, to whom incident reported.

Keeping such records allows the organisation to monitor health and safety and, if there is ever a court case, all the facts can be presented as they have all been written down.

Other health and safety records include:

- dates on which fire extinguishers were checked
- times when pool water was tested
- lifeguard training and qualifications.

Internal customer records

As well as keeping records for external customers, many leisure and tourism organisations keep internal customer records. These include records on all employees, including name, address, bank details, National Insurance number, staff training details, holiday entitlement and sick leave.

For example, if employees are absent due to illness they will be expected to complete a self-certification sickness note showing how many days they were off sick. Likewise, when

ANNUAL LEAVE APPLICATION FORM

This form should be submitted at least 14 days prior to the leave date requested.

NAME: Lisa Cheung   POSITION: Administrative Assistant

START DATE: 20/9/02   FINISH DATE: 27/9/02
(Inclusive dates)

NO. OF WORKING DAYS: 6

When completed please pass to your supervisor, or Duty Manager. The bottom section of this form will be returned to you indicating whether your leave has been granted.

SIGNATURE OF APPLICANT: Lisa Cheung   DATE: 9/8/02
SIGNATURE OF SUPERVISOR: M. Smith   DATE: 9/8/02
SIGNATURE OF MANAGER: Z Van de Merwe   DATE: 12/8/02
SIGNATURE OF ADMINISTRATOR: Inara Vinegars   DATE: 12/8/02
LEAVE GRANTED: YES / ~~NO~~   LEAVE DAYS REMAINING: 10

Internal customer (staff) record

taking annual leave employees may have to complete a leave request form which has to be handed in four weeks before the date they will start their leave. All leave forms are authorised by the departmental manager.

Creating customer records

Accurate records are an essential part of good customer service. You will need to know how to create customer records either on a computer system or manually.

Any information you keep on record on computer is covered by the 1998 Data Protection Act.

Computer systems have mainly taken over from manual systems for keeping records and are used in libraries when bar coding books and in pubs for stock control.

Manual systems which are still in use include accident report forms, maintenance sheets, and card index records.

Whichever system is used to keep records it must be:

- accurate
- clear
- legible
- up to date
- easily accessible.

Finding and changing existing records

You will need to know how to find and alter customer records because customers' details change – for example change of address, they get older, they have children.

Customers' records may be kept on a computer, in filing cabinets, in diaries, daybooks or on record cards. They must be easily accessible so it might be an idea to keep them all centralised, either on a computer database or in a filing cabinet.

If finding records has to be quick, then changing them has to be accurate. If a customer changes address, and the new address is not taken down properly, then all future correspondence with the customer will be lost, which could mean a loss of business for the organisation.

Accuracy and confidentiality

Customer records need to be accurate, so if you enter information the details must be correct and double checked if necessary. Imagine if you made a customer ten years older than he or she really was. That could lead to all sorts of complications.

Customers give information about themselves in the knowledge that this information will not be passed on to other people. It is essential therefore that records are kept secure and that only authorised personnel have access to them.

You also need to be aware of the Data Protection Act which limits the amount and type of information you can place on computer about people.

Organisations are also required to inform the Data Protection Commission that they will be storing information about customers on computer systems.

Fact file

The Data Protection Act 1998 gives people the right to know exactly what information is held about them and the right to refuse to provide information.

Customer service – a summary

- People shop around for similar products which are more or less priced the same. Excellent customer service can make 'browsers' stay, buy and return so that they become regular customers.
- First impressions are lasting impressions. It takes only three seconds for a customer to gain an impression. Make sure it's a good one.
- Different customers have different needs. Identifying and meeting these needs will enhance the image of both you and your organisation.
- Internal customers (your colleagues) are just as important as external customers. Good teamwork, cooperation and support between internal customers lead to excellent customer service for external customers.
- Dealing with customers takes skill, personality and patience. This is one of the most enjoyable parts of working in leisure and tourism.
- A complaint handled properly and professionally can, in fact, lead to repeat business.
- Customers demand high standards of service – treat them as you would like to be treated – put yourself in their shoes.

Check your knowledge

1. What is the main reason for leisure and tourism organisations keeping customers' names and addresses?
2. Why do organisations keep records of accident reports?
3. Why do leisure and tourism organisations keep customer records?
4. Give two methods of storing information.
5. Why is it important to ensure the security of information about customers?

Unit 3 Assessment

This unit is assessed through your portfolio work. The mark for this assessment will be your mark for the unit.

Scenario: As part of your week's work experience at a leisure and tourism organisation of your choice, you have to produce a review of the customer service provided by the organisation.

Your review has to include the different aspects described below.

To achieve grades GG, FF, EE you have to:

1. Describe at a basic level what is meant by customer service.
2. Describe at a basic level how the organisation meets the needs of a variety of customers and deals with complaints.
3. Describe at a basic level the benefits of effective customer service to the organisation.
4. Describe two examples of customer service records used by your chosen organisation.
5. Communicate clearly with a variety of customers, listening carefully and responding appropriately.
6. Describe simply how you have handled a customer complaint.

To achieve grades DD, CC, BB you will need to:

1. Explain why customer service is important to your chosen organisation and use examples.
2. Describe with examples how the organisation meets the needs of its internal and external customers and explain the complaints procedure.
3. Explain fully the benefits of effective customer service procedures to the organisation.
4. Deal confidently with a variety of customers, demonstrating good presentation and communication skills.
5. Effectively handle a customer complaint, following the procedures of the organisation.

To achieve grades BB, AA, AA* you will have to:

1. Produce a thorough and knowledgeable analysis of customer service in your chosen organisation.
2. Evaluate the ways the organisation meets the needs of all its customers and analyse its complaints procedures.
3. Recommend improvements in customer service procedures to increase the benefits to the organisation.
4. Suggest alternative ways the organisation could use its existing records in order to improve customer service provision in the organisation.
5. Communicate successfully and confidently with customers, listening carefully and providing a full and effective response.
6. Evaluate your own performance in customer service situations you have undertaken, including the handling of complaints made by customers.

Appendix

Work experience

The value of work experience

Work experience may offer you your first opportunity to go out into the big wide world and experience what it is like to work for a living, although you won't be paid for it. The benefits you will derive from your work experience will far outweigh the lack of wages.

Work experience can help you develop new skills, give you an idea about your future career, allow you to work closely with people of different ages, improve your ability to work independently and as part of a team, discover talents that you didn't know you possessed and meet people who may have very different attitudes and values.

Making contact

There are a couple of ways to make contact with a company or organisation where you would like to do your work-experience placement.

Firstly, your school, possibly through your careers teacher, may organise your placement. Secondly, you can contact the company yourself, which will probably be more beneficial to you. This gives you a sense of responsibility and will get you into the frame of mind of being proactive (making things happen).

The phone call

Once you have decided where you want to work, contact the organisation (preferably after discussing your plans with your tutor).

If you contact the organisation by telephone there are a few important things to remember:

- Know what you want to say. It might be a good idea to write down what you want to say, e.g. 'My name is Peter Hayward and I would like to speak to Mr Smith the manager about the possibility of doing some work experience at Lunn Poly'.
- Speak clearly and be positive. Remember, 'Smile when you dial, don't phone a groan'.
- Sell yourself. In other words be enthusiastic.

The interview – personal preparation

You may be invited for an interview before you start your work experience. This may be your first interview so naturally you will be nervous. Here are some helpful hints to ensure your interview will go well:

- Be yourself.
- Arrive early.
- Look your best. Remember first impressions are lasting impressions, so make sure your shoes are well polished, your hair is tidy and smart, your nails are clean and tidy, your make-up is not excessive, and your clothes are very smart (i.e. no jeans and T-shirts).
- Prepare answers to questions you are likely to be asked such as: Why do you want to come here for your work placement? What are your strengths? What do you know about our organisation?
- Prepare some questions that you would like to ask, such as: What hours will I work? Who should I report to on my first day? Who will be my supervisor? What should I wear? Is there anything I need to bring with me?
- Take with you as much information as possible about your course, so that your organisation or company knows what you want to achieve from your work experience.

Work experience in practice

You have been accepted for a work placement. Make sure you arrive on time throughout your placement. Everything will be new and you will be introduced to so many people that you will forget their names. Take a notepad to write down names, places, procedures and duties. Your notes may come in useful if you have to write a report at the end of your placement.

Your first day

Were you prepared? Write an account of your first day on your placement. You may want to use the following questions to help:

- Was it what you expected?
- Were you shown around?
- Who told you what to do?
- What did you do?
- How did you feel at the end of the day?
- What did you do for lunch?
- How do you feel about tomorrow?
- Did anything surprise you?
- Who did you meet?

General information

As your work placement progresses it is a good idea to keep a record of what you have done. Your record could include:

- people you have spoken to, e.g. staff, customers
- equipment you have used, e.g. photocopier, fax machine

- skills you have learned
- problems you have solved
- people you have worked with
- tasks you were set
- skills you have gained/improved
- what you liked/disliked.

Checklist

The following checklist will help you when you write up your report of your placement.

I arranged and attended an interview before my placement, and my employer has confirmed this	❏
I organised my own transport, using a timetable and calculating fares and times, and I have evidence to prove this	❏
I have evidence to show that I researched the health and safety rules of the company	❏
I have recorded all the jobs I have done, including details of equipment used, and people worked with and have signatures to prove this	❏
I have used information technology during my placement and have copies of work, receipts etc. to show this	❏
I have completed a review of my first week. I set targets for my second week, and had these signed	❏
I have recorded the visit of my teacher and have completed a witness testimony that he/she signed	❏
I have completed a review and evaluation with my supervisor, which he/she signed	❏
I have written a thank-you letter to the company	❏

Work experience – A final word

The most important thing is to enjoy your work experience. If you chose your work placement you should have chosen a place where you want to work and so be motivated and enthusiastic about it. The experience and knowledge you gain can serve you well, both when you return to school and when you start your career.

Building your portfolio

Having studied this book and all the information you have gathered from visits and talks by guest speakers you will have realised that there is a lot of work involved in this course. Your portfolio is a collection of all this evidence to show that you have gained the necessary knowledge throughout your course.

Unit 1 is examined by an external assessment and Units 2 and 3 are assessed by portfolio evidence.

Presenting your portfolio

Your school may provide you with an A4 lever-arch file. If not, you should buy your own as it will be a worthwhile investment. Coloured dividers are also a good investment as they are an effective way of separating each unit. On the front of each divider put the unit number and unit title. As mentioned in the book, first impressions are lasting impressions so it is also a good idea to design a front cover for your portfolio which includes your name, school, subject, dates and relevant Clip Art. You are now ready to build up some evidence for your portfolio.

Unit 1

This is quite large in comparison to the other two units. Although you will be assessed externally in the form of a one-and-a-half-hour exam you still need to collect the evidence from which to revise.

The unit is divided into three sections so it is worth using your dividers to separate the unit into:

1. The leisure industry
2. The travel and tourism industry
3. Links between leisure and tourism.

Any work that is set by your teacher needs to be included in the relevant sections. This may include practice tests, handouts, past papers, brochures, homework or any other tasks you have been set for which you have collected evidence.

All this information will help when it comes to revision. It may be worth asking your teacher for a copy of each unit specification to include in your portfolio so you know exactly what you have to cover.

Self-organisation of your portfolio is absolutely essential to ensure success.

Unit 2

This unit can be divided into the following sections (again using your dividers):

4. What is marketing?
5. Target marketing
6. Market research

7. The marketing mix
8. Swot analysis
9. Promotional campaigns.

This unit differs from Unit 1 in that it is assessed purely by portfolio assessment. You will be given certain tasks by your teacher which will go towards the evidence needed to pass this unit, such as producing an investigation into the marketing activities of two organisations from the leisure and tourism industry.

Your final piece of work will be assessed by your teacher and you will be given a grade. This work will then be moderated by an examiner from the examination board so it is important that your work covers the tasks set in the right amount of detail and in the right format, not necessarily in essay form but perhaps in the form of a poster or even a video. Whichever way you have completed the task it forms part of your portfolio assessment.

Unit 3

Again, Unit 3 is assessed purely by portfolio assessment so the unit can be divided into the following sections (using your dividers):

10. What is customer service?
11. Different types of customer
12. External and internal customers
13. Benefits of customer service
14. Communicating with customers
15. Personal presentation
16. Handling complaints
17. Keeping customer records.

Your main task will be to produce a review of the customer service provided by a selected leisure and tourism organisation. Again it could be presented in different formats, depending on how your teacher instructs you.

Producing your portfolio

Your teacher will offer advice about how to approach the tasks you are set and will supervise your work as you progress. You will have to reach your own judgements and conclusions – your teacher won't do that for you.

There are a few other points you need to remember when carrying out your portfolio work:

- Don't copy straight from books. This is known as plagiarism and can be spotted easily. Try to put your work into your own words.
- If you do use a quotation or a chart from a source of information you must say where you got it from, i.e. title, date, page number. This is known as referencing material.
- Quotations must be clearly marked and a reference provided wherever possible.

Portfolio building – a final word

The material within your portfolio and the way it is organised is connected directly to your success in the course. Try to remember the expression 'self-organisation leads to success'.

Take pride in your work and show it off at home. This will give you a good opportunity to practice for when you have to present it to your teacher and external examiner.

Index

A
advertising 131, 136–7, 145
  brochures 137–8
  Internet 139–40
  media 147
  merchandising 138–9
  point-of-sale 138
  posters 138
  videos 139
after-sales services 124–5
age, and leisure 7–8, 46
air travel 71
  air taxis 71
  charter 71
  employment 85
  long-haul 69
  scheduled 71
  short-haul 68–9
Alton Towers 29, 88
Areas of Outstanding Natural Beauty 20, 77
art galleries 17
attractions 57, 65–6, 78

B
bank holidays 6, 9
bingo halls 17–18
Blackpool 81–2
bookshops 44
brand image 145, 178
brand names 123–4
British Tourist Authority 62
brochures 137–8
business tourism 58, 169–70

C
camping 21
catering facilities 31–2, 65
Channel Tunnel 72
children
  holiday play schemes 24–5
  holiday reps 85, 165
  play areas 24
cinemas, attendance 4–5, 38
city breaks 69–70, 77–8
coach drivers 84
communication skills 83, 182
  body language 185–6
  groups 183
  language 182–3
  listening 186–7
  speech 183–4
  telephone 192–3
  writing 193–4
community centres 40
complaints, dealing with 160–1, 195–7
computers
  access 6
  games 6, 44
conference organisers 84
conferences 58
Cook, Thomas 6, 56, 67
countryside recreations 18–23
  environmental impact 21, 22, 78–83
cultural holidays 69
currency exchange 60–1
customer satisfaction 99, 122–3, 124–5, 174, 177
customer service
  and competition 178
  complaints 160–1, 195–7
  extra 161
  importance of 153, 154–5, 156, 173–4
  problems 160
  provision 157–8, 160
  training 153, 157
customers
  attracting new 146
  basic needs 169
  communication with 144–5, 182–7
  cultural differences 166
  external 171
  groups 164–6
  identifying needs of 162–3, 169
  individual 162–3
  internal 171–2, 178–81
  loyalty 154, 173–4, 177
  meeting needs of 99, 155–6
  motivating 145
  records 198–200
  with special needs 167–8
  staff motivation 174
cycling 19

D
Data Protection Act (1998) 200
direct marketing 131–2
discos 5
domestic tourism 55, 75–8

E
eating out 5, 38–40
  catering 31–2, 65
Eden Project 30
employment
  air cabin crew 85
  coach drivers 84
  conference organisers 84
  internal customers 171–2, 178–81
  job satisfaction 180–1
  leisure centres 52–3
  museums 17
  personal appearance 188–91
  resort representatives 85, 164–6
  skills needed 83–4, 182–7
  tour guides 85
  tourist information centres 89
  travel consultants 84
English Tourism Council 6
  customer service 62, 174
entertainment
  arts and 14–17
  cultural diversity 18
environmental issues, tourism 21, 22, 78–83
ethnicity
  facilities 47, 48
  and leisure 106–7
euro 61
external customers 171

F
facilities 3
  additional 12

meeting needs 33–4
families
  facilities for 9
  working days 48
ferries 73
first impressions 188–90, 191–2
fitness instructors 52
fly-cruises 69
football, public image 41

G
gender, and leisure 49, 104–5
ground staff 53
guiding services 63, 85

H
health and safety records 198
healthy lifestyle 32–3, 36
Heritage Coasts 19, 75–6
holidays 56, 68–70
  domestic 68
  history of 6, 56, 67, 75
  independent 67
  package 67
  paid 6, 9
home improvement [DIY] 22–3
hotels
  accommodation options 64
  grading 65
  health facilities 36
  location of 129–30
  types of 64–5

I
income, and leisure 49, 51–2
incoming tourism 55, 166
internal customers 171–2, 178–81
Internet
  advertising 139–40
  market research 119–20
  travel services 63

J
job satisfaction 180–1

L
Lake District 79
languages, foreign visitors 166
Legoland Windsor 43
leisure 2
  age-related 7–8, 46
  and gender 49, 104–5
  home-based 44
  income and 51–2
  and lifestyle 32–3
  religious constraints 8, 47
  and socio-economic groups 49, 105–6
  time availability 7–8
  trends 100
leisure assistants 52
leisure centres 34–5, 46
  additional facilities 45
  equipment sale/hire 45
  functions of 45
  programmes 35–6
  user charges 45
leisure industry
  development 8–9
  fashion 50–1
  history of 6–7
  interrelationships 33
  population-related 32
  structure 3–4, 9
  and tourism 87–9
leisure shopping 28
libraries 36–7, 44
life cycle categories 104
lifeguards 53
lifestyle, classification 106
location
  hotels 129–30
  tour operators 130
  travel agents 61, 130
London Marathon 12, 66
Long-distance Footpaths 19–20

M
market research 100, 108–9
  Internet 119–20
  observation 118–19
  personal surveys 115–18
  postal surveys 111–13
  primary 110
  qualitative 110
  quantitative 110
  secondary 110
  telephone questionnaires 113–15
market segments 102–3
  age-related 103–4
  brand names 124
  ethnicity 106–7
  gender-related 104–5
  life-cycle related 104
  socio-economic groups 105–6
marketing 96–7
  aims 97
  campaigns 100
  decisions 121–2
  direct 131–2
  mix 121–2
  profits 97–8
  target 102, 135–6, 146

Meadowhall shopping centre 28
messages 158–9
museums 16–17, 65–6
music, listening 5

N
National Parks 20–1, 54, 76–7, 79, 83
National Trails 19
nightclubs 18

O
observation
  direct 118
  participant 118–19
Olympic Games 13
outgoing tourism 55

P
package holidays 67
park rangers 54
performance, SWOT analysis 141–2
personal appearance 188–91
personal surveys 115–18
physical recreation 10–11
place 129
point-of-sale materials [POS] 138
portfolio 205–7
postal surveys 111–13
posters 138
prices
  calculating 127, 128
  cost-plus 128
  discounted 128–9
  market-led 128
  one-off 128
  peak/off-peak 128
problems, dealing with 160
products 3, 44–5, 122
  after-sales services 124–5
  brand names 123–4
  customer service 122
  development 100, 123, 125
  life-cycle 125–6
  promotion 99–100
  services as 122–3
profits 97–8, 127
  social 98
promotion 131
  advertising 131, 136–40, 146–7
  customer communication 144–5
  demonstrations 134–5
  direct marketing 131–2
  discounts 135

evaluation 148–9
personal selling 133–4
public relations 132
SMART objectives 143–4
sponsorship 134
target marketing 135–6
techniques 146–7
public relations (PR) 132, 178
pubs 38–9

Q
questions
closed 116, 187
open 116, 186–7

R
rail travel 72
reading 4, 36–7, 44
reception areas 191–2
religion, and leisure 8, 47
repeat business 99, 174, 177
restaurants 5, 39
fast-food 39–40, 44
managers 54
road travel 73
buses/coaches 74, 84
private cars 74–5
taxis/hire cars 74
rural facilities 18–23, 40, 50

S
sales
displays 133–4
personal 133
skills 133–4
seaside holidays 75
self-catering accommodation 64, 65
services 3, 44–5
as products 122–3, 154–5

short-break holidays 69–70
sightseeing 56
SMART objectives 143
social issues, tourism 78, 80–2
socio-economic groups, and leisure 49, 105–6
special interest holidays 69
special needs, catering for 47–8, 167–8
sponsorship 11, 134
Sport England 10
National Centres 42–3
sports 4, 10
business 11–12
events 58, 66
extreme 7
spectators 57–8
venues 40–2
staff motivation, by customers 174
steam railways 72
SWOT analysis 141–2

T
target markets 102, 135–6, 146
telephone questionnaires 113–15
telephone skills 192–3
television, viewing 5
theatres 14–16
theme parks 29, 43, 78
tour operators 61–2
employment 85
location of 130
tourism 55–6
business 58
environmental issues 78–83
importance of 26–7, 56
and leisure industry 87–9
policies 56

social issues 78, 80–2
trends 100
tourist attractions 6
tourist information services 62–3, 89, 163
training, customer service 153, 157
transport industry 55, 66–7, 70
travel
air 68–9, 71
choice 66
ferries 73
rail 72
roads 73–5
travel agents 59–60
business 60
employment 84
independent 60
location of 61, 130
multiple 60
online 63
retail 60

U
urban tourism 77–8

V
video rentals 37–8, 44
visiting friends or relatives (VFR) 57
visitor attractions 25–6

W
walking 5, 19–21
work experience 203–5
working hours, European Directive 172
writing skills 193–4